European Studies in Social Psychology

Advances in the social psychology of language

European studies in social psychology

Editorial Board: J. M. F. JASPARS, University of Oxford; WILLEM DOISE, Université de Genève; COLIN FRASER, University of Cambridge; SERGE MOSCOVICI, Ecole des Hautes Etudes en Sciences Sociales; KLAUS R. SCHERER, Justus-Liebig-Universität Giessen; HENRI TAJFEL, University of Bristol; MARIO VON CRANACH, Universität Bern.

The series is jointly published by the Cambridge University Press and the Editions de la Maison des Sciences de l'Homme, in close collaboration with the Laboratoire Européen de Psychologie Sociale of the Maison, as part of the joint publishing agreement established in 1977 between the Fondation de la Maison des Sciences de l'Homme and the Syndics of the Cambridge University Press.

It consists mainly of specially commissioned volumes on specific themes, particularly those linking work in social psychology with other disciplines. It will also include occasional volumes of 'Current Research'.

Cette collection est publiée en co-édition par Cambridge University Press et les Editions de la Maison des Sciences de l'Homme en collaboration étroite avec le Laboratoire Européen de Psychologie Sociale de la Maison. Il s'intègre dans le programme de co-édition établi en 1977 par la Fondation de la Maison des Sciences de l'Homme et les Syndics de Cambridge University Press.

Elle comprend essentiellement des ouvrages sur des thèmes spécifiques permettant de mettre en rapport la psychologie sociale et d'autres disciplines, avec à l'occasion des volumes consacrés à des 'recherches en cours'.

Already published:

Social markers in speech, edited by Klaus R. Scherer and Howard Giles

Forthcoming:

The analysis of action: recent theoretical and empirical advances, edited by Mario von Cranach and Rom Harré
Social identity and intergroup relations, edited by Henri Tajfel

Advances in the social psychology of language

Edited by
Colin Fraser
Lecturer in Social Psychology in the University of
Cambridge and Fellow of Churchill College

and
Klaus R. Scherer
Professor of Psychology, Justus-Liebig-Universität Giessen

Cambridge University Press
Cambridge
London   New York   New Rochelle
Melbourne   Sydney

Editions de la Maison des Sciences de l'Homme
Paris

Published by the Press Syndicate of the University of Cambridge
The Pitt Building, Trumpington Street, Cambridge CB2 1RP
32 East 57th Street, New York, NY 10022, USA
296 Beaconsfield Parade, Middle Park, Melbourne 3206, Australia

© Maison des Sciences de l'Homme and Cambridge University Press 1982

First published 1982

Printed in Great Britain at the University Press, Cambridge

Library of Congress catalogue card number: 81-15551

British Library Cataloguing in Publication Data
Advances in the social psychology of language.
 – (European studies in social psychology)
 1. Psycholinguistics – Addresses, essays, lectures
 2. Social psychology – Addresses, essays, lectures
 3. Sociolinguistics – Addresses, essays, lectures
 I. Fraser, Colin II. Scherer, Klaus, R. III. Series
 401'.9   P37

ISBN 0 521 23192 2 hard covers
ISBN 0 521 29857 1 paperback

Contents

Contributors

MICHAEL ARGYLE
   Deparment of Experimental Psychology, University of Oxford
JENNY CHESHIRE
   School of Modern Languages, University of Bath
DAVID D. CLARKE
   Department of Experimental Psychology, University of Oxford
COLIN FRASER
   Social and Political Sciences Committee, University of Cambridge
HOWARD GILES
   Department of Psychology, University of Bristol
THEO HERRMANN
   Fachbereich Psychologie, Universität Mannheim
RAINER KRAUSE
   Fachrichtung Psychologie, Universität des Saarlandes
W. P. ROBINSON
   School of Education, University of Bristol
KLAUS R. SCHERER
   Fachbereich Psychologie, Justus-Liebig-Universität Giessen
JITENDRA N. THAKERAR
   Department of Psychology, University of Bristol
C. G. WELLS
   School of Education, University of Bristol

1. Introduction: Social psychological contributions to the study of language

COLIN FRASER and KLAUS R. SCHERER

In his review of the relationship between the psychology of language and social psychology, Engelkamp (1978) points out that one might expect a very close relationship between these two intellectual enterprises since language is a social and cultural phenomenon and since much of social behaviour consists at least in part of speech behaviour. Engelkamp proceeds to show that contrary to what one would expect, there seems to be very little contact between the psychology of language, or psycholinguistics, and social psychology. As a rough measure of the respective impact of these fields on each other, he examined the subject indices and tables of contents of textbooks on the psychology of language and on social psychology. His conclusions are quite clear-cut: The psychology of language which has seen an explosive development since the 1960s is virtually never quoted in social psychological textbooks. Similarly, social psychological aspects of language use are virtually never dealt with in textbooks on the psychology of language. Engelkamp's explanation for this regrettable state of affairs is that psycholinguists are overly oriented towards cognitive processes whereas social psychologists, even when they use cognitive labels, are mainly concerned with affective or motivational phenomena. Although we certainly accept Engelkamp's conclusion that at present there is regrettably little contact between the psychology of language and social psychology, we do not fully agree with his analysis of the reasons for this sorry state. We do recognize that psycholinguistics has been overly cognitive and insufficiently social and would add that this state of affairs can be readily understood, given that psycholinguistics was the offspring of an individually oriented psychology, just beginning its cognitive revolution in the late 1950s, and of a linguistics apparently transformed by its transformational grammarians. Its parents inevitably directed the infant towards the study of syntactic and semantic aspects of language, knowledge and structure, to the neglect of the pragmatics of language use. The relatively recent burgeoning of interest in pragmatics, speech act theory, discourse analysis, the ethnography of speaking, and in sociolinguistic approaches in general has made large areas of linguistics much more social than they had been for decades and it is hard to imagine that, at least in limited respects, the psychology of language will not move in the social direction currently being followed by language studies in general.

The study of language has rediscovered the social through the efforts of linguists, developmental psycholinguists, language philosophers, ethnographers, ethnomethodologists, and many others, amongst whom social psychologists have been conspicuous by their relative absence. The prime reason for this, and for the lack of influence of social psychology on the psychology of language, is not the debatable argument of Engelkamp but the fact that there has not been a social psychology of language, a fact which is particularly clear if one looks at what, at least until recently, has been the dominant approach to social psychology, North American experimental social psychology. Whether one believes social psychology to be the study of the individual as influenced by other individuals, or of face-to-face interaction, or of the relations between individuals and the societies they live in, language would appear to lie at the heart of its concerns. Influence, interaction, ideology all depend on language and its related systems, which together make up speech and communication. Yet social psychology has managed to construct itself as a discipline while, for the most part, studiously avoiding the systematic study of language.

It is true that we have of course used language as a medium for stimulus input and for response measurement. It is also the case that, in studying social influence processes, persuasive communication, and the like, we have been concerned with some of the consequences of language, albeit at two or three steps removed. But social psychology has not been interested in language as an object of study in its own right, and the occasional handbook or textbook which appears to call this claim into question (e.g. Brown 1965; Maccoby, Newcomb & Hartley 1947) turns out to be an exception. Brown (1965), for example, is such a splendid exception that he not only proves the rule but makes the rule look baffling.

It *is* a puzzle why social psychology has ignored what should be one of its central concerns. It cannot be explained away as an understandable deficit on the part of a young and immature field of scientific endeavour, for, in social psychology as in psychology, language and speech held a prominent place in the canon of the discipline in the early days of its development. In his monumental *Voelkerpsychologie* (1900–20), Wilhelm Wundt, for example, put language at the top of the list of social psychological phenomena which concerned him. Doubtless some future philosopher of the social sciences will produce an explanation of the puzzle. It will be a complex explanation. Here, we can only tentatively suggest a few of the strands that might enter into it.

The disappearance of language from social psychology's agenda must have had something to do with the impact of behaviourism and positivism on psychology and the social sciences. Presumably as they started to have their effects during the 1920s and 1930s, it came to be felt that phenomena as mentalistic and as messy as those of language were, for a variety of reasons, inappropriate for the incipient objective sciences. In time that feeling must have played a part in creating the mutual ignorance which developed between the social sciences and linguistics, some of whose founding fathers, such as Sapir, had been much impressed by the importance of social psychological aspects of language and language use. But when, in the late 1950s and early 1960s, linguistics and the social and behavioural sciences rediscovered each other's existence, and most disciplines rushed to create their own brand of hyphenated linguistics, why did social psychology alone choose to look away? The most likely explanation is that, at just that time, the dominant American social psychology had decided to undergo its own latter-day methodological purification, namely the creation of an avowedly experimental social psychology. If you have just decided that rigour and respectability are what are required, that is not the time to face up to the intricacies and scope of language; better to net a few minnows than to risk grappling with an octopus.

In the past decade, dissatisfaction with the paradigms of mainstream experimental social psychology has been pervasive, and the resulting critiques of social psychology's scope and methods should have cleared the way for the re-emergence of language and speech as a central concern, and indeed there have been signs of this. Interestingly, however, amongst American social psychologists speech and communication are being studied almost exclusively as non-verbal communication. Language is still being circled around nervously, which may be a sign of a touching humility and misguided reluctance to stake a claim in an already populated field, or it could be a reflection of a desire for quick pickings from virgin territory.

Those then are some threads that one day may be woven into a complex answer to our puzzle. But at least one additional strand remains to be added. What has been claimed of American social psychology has been noticeably less true of its emerging European counterpart, in which there has been an ever increasing concern with social psychological aspects of language throughout the past twenty years (Rommetweit 1966; Moscovici 1967; Robinson 1972; Giles & Powesland 1975), with the consequence that the past few years have seen the emergence of a productive European social psychology of language (Blakar 1980; Giles 1977; Giles, Robinson & Smith 1980; Rommetweit 1974; Scherer & Giles 1979). It might be argued that this reflects the weaker hold of experimental social psychology in Europe, but the fact that much of the European work has used experimental methods suggests that other factors may be more important. We would suggest that the everyday salience of language, and language variations, is one of them. If one travels from one European country to another, or if one lives in a bi- or multilingual society, or even in a predominantly monolingual nation where regional and class dialects are pervasive, then it is hard for a European social psychologist not to recognize the theoretical and practical significance of language. It is striking that the most obvious exception to North American social psychology's lack of interest has been the work of Wallace Lambert and his associates (e.g. Lambert et al. 1960; Taylor & Simard, 1975) in bilingual, politically volatile Montreal. We have to concede that in the everyday America inhabited by some social scientists in disciplines other than social psychology language must also be salient. Perhaps it is particularly in the America of the experimental laboratory, peopled only by English-speaking assistants and sophomores, that language can become so unproblematic and taken for granted that it can be ignored for decades at a time.

Having explained away the absence of a social psychology of language, let us now turn to its presence, in the form of five substantial accounts of important sets of ideas and studies which we feel are particularly suitable illustrations of the fruitfulness of including social psychological considerations in the study of language and language use. The unorthodox structure of the volume is deliberate. As editors, we feel that, for both authors and readers, a particularly attractive, yet underused format is one where contributors can extend themselves well beyond the scope of a journal article or short contribution to an edited volume, without having to produce a monograph. Such contributions permit the presentation of an integrated review of a range of ideas or of a set of studies or, as in each of the cases here, some combination of the two. The nearest to a model for this book is the series of *Advances in Experimental Social Psychology* edited by Leonard Berkowitz. Our 'advances', however, are all on one theme and they employ a mixture of observational and strictly experimental methodologies.

Within the overall theme of the social psychology of language, we have solicited five contributions which, on the one hand, share the characteristic of being, in our view, important advances in the social psychological study of language and communication. On the other hand, they have been deliberately chosen to provide a diversity of illustrations of the potential of a social psychology of language.

We shall briefly use each of the contributions in turn as an example of how a particular substantive area which could be seen as falling within either psycholinguistics or sociolinguistics can and perhaps should be approached from a social psychological perspective. We should emphasize that by 'social psychological perspective' we mean a very broad set of considerations that are studied not only in social psychology but also in sociology, anthropology and other social sciencies. However, we believe that the social psychological approach that is illustrated in all of the chapters in this book is characterized by attempts to look at the mediation between social factors and individual behaviour by studying the way in which social and situational factors interact with the cognitive, affective and motivational organization of individuals producing language behaviour. Furthermore, in all of the contributions in this volume, the importance of empirical investigations using a combination of experimental and observational models of research is highlighted.

Developmental psycholinguistics is probably one of the fastest growing disciplines at the present time. Yet, here too one finds that social factors in language acquisition are often overlooked or neglected. In chapter 2 of this volume, Wells and Robinson show in a careful review of the evidence on the role of adult speech in language development that environmental differences in the speech addressed to the language learning child significantly affect the course and rate of learning. In particular, they stress the importance of investigating the relationship between the utterances of adults directed at children in normal conversation and the situation in which conversation occurs. As major tasks for the future, they identify the development of an appropriate methodology for investigating conversation in social interaction, as well as attempts to unravel the development of communicative competence. In evaluating the evidence available to date on factors that affect the development of language, they stress the importance of communicative functions of utterances and the part they play in a child's socialization.

In chapter 3, the focus is on speech pathology, particularly stuttering. As in other areas of the psychology of language, clinical psycholinguistics often suffers from a neglect of both social and affective factors, which may contribute to speech disturbances or may even be at the core of the problems. In his chapter, Krause proposes a theory that links the aetiology of stuttering to socialization processes concerning the expression of affect. He points out that many of the existing explanations of the origins of stuttering, as well as many of the therapeutic techniques that are presently being used in clinical psychology, lack supportive evidence or, in the case of therapies, lasting success. He regards the failure to understand the nature of conversational language as one of the most important drawbacks to the study of the development of stuttering and of appropriate therapeutic techniques. Using data from a long-term study on Swiss stutterers as an example, he attempts to show that inadequate strategies of affect management, particularly over-control of emotional arousal, may be a crucial factor in the aetiology of stuttering. He suggests that over-control of the child's expression of affect by the parents might be the major source of the problems stutterers seem to have in expressing their emotions appropriately in social interactions. The data Krause presents suggest that stutterers cannot function normally in conversation because of their affect expression problems. In some cases, they may actually try to avoid contact with their interlocutors, often by dominating the floor. Krause describes a number of important consequences for the regulation of both the conversation and the relationship between a stutterer and his interlocutor which result from inadequate conversational skills. In the light of his findings, Krause proposes techniques for stutterer therapy which consist of encouraging the expression of affect, rather than reducing arousal as suggested by most current therapeutic techniques.

The chapter by Herrmann emphasizes that language behaviour can only be understood if it is studied in terms of the situation in which it occurs. Herrmann and his associates have been able to show in a series of ingenious experiments that both the encoding and the decoding of verbal material is highly dependent on situational cues. Herrmann demonstrates that speakers generally select only some propositional components of mental structures for encoding, i.e. only a part of the whole is encoded. Yet, the listener generally has no problem in decoding the meaning of the utterance in terms of the whole mental structure that underlies the speaker's utterance. Speakers, by means of their prior learning experiences, utilize situational cues in the conversation setting in selecting those components of propositions that are minimally necessary to provide sufficient information for their interlocutors and to permit attainment of the goal specific to the episode. Again, as in earlier chapters, the importance of the communicative functions of utterances and their embeddedness in social and situational settings lies at the core of the discussion in this chapter. The empirical material that Herrmann and his associates have brought together clearly shows that language behaviour cannot be treated as simple encoding and decoding of verbal strings. One of the major contributions in the chapter by Herrmann is the demonstration that it is possible to specify a set of rules that describes the effect of situational cues on encoding and decoding behaviour. In a set of eight postulates Herrmann proposes a theoretical framework amenable to experimental study. As he himself has demonstrated, it can be extremely fruitful to use experimental techniques to test theoretical propositions about the role of social factors in language behaviour.

In chapter 5, Clarke & Argyle review some of their work on the structure of conversation sequences and the skills that interaction partners must possess in dealing with conversational situations. They are able to show that conversations are highly structured events that cannot be described by simple chain-like models. The interlocutors in a conversation follow a very complex hierarchical rule structure in intermeshing their contributions to the conversation. One of the central issues introduced in this chapter is the social skills model that has been proposed by Argyle. Obviously, the ability to converse is one of the most important of social skills and one of the major indicators of social competence. As in earlier chapters, the importance of the situation in which conversation takes place is highlighted in the chapter by Clarke & Argyle. The nature of the episode or situation strongly determines the kind of sequencing that will result, and special skills are required to deal with different situations.

As was noted earlier, a very active area of language research is that of sociolinguistics. However, as Giles and his associates have argued on a number of occasions, there is more to the social study of linguistic behaviour than the demonstration of static differences between various social groups or strata. The chapter by Thakerar, Giles & Cheshire provides excellent examples of the dynamic nature of linguistic adjustments in social situations. The basis of the chapter is accommodation theory, a social psychological theory postulating that partners in interaction will tend to converge in many aspects of their speech behaviour if they like or value each other, and tend to diverge if they wish to distance or dissociate themselves from each other. In chapter 6, a number of new empirical results bearing on convergence and divergence phenomena between speakers of different status are reviewed. Furthermore, an important distinction is drawn between psychological and linguistic convergence, or between intended and observable convergence. This chapter shows the importance of a social psychological approach to studying social factors in language. It is not sufficient to postulate effects of different social variables on language behaviour. An important contribution of the social psychologist is to investigate ways in which the effects of social and situational variables are mediated by cognitive, affective, and motivational processes in individuals.

The programmes of research presented in this volume make up only a small sample of current work in Europe on the social psychology of language. But small though the sample is, we are confident that the individual chapters, almost as case studies, will demonstrate how language and its use can be profitably studied from a social psychological vantage point. The implications are twofold. First, without social psychological analyses, both a psychology of language and a sociolinguistics are bound to remain incomplete. Secondly, at any rate in Europe, a social psychology of language is not only possible but is alive and thriving.

References

Blakar, R. M. 1980. *Studies of familial communication and psychopathology*. Oslo: Universitetsforlaget.
Brown, R. 1965. *Social psychology*. Glencoe, Ill.: The Free Press.
Engelkamp, J. 1978. Zur Beziehung von Sprachpsychologie und Sozialpsychologie. *Zeitschrift für Sozialpsychologie*, 9, 288–98.
Giles, H. (ed.) 1977. *Language, ethnicity and intergroup relations*. London: Academic Press.
Giles, H. & Powesland, P. F. 1975. *Speech style and social evaluation*. London: Academic Press.
Giles, H., Robinson, W. P. & Smith, P. M. (eds.) 1980. *Language: social psychological perspectives*. Oxford: Pergamon.
Lambert, W. E., Hodgson, R. C., Gardner, R. C. & Fillenbaum, S. 1960. Evaluational reactions to spoken language. *Journal of Abnormal and Social Psychology*, 60, 44–51.
Maccoby, E. E., Newcomb, T. M. & Hartley, E. L. (eds.) 1947. *Readings in social psychology*. New York: Holt, Rinehart & Winston.
Moscovici, S. 1967. Communication processes and the properties of language. In L. Berkowitz (ed.) *Advances in experimental social psychology*, vol. 3. New York: Academic Press.
Robinson, W. P. 1972. *Language and social behaviour*. Harmondsworth: Penguin Books.

Rommetweit, R. 1966. Linguistic and non-linguistic components of communication. Notes on the intersection of psycholinguistic and social psychological theory. Paper presented at Royaumont Conference on Experimental Social Psychology.

1974. *On message structure.* London: Wiley.

Scherer, K. R. & Giles, H. (eds.) 1979. *Social markers in speech.* Cambridge: Cambridge University Press.

Taylor, D. M. & Simard, L. 1975. Social interaction in a bilingual setting. *Canadian Psychological Review,* 16, 240–54.

Wundt, W. 1900–20. *Voelkerpsychologie,* vols. 1–10. Leipzig: Engelmann.

2. The role of adult speech in language development

C. G. WELLS and W. P. ROBINSON

1. Introduction

After setting the study of the language development of young children in its immediate historical context, we report and review attempts to describe those characteristics of the speech of adults which are peculiar to their interaction with young children. While the achievement of successful communication appears to be a major reason why adults make such adjustments, it is not the sole reason. Regardless of the nature of these reasons, we can ask about the consequences for children's learning. Although only a very small number of experiments have been conducted to show how adult speech might relate to children's language development, a growing body of naturalistic studies has achieved some success in demonstrating correlations between maternal behaviour on the one hand and the quality and rate of children's language development upon the other.

These results from investigations of individual differences are consistent with those that used socially based differences as the point of departure. Socio-economic status (SES) is exploited to illustrate this consistency. SES differences in maternal ways of answering children's questions, regulating their behaviour and instructing them how to play games are shown to be associated with predictable differences in the speech performance and learning of children. These studies have been carried through to demonstrations of within-SES co-variation between mothers and children.

Action-oriented research with socially disadvantaged and mentally retarded children provides further data requiring integration with the more academically oriented studies reviewed in the earlier sections of this chapter. While some of the action-oriented researchers have explicitly acknowledged their commitment to Skinnerian principles of learning for the construction and implementation of their programmes, academic researchers have been reluctant to comment upon the theories of child development and learning which might explain how and why some kinds of adult interaction may be more facilitative than others for children's language development. In the concluding section we note that these issues have to be faced and offer some comments upon that almost taboo topic.

The last twenty years have seen vigorous activity in the study of children's linguistic development – a hurrying and scurrying initially set in motion by the exciting possibilities that the new, transformational theory of grammar (Chomsky 1959, 1965) seemed to offer of being able to chart and explain the course of that development. Approached within this framework, the study of language development was restricted to the acquisition of syntax and morphology, and transformational rather than other types of rule became the major focus of attention. Wonder was expressed both at the abstractness and complexity of the rules that the child was credited with acquiring and at the short space of two or three years in which this remarkable feat was accomplished (McNeill 1966). With classical conditioning, instrumental conditioning and learning by imitation rejected as incapable of explaining how a normal speaker/hearer comes to be able to produce and comprehend an indefinitely large number of new, but grammatically acceptable, sentences, there seemed to be no alternative but to attribute a central role in development to the Language Acquisition Device (LAD) – i.e. to an innate endowment of knowledge of linguistic universals. Equipped in this way, the child only needed to have his LAD triggered by speech in his environment to learn the particular human language to which he was exposed (Lenneberg 1967). The precise characteristics of this speech – the Primary Linguistic Data – were considered to be unimportant.

By the end of the 1960s, however, the initial enthusiasm had begun to waver and during the 1970s a rather different – though less clearly defined – picture of language development gradually emerged, one which is based upon a much broader definition of language and of the factors that affect its development. Nevertheless, it would probably still be true to say that Chomsky's hypothesized innate LAD has been the single most important influence on the study of child language during this period, firstly as a radical alternative to behaviourist explanations, such as those sketched by Mowrer (1960) and Skinner (1957), and then subsequently as a powerful stimulus to empirical investigations designed to test the arguments upon which the proposal for LAD was based.

An early constructive reaction was heard as early as 1966 when, in discussing McNeill's (1966) exposition of the role of LAD, Donaldson suggested that the similarities found between children from different linguistic communities in the types of structured utterances that they first produce at about the age of 18 months need not result from the application of innate knowledge of syntactic universals, but might be based upon the cognitive schemata that develop universally as a result of the characteristic types of interaction that take place between the human infant and his environment during what Piaget has called the sensori-motor stage of intellectual development (Donaldson 1966). The argument for the cognitive basis of language development has been subsequently developed by Macnamara (1972) and Slobin (1973). Brown, also, having reviewed the available evidence from studies conducted on children learning a variety of languages, concluded that 'the first meanings [to be expressed] are an extension of the kind of intelligence that Jean Piaget calls sensori-motor' (Brown 1973: 198).[1]

The definition of the end-state of learning as grammatical competence also came under attack from those, such as Hymes, who pointed out that the knowledge that the child was acquiring included knowledge of when, where and how to speak and of how to produce utterances that, as well as being well-formed, were appropriate to the context in which they were uttered – in fact 'communicative competence' (Hymes 1972). This line of research has been developed in some detail by Ervin-Tripp (1973) and Bates (1976). Going still further, Halliday (1977) rejected the competence–performance distinction altogether, arguing instead for a view of language as 'resource' – a 'potential for behaviour' – and it is in terms of increasing potential for meaning that he describes his own child's language development (Halliday 1975b).

If language is behaviour, however, it is a particular kind of behaviour,

---

[1] To be fair to Chomsky, he had never suggested that the 'faculty of language' was isolated from other cognitive faculties: 'we do not, of course, imply that the functions of language acquisition are carried out by entirely separate components of the abstract mind or the physical brain . . . In fact, it is an important problem for psychology to determine to what extent other aspects of cognition share properties of language acquisition and language use' (1965: 207, n. 32). However, the relative insignificance that he seems to attach to factors other than syntactic knowledge is indicated by the following passage from the main body of the text: 'That the latter [evidence from language] is a prerequisite for language acquisition seems to follow from the widely accepted (but, for the moment, quite unsupported) view that there must be a partially semantic basis for the acquisition of syntax or for the justification of hypotheses about the syntactic component of a grammar. Incidentally, it is often not realized how strong a claim this is about the innate concept-forming abilities of the child and the system of linguistic universals that these abilities imply' (ibid.: 32).

which typically occurs in interpersonal interaction, with communication as its goal. Chomsky has resolutely refused to accept communication as the 'essential function' of language (e.g. Chomsky 1976), but the importance of prelinguistic interpersonal communication as the nexus from which language develops has become very apparent from the work of Trevarthen (1974) and Stern (1977), on early mother–child interaction, and of Bruner (1975) and Carter (1974) on communication at the end of the child's first year. In the second year, as Halliday (1975b), Dore (1975) and Wells (1975) have all shown, the function, or illocutionary force, of the one-word or early structured utterance is more salient than its propositional content, and shows a continuous development from the socially and pragmatically effective communicative behaviours of the prelinguistic period.

With the recognition of the importance of the conversational context in which language development takes place has come a need to examine more carefully the contribution of the other participant in the conversation, typically the mother, father or other caretaker, and considerable attention is now being given to the structure of early conversation. Dore, Gearhart & Newman (1978), for example, have drawn upon speech act theory (Searle 1969, 1975) to characterize nursery school conversation, whilst Garvey (1977) and Wootton (1981) have, in their different ways, employed the approach of the conversational analysts to describe particular features of adult–child conversation. Wells, Montgomery & MacLure (1979) and Wells, MacLure & Montgomery (1981) have combined both these approaches in their attempts to describe adult–child conversation systematically, and to investigate the different kinds of opportunity for learning that different styles of conversation provide.

Interest in adult speech to children did not have to wait for the emergence of conversationally oriented studies, however. Already in the late 1960s and early 1970s a number of studies had been undertaken in order to test the validity of some of the claims made by the innatists about the insignificance of the child's linguistic environment for his language development. In arguing for a 'rich' innate LAD, Chomsky (1965) repeatedly stressed the deficiency of the primary linguistic data to which the child was exposed. Not only was it presumed to be restricted in scope – a small and random selection of the potentially infinite number of sentences in the language – but it was also 'degenerate' – containing many deviant expressions, false starts, hesitations and other performance degradations. Making the same point in commenting on work in child language, Chomsky (1964) appealed to tape recordings of the speech of participants at a conference to support his contention. The first studies of adult input, therefore, were essentially descriptive, carried out to show that, by comparison with normal speech between adults, the speech addressed to children was, on the whole, well-formed, simple and semantically highly redundant, and thus well adapted to the needs of the language learner.

As will be seen in the next section, these aims were convincingly achieved. But that, in itself, does not seriously weaken Chomsky's argument. As he points out, these primary linguistic data may play either or both of two roles (in addition to that of determining which language the child will learn): they may have the function of initiating or facilitating the operation of the innate LAD or, once the process has been triggered, that of influencing the direction that learning takes. To demonstrate that adult input is well adapted to the learner's requirements may be relevant for a consideration of the first of these roles, but does not have any necessary bearing on the second. 'It would not be at all surprising,' he argues, 'to find that normal language learning requires use of language in real-life situations, in some way. But this, if true, would not be sufficient to show that information regarding situational context . . . plays any role in determining how language is acquired, once the mechanism is put to work and the task of language learning is undertaken by the child' (1965: 33). In addition to demonstrating the adaptedness of adult speech to children, it is still necessary, therefore, to show that presence or absence of some (or all) of its characteristic features affects the course of development. And even if that can be achieved, there remains the still more difficult task of providing an account of *how* this effect is achieved.

The first major part of this chapter will consider each of these issues in turn. In the second major part we examine the contribution to them of studies of socio-economic status differences and special educational programmes.

2. The characteristics of adult speech to young children

Interest in the modifications that adults introduce into their speech when addressing young children is not just a recent phenomenon. Ferguson (1977) makes reference to written observations dating as far back as the first century B.C. But until the late 1960s the interest was largely of an anthropological kind and not concerned directly with the question of the role of such modified speech for the language learning child. However, from these earlier studies, it became clear that Baby Talk (BT) is a widespread and possibly universal phenomenon and that the ways in which it differs from speech amongst adults show considerable cross-linguistic similarity.

The use of special lexical items, e.g. *bunny* for *rabbit*, the simplification of words judged to be difficult to pronounce, e.g. *tummy* for *stomach* and syllable reduplication (e.g. *gee-gee*) are perhaps the most obvious features of BT but, as recent studies have shown, systematic modifications are to be found at all linguistic levels. The following are some of the most-well documented features:

1. *Manner of delivery.* BT is slower than normal speech (Broen 1972; Drach 1969; Sachs, Brown & Salerno 1976), generally more fluent (Broen 1972; Remick 1976) and clearly pronounced (cf. Ferguson 1977 for cross-linguistic discussion).

2. *Formal simplicity.* Utterances addressed to young children are typically shorter than those addressed to other adults (Drach 1969; Fraser & Roberts 1975; Phillips 1970, 1973; Snow 1972) and syntactically simpler. This latter characteristic has been assessed in a variety of ways, including pre-verb length (Snow 1972), complexity of verb phrase (Phillips 1970, 1973; Remick 1976; Sachs et al. 1976) and percentage of complex sentences (Drach 1969; Phillips 1970, 1973; Sachs et al. 1976; Snow 1972).

3. *Prosody.* BT has been found to be generally higher in pitch than speech to older children or adults, and to make greater use of the pitch range, particularly the upper end (Garnica 1977; Remick 1976). The impression is thus of an exaggerated use of intonation. Garnica (1977) also found a greater than usual use of rising tones.

4. *Semantic simplicity and redundancy.* Utterances in BT tend to be restricted to the small set of semantic relations that children themselves express in their earliest utterances (Snow 1977a); they are also lexically restricted (as assessed by type–token ratio) (Broen 1972; Drach 1969; Phillips 1970; Remick 1976). There is much repetition of words, phrases and whole utterances (Ferrier 1978; Kobashigawa 1969; Snow 1972) and topics tend to be restricted to events in which the participants are engaged or to perceptible features of the immediate situation (Moerk 1972; Phillips 1970). BT thus tends to be highly redundant in context.

5. *Function.* Speech to young children has been found to contain a high proportion of imperatives and interrogatives and a relatively low proportion of declaratives (Drach 1969; Sachs et al. 1976; Snow 1972). From this it may be inferred that a high proportion of such speech has the

pragmatic function of controlling and directing the child's behaviour and of sustaining the interaction.

The majority of the studies cited above involved speakers of English, but in an earlier work, Ferguson (1964) had gathered together findings on BT, in six languages, and more recently several of the findings discussed above have been replicated in studies of various other languages, including Berber (Bynon 1977), Latvian (Rūķe-Draviņa 1977) and Luo and Samoan (Blount 1972). Studies of languages other than English have also shown that the use of BT is not restricted to mothers – as the alternative term for the same register, 'motherese', might seem to suggest – but is found to varying extents in the speech of all caretakers (Blount 1977a, b). However, where the speech of fathers and mothers has been compared for American English-speaking families, some differences have been found which suggest that fathers make fewer adjustments in the direction of BT (Berko Gleason & Weintraub 1978), but this is confounded with the different roles that fathers, as compared with mothers, tend to adopt in interacting with their children (Engle 1980).

Older children have also been found to modify their speech in ways similar to adults when talking to younger children. Anderson & Johnson (1973) found that an 8-year-old girl, talking to an adult and to younger children aged 5 and 3 years and 18 months, showed a progressive decrease in syntactic complexity and an increase in pitch with decreasing age of the addressee. Indeed, systematic modification has been found in children as young as 4 years: Shatz & Gelman (1973) observed sixteen 4 year olds talking to 2 year olds and to adults in two different situations, and in both situations their speech to 2 year olds was shorter, simpler and more repetitive than that to adults.

From these studies it can be concluded with some confidence that all mature speakers, and even relatively immature ones, will employ some of the features of BT when interacting with young children, although which features are selected and the extent of the modification depends on specific characteristics of the interaction. Age and status of the person interacting with the young child have already been mentioned as important determinants. The characteristics of the activity in which the participants are engaged have also been shown to be influential. Snow, summarizing a number of studies in which these were varied, concludes that 'task difficulty has little effect on mothers' speech, but kind of activity has a large effect' (1977a: 36). In particular, 'mothering' activities tend to elicit simpler speech than others, whilst the most complex speech occurs in the context of looking at a book together. The gender of the child has also been found to be a significant variable. Cherry & Lewis (1978) found that (American) mothers tend to interact differently with boys and girls, acknowledging more of the girls' utterances and addressing more and longer utterances to them. Girls were also asked more questions whilst boys received more utterances with a directive function.

However, most strongly associated with changes in the use of BT is the stage of development of the child being addressed (Cross 1977; Ellis & Wells 1980). Phillips (1973) found that the full range of BT features did not occur in mothers' speech until the children themselves began to speak, and Snow (1977b), although not finding such sharp changes in length and complexity at the onset of speech in the children she studied, did find changes in the content and function of maternal utterances at a rather earlier age. She interpreted these results in terms of the mothers' perception of a change in the sorts of conversation it was possible to have with their children. This interpretation is corroborated by Bingham (1971), who found that mothers would adopt a characteristic BT style even before their infants began to speak, if they believed that the infants were cognitively advanced and able to understand more than they were yet able to express.

3. Baby talk as a response to characteristics of the child

From these various studies it is clear that BT consists of a complex of features which, rather than being used in an all-or-nothing fashion, are adjusted in relation to the child's increasing maturity. What is it about the child that signals the density of BT that is appropriate? Apparent age is no doubt a rough guide for unfamiliar adults, since within particular cultures there are social expectations about the capabilities of children at different stages of development, with consequent implications for appropriate adult behaviours (Grimshaw 1977). These can be very different from one culture to another. Blount (1972), for example, found that Luo and Samoan children received very little speech from their parents of a form that suggested they were treated as equal conversational partners; black children in the United States, by contrast, were consulted much more about what they wanted and generally received speech that indicated they were considered much more as conversational equals.

Age-related status is by no means the only factor that influences adult speech, however. Within an English-speaking culture, at least, there is considerable evidence that the form of BT that is used occurs as a response to the characteristics of the particular child being addressed, rather than as a response to the stereotype 'ideal' of a child of a particular age. In a comparison made by Snow (1972) between the speech of mothers addressing children who were physically present and that of mothers imagining they were addressing children of the same age, the presence of the children actually reacting to the mothers' speech was found to elicit a simpler and more redundant speech style. It seems, therefore, that the children themselves provide many of the cues that others use in deciding how to speak to them.

One obvious cue is the speech of the children themselves. Several of the features of BT have been found to vary quite systematically with increasing maturity of children's production, such as average length and formal complexity (Ellis & Wells 1980) and the range of semantic relations expressed (Snow 1977a). However, the relationship between adult speech and the children's level of comprehension appears to be even stronger and applies to discourse features as well. Indeed, on the basis of a study of the speech addressed to a group of rapidly developing children aged between 19 and 32 months, Cross (1977) concluded that, in many respects, the speech of these mothers was quite 'finely-tuned' to their children's receptive abilities, as measured by a series of comprehension items that were interspersed in the conversation.

Studies such as those just cited draw their conclusions from correlations between the frequencies of certain BT features in adult speech and measures of the children's communicative abilities. As a result, they might be taken to imply that adults make a global adjustment to their children's level of development. But such an interpretation is far too static. Finely tuned adult speech does not consist of utterances which are uniformly simple in form and semantically redundant. Rather it is influenced by the particular purpose of the interaction and the context of activity in which it occurs and is characterized by a dynamic utterance-by-utterance adjustment to the communicative demands of the conversation, as these are assessed on the basis of the continuous feedback that the adult receives in the form of the child's behaviour, both verbal and non-verbal. The result is that the density of BT features varies from utterance to utterance, oscillating around a mean which changes as a function of the particular context and of the child's gradually increasing ability to participate fully in the interaction. This can be seen in the following extracts from conversations between Gerald and his mother. (See Appendix for meanings of symbols in extracts.)

Extract 1
Gerald (18 months) has found a box which is used as Teddy's bed.
Gerald: Teddy(v)
　　　 Teddy(v)

| | Mother: | That's Teddy's bed isn't it?
Where's Teddy?
I think Teddy's downstairs
I think we took him down with us |

Gerald:　A box
　　　 A box

| | Mother: | A box yes
Teddy's bed isn't it?
Wait a minute
Let's go and see if we can find Teddy |

Extract 2
Gerald (21 months) is helping Mother make a soufflé.

| | Mother: | D'you want to grease the pan for me? |

Gerald:　Grease
　　　 Grease ə pan

| | Mother: | Do you? |

Gerald:　Grease ə pan

| | Mother: | Here it is
You grease the pan then
Roll that bit of butter round it for me
Roll it round and round
All over the pan

. .

Give me that
　　　　　　　[M. takes the whisk]
That's it |

Gerald:　No eating (= it's
　　　　　not for eating)
　　　 No eating

| | Mother: | No, not for eating
It's not very nice to eat neat
　　　　margarine or whatever |

Gerald:　Marg.ine

| | Mother: | You rub it
You rub it round and round
That's it |

Extract 3
Gerald (24 months) is climbing in and out of a cardboard box.

Gerald: I am boxing with Teddy
          (= I am getting into
          the box with Teddy)

                              Mother: (laughs)
                                        You don't quite fit in – both of you in
                                            that little box

                    (some minutes interruption)

Gerald: Mummy(v)
          <Where's Gerald?>
                              Mother: Hello Gerald
                                        What are you doing?

Gerald: This
              * *
          This are –
          This one's broken
                              Mother: Yes it is
                                        That's right

Gerald: Teddy's broken this box

                              Mother: I don't know if Teddy broke it
                                        I should think that it's you getting in
                                            that was the final straw

                                        That's what I should think
                                        It broke in the end because Gerald
                                            got in
                                        Don't you think?

Gerald: Like a house
          (= it's like a house)
                              Mother: It is like a house

4. The motivation for adults' speech adjustments

It is sometimes suggested, at least by parents, that their reason for using
BT is to teach their children to talk. Certainly some conversational sequences seem expressly designed to this end, in particular 'what's that?'
routines when looking at a picture book or set of toys. Brown long ago
remarked that 'the most deliberate part of first-language teaching is the

business of telling a child what each thing is called' (1958: 14) and more recently Ninio & Bruner (1978) have emphasized the collaborative nature of these ritualized dialogues, concluding that such routines are the major mechanism through which labelling is achieved.

However at no stage is labelling the most frequent function of adult speech to children; moreover, although important, it is only one aspect of language use that children have to learn. Whether other aspects of language, such as phonological and grammatical structure, are to be viewed as being deliberately taught will depend on what is to be counted as 'teaching'. Certainly, if 'teaching' is defined as deliberate and systematic instruction, then most adult speech does not meet this criterion. It might nevertheless be argued that the simplification of adult speech that has been reported in most studies of BT does serve a teaching function, even though it may not be produced with that intention in mind. Newport, Gleitman & Gleitman (1977), however, were not convinced that the sort of speech they observed mothers to produce was simple in the way in which a teaching curriculum might be expected to be; neither did they find compelling evidence 'that mothers tune their syntactic complexity to the growing language competence of their children through [the] crucial age of syntax acquisition, the period from one to two and a half years' (1977: 123–4). Furrow, Nelson & Benedict (1979), on the other hand, found that on a number of syntactic measures adult speech did increase in complexity with the child's developing maturity, and they conclude that 'motherese' is, in fact, an effective teaching language.

However, like most other researchers, they do not attribute to adult users of BT an intention actually to teach language. Much more probable is that the formal simplicity of BT is an outcome of parents' attempts to achieve successful communication by modifying the encoding of their intentions in order to make them more readily intelligible to conversational partners who are severely limited in what they can understand, both linguistically and cognitively. If the typical form of adult speech to children does spring from an intention to teach them, it is probably from the adults' intention to help the child to explore and understand the world of objects and events which he shares with them; and one part of this undoubtedly involves learning how language is mapped on to the categories and relations which provide the structure for his non-linguistic experience.

Certainly such an explanation could account for many of the characteristics of BT that have been reported in the earlier part of this chapter. For example, Snow's (1977a) finding that the majority of adult utterances to 2 to 3 year olds are restricted to the meaning relations that are the first to be expressed by children is one form of simplification that could be explained in these terms; the relatively lower number of contractions, copulas, pronouns and verbs that Furrow, Nelson & Benedict (1979) found in the speech addressed to 18-month-old, as opposed to 27-month-old, children, would be another. Similarly, the higher incidence of repetitions in the speech to less advanced children could be explained as being triggered by their greater lack of understanding (Berko Gleason 1977), whilst the increase, with age, in the proportion of utterances referring to objects and events outside the immediate context of utterance (Cross 1977; Ellis & Wells 1980) could be related to their developing understanding of the world of experience beyond the here-and-now. Furthermore, since, from this point of view, it is children's receptive, rather than their productive, ability that is seen as influencing the speech that adults address to them, further support for this explanation is found in Cross's (1977) finding that it was with children's comprehension that the variables in adult speech were most strongly related.

Somewhat more direct evidence for the primacy of the goal of successful communication as the determinant of many of the features of BT comes from Garnica's (1977) study, which is one of the few that have actually investigated adults' reasons for adopting this register when addressing young children. Rather than speculate about motives, she asked the mothers in her study whether they were aware of modifying their speech when addressing their children and, if so, why they thought they made those modifications. Two groups of mothers were involved, twelve with 2-year-old and twelve with 5-year-old children. The questions were put to the mothers after they had carried out three tasks, first with the investigator and then with their own children. Garnica's interest was in certain prosodic and paralinguistic aspects of these mothers' speech, and the questions to them were also angled in this direction. Nevertheless, the answers they gave would probably also apply to other features of BT. The mothers of the 2 year olds all reported being aware of modifying their speech in terms of slower pace, higher pitch and expanded pitch range, particularly when trying to gain their children's attention. They believed that they modified their speech in these ways because it made their communication with their children more effective. Of the second group of mothers, whose children were 5 years old, all those who were aware of making modifications reported that they introduced the features in question in specific situations, most commonly when they were experiencing, or were likely to experience, difficulty in communicating with their children. All the subjects agreed that the most effective means of gaining a child's attention was to change one's voice so that it would contrast with the ongoing level of speech.

There is thus a considerable amount of evidence (albeit much of it indirect) for the view that BT takes the form it does as a result of adults' attempts to be understood by less mature conversational partners. If this explanation is correct, then it follows that modifications that lead to more successful communication are also modifications that lead to 'primary data' from which it may be easier for children to learn. In this sense it would be the case, as Snow (1972) suggests, that BT 'in many ways seems quite well designed as a set of "language lessons"' (quoted in Ferguson 1977: 233).

Important though the desire to be understood may be, as a determinant of the way in which adults talk to young language learners, it is not a complete explanation, because it ignores other important aspects of communication – notably the part that the child contributes to the interaction. Some of the features of BT almost certainly have their origin in the adults' attempts to elicit conversational contributions from the child and to support and extend those contributions that are forthcoming, so that both participants can experience the satisfaction of jointly constructing sequences of interaction. This is certainly one of the chief characteristics of maternal behaviour when the infant is in the prelinguistic stage, where the aim seems to be to establish intersubjectivity of awareness, first with respect to the parties in the interaction, and then to the objects and events in their immediate environment (Stern 1977; Trevarthen & Hubley 1978). Naturally, at this stage, the infant's repertoire of contributions is severely limited, but both Stern and Trevarthen stress the importance of the mother being both responsive to the infant's initiatives and sensitive to his lead in the timing and intensity of the unfolding interaction. At a somewhat later stage, as Bruner has shown, adults use routine situations of joint activity, such as bath-time, or playing with mechanical toys, to provide a scaffolding within which the young child can learn to play his part in building up sequences of interaction and discover the significance of his contributions from the feedback that he receives within these familiar routines (Bruner 1975, 1978; Ratner & Bruner 1978).

Features of BT that seem to perform a somewhat similar function when the child has begun to talk are the high frequency of imitations, expansions and extensions of the child's preceding utterance (Cross 1977), and the use of questions, tags and high pitch to encourage the child to make a further contribution (Wells, MacLure & Montgomery 1981). The following example illustrates many of these features as the mother sustains and develops the child's ostensive initiation.

Extract 4
Mark (23 months) can see some birds in the garden.

Mark: 13' /ɛəæt/ (= look at that)
         23' Birds / 34 'Mummy(v)

                    Mother: 213 'Mm

Mark: 23 'Jubs (= birds)

                    Mother: What are they 34 'doing?

Mark: Jubs 13 'bread

                    Mother: Oh 213 'look
                               They're 343 'eating the 12 'berries /
                               14 'aren't they?

Mark: 24 'Yeh

                    Mother: 2 'That's their 213 'food
                               They have 343 'berries / for 23 'dinner

Mark: 24 'Oh

                                        (from Wells 1981)

Finally, we should not ignore the extent to which the characteristics of adult speech are determined by the restrictions on the range of activities in which the child can participate by virtue of his physical immaturity. This goes quite a long way to explaining the limited vocabulary used by adults, and hence the high type–token ratio. It may also provide a partial explanation for the restricted range of semantic relations in adult speech (Snow 1977a). It is interesting to note that, whilst supporting Snow's findings in broad outline, Wells (in preparation) found that the relative frequency of expression of these meaning relations is not constant over the period covered by Brown's (1973) Stages I–III. Different meanings reach their highest frequency at different points, in some cases before and in others just after the children have shown that they have mastered the expression of the same meaning. No doubt the introduction of new meanings in adult speech in part reflects the adult's estimate of the child's increasing cognitive understanding of his environment, but there is some indication that it also occurs in response to the child's increasing motor co-ordination: the peak in the adults' references to agentively caused change of location, where agent and object are co-referential (e.g. 'going' and 'coming'), occurs soon after the child has mastered upright locomotion, whilst the peak in references to functions such as eating and drinking occurs some time later, when the child is able to perform these functions for himself.

The characteristics of BT thus appear to be multiply determined. As we have seen, some features of BT serve to attract the child's attention, whilst others seem to be designed to make the adult's message easy to understand, once the child's attention has been gained. Yet other characteristics can be accounted for in terms of the need to elicit, and provide feedback to, the child's contributions. However, at the most general level, they can all be explained as occurring in the interests of promoting conversational interaction and as a response to the immaturity of the conversational partner to whom BT is addressed. Furthermore, it has been claimed, these characteristics also have the effect of facilitating the child's mastery of the language system and of the interactive uses to which that system is put. In the following section we shall consider those studies which have attempted to test that claim.

5. Experimental manipulations of adult input

The effects of adult speech adjustments on children's language development have been investigated both experimentally and naturalistically. We shall start by considering the former, in which, by means of small-scale attempts to induce the learning of one or two linguistic units or structures, the emphasis has been on explaining the mechanisms of change rather than on substantially modifying the course of development. To date, these have been few in number, mainly perhaps because the dominating psycholinguistic perspective has had no theory of developmental change associated with it.

In one of the first such studies, Cazden (see 1972 for a published resumé) contrasted the efficacy of syntactic expansion and semantic extension as possible means by which an adult might facilitate language development. Three groups of four black children aged 28–38 months were matched on initial level of language development and assigned to one of three conditions. For forty minutes per working day for three months each utterance of the syntactic expansion group was filled out by a specially trained tutor, e.g. 'Dog bark' was reflected back as 'Yes, the dog is barking.' In the semantic extension group, the child's remarks were followed by utterances that maintained semantic cohesion and elaborated the topic in some way, e.g. 'Yes but he won't bite.' The third, control, group in the same day nursery received no special treatment.

Six linguistic measures were employed to check the effects of the different treatments: Mean Length of Utterance (morphemes), a noun phrase index, complexity of verbal group, a copula index and an index of sentence type. The situation in which these were sampled is not mentioned. Cazden reports that semantic extension was facilitatory and syntactic expansion was not, but for which variables is not stated.

Because this experiment is widely reported and its results occasionally elevated to the status of proving that syntax cannot be taught, it is worth noting some weaknesses in the design. Four children per group places great strain on any statistical test of dissociation: real effects may have been produced which nevertheless went undetected. No measure of completeness of syntax was used as a dependent measure, although any hypothesis of observational learning would have to treat this as the language feature most likely to be influenced. But most serious is the unnatural nature of the treatment. As Brown, Cazden & Bellugi (1969) point out in their discussion of this experiment, where every child utterance is expanded, a certain proportion of the adult utterances is likely to be based on an incorrect interpretation of the child's intention and thus a source of confusion to him rather than a helpful model. The complete absence of new, but related, semantic material in the adult utterances is another reason for considering this form of feedback less than satisfactory. As will be seen below, in the naturalistic studies that have investigated these features of adult speech, it is semantic extension rather than syntactic expansion which has been found to be the more strongly associated with overall child progress – although a combination of the two is better still.

Nelson, Carskaddon & Bonvillian (1973) devised what might be evaluated as a more natural means of achieving syntactic expansion. As well as repeating back syntactically incomplete utterances in their expanded forms, they also recast the syntax of other utterances while preserving semantic content, e.g. creating questions for the child out of his statements. This treatment was administered daily through eleven weeks of sessions in the form of 20-minute conversations about pictures; over 400 recastings were involved. Nine nursery-age children were in the main experimental group. A second comparable group was provided with a similar number of equivalent syntactic forms in the same context, but these were not changed versions of their own utterances; the experimenter's replies excluded content words in the child's preceding utterance, but maintained semantic continuity. A control group from the same day nursery was used as a baseline for comparison on the six language measures used: two measures of MLU, a noun phrase index, verbal phrase elements, verb auxiliaries, and performance on a sentence imitation test. The results pointed to the efficacy of recasting in respect of differential gains on the sentence imitation test and the use of more complex phrases.

Nelson (1977) developed this line of argument further with a recasting treatment applied differentially either to questions or verbs in similar sessions with two groups of children aged 28–29 months, whose spontaneous speech had shown four forms of the kind offered. In the case of questions, the recastings involved tag forms and negatives; in the case of verbs, it involved compound verbs, future tenses and conditionals. While progress on the more general measures did not discriminate between the two groups, each showed some significantly selective progress on the forms for which they had experienced recasting.

These two studies imply both that syntactic development can be facilitated, if appropriate techniques are supplied to appropriate forms, and that recasting is such a technique for the forms and children studied. On the other hand, offering recastings of hypothetical counter-factuals (if it had not been the case that . . .) to children at this stage of development might not have led to their acquisition; similarly, recasting may not be a suitable device for older children or for other features. But that is a question for further investigation.

Nelson & Bonvillian (1978) have also been active in examining treatments that enable children to learn the names of objects which instantiate concepts labelled in adult speech by nouns. Using real words rare in child conversation (*hedgehog*(?), *pulley*) and artificial names (*fiffin*, *wangsop*), they have established that relatively infrequent naming of these objects by mothers can lead to successful naming over six months by 2 year olds. If the maternal naming was restricted to only one exemplar, 19 per cent of the objects and 58 per cent of the concepts could be named, but if two or four were present these figures rose to 43 per cent and 83 per cent respectively; generalization was also greater with more exemplars.

Miller (1977) refers to an unpublished study by Bartlett & Carey in which these authors injected the word *chromium* into one discriminating utterance to each of fourteen 3-year-old children in a nursery classroom. The authors used it as a substitute for *olive* to identify the colour of one of three cups and trays in the room. One week after this, six of the children pointed to the olive chip when asked to point to the 'chromium' one. The authors did not use the word again for five weeks: eight produced a response when asked the colour of an olive chip different from the term they had used before the 'chromium' experience. Subsequent exposure to the word and its consequences suggested the existence of two directions for learning: one group assumed *chromium* was a synonym of *green* and had not 'solved the problem' after 15 weeks, the other achieved comprehension of *chromium* as *olive*, but did not fully master production, even though they occasionally used it spontaneously. What Miller infers is that learning new words may have a quick initial take-up of both its sound and rough semantic domain, followed by an extended period of working out the precise semantics. While in one sense it is necessarily true that if a child does not hear a word, he cannot learn it, it has been suggested that frequency of experience may be irrelevant. What Miller's example and Nelson & Bonvillian perhaps show is that some minimal exposure to appropriate use is both necessary and sufficient, if maintained over time.

Experiments have also been carried out to test the efficacy of elicited imitation as a method of training. Malouf & Dodd (1972), for example, found that the learning of an adjective order syntactic rule by 6- and 7-year old children could be facilitated by both elicited imitation and syntactic expansion, and investigators working with children with varying degrees of mental retardation have constructed whole education programmes for language and other development in which elicited imitation plays a central role (see below). The efficacy of imitation was studied by Ruder, Smith & Hermann (1974) who attempted to evaluate the differential efficacy of imitation and comprehension procedures in the teaching of Spanish nouns. Imitation training required repetition of the word said. Comprehension training consisted of the child pointing to one of three pictures after hearing the word. Neither procedure in itself led to successful production of the words in response to the relevant pictures. When the procedures were switched for half of the items from each set, comprehension following imitation was ineffectual, but imitiation following comprehension led to rapid success. The authors draw the conservative conclusion that training which includes both imitation and comprehension is required to achieve production.

Whitehurst (1974) has also argued that what he calls delayed selective imitation can play a role in the mastery of syntactic structures. Pointing to the narrowness and strictness of the definition of 'imitation' sometimes employed and noting that the young child might not reveal his learning for days (or even weeks), he devised a short training in the comprehension of indirect–direct object sentences for 4 year olds who did not understand these initially. Elicited imitation with corrective feedback sufficed to enable children to use this construction productively in subsequent descriptions of similar but different pictures.

Investigators working with children of varying degrees of mental retardation have generally concentrated their efforts into the construction of whole educational programmes for language and other development, but some experiments that attend to the learning processes themselves have also been reported.

Elicited imitations with correcting feedback have been used with mentally retarded children to equip them with well-articulated phonemes (Baer, Peterson & Sherman 1967), the plural morpheme (Baer & Guess 1973; Guess et al. 1968), past tense morphology (Schumaker & Sherman 1970), phonic reading capacity (Lovitt & Hurlbut 1974), unreversed letters in writing (Smith & Lovitt 1973) and accuracy in spelling (Lovitt, Guppy & Blattner 1965).

What these studies show is that specific training procedures can be effective in bringing about learning of specific linguistic forms or features by children with the developmental characteristics investigated. Whether or not the learning achieved by means of these procedures transfers into the everyday speech of the children concerned is, of course, a different question – and no evidence has been presented to show such generalization – but it does not affect the issue of the learning itself or of the potential relevance of the training procedures used. Similarly, from the fact that everyday life provides a much messier environment than the conditions of the laboratory, it does not follow that principles of imitation, feedback or reinforcement are either irrelevant or unimportant. Indeed Clark & Clark (1977) have recently put forward a strong case for the importance of spontaneously occurring imitations and, as will be seen below, expansions and extensions – which can be seen as forms of feedback and reinforcement – have been found by several investigators to be associated with children's differential rates of learning.

Nevertheless, because the unscheduled nature of spontaneous conversation more or less precludes the possibility of testing hypotheses about the learning of specific features of language, observational studies have tended to investigate rather different questions, such as: do features of BT, as they occur in spontaneous conversation, have a significant effect on children's rate of language development and, if so, which features are of most importance? It is to a consideration of these 'naturalistic' investigations that we shall now turn.

6. Naturalistic studies of the effects of BT

From the naturalistic studies already discussed, it might be supposed that, as well as being universal, BT was experienced very similarly by all children. If this were so, it would not be possible to answer the question just posed on the basis of such studies. However, this is certainly not the case. Not only are there substantial differences between cultures in the beliefs that are held about appropriate ways of talking to young children (Ferguson 1964) and in the way in which the caretaking role is allocated (Blount 1972), but there are also quite large individual differences between caretakers within particular cultures in the ways in which they fulfil this role with respect to their style of linguistic interaction. Furthermore, as we have seen, there is variation over time in response to the child's growing competence as a communicator.

By comparing the speech addressed to individual children, or groups of children, and relating such differences as emerge to differences in the children's learning, it is possible to identify those features of BT which are most strongly associated with children's progress and thus prima facie candidates for consideration as facilitative of the learning process. Research on this issue has so far been restricted to within-group variation with respect to children learning English – largely, no doubt, due to the difficulty of comparing progress across different languages – and has been mainly concerned with the speech of mothers when their children are at the two- and three-word stage of development. In addition, children's progress has been defined almost exclusively in formal terms, being measured on such parameters as Mean Length of Utterance (MLU), ratio of verbs or noun phrases per utterance, inflections per noun phrase and so on. Comprehension of the speech addressed to them or the purposes for which they were using language have received much less attention. Despite these limitations, however, the results of the four studies that have so far been published are of considerable interest both for their substantive findings and for the methodological issues that they raise. (See table 1 for a summary of the results to be discussed.)

The first study to be considered here was carried out by Newport et al. (1977) with fifteen mother–daughter pairs, all middle class. Two naturalistic observations were made six months apart, and at the time of the first observation the children fell into three age groups: 12–15 months, 18–21 months, and 24–27 months. Children's progress over the six-month period was measured in terms of gain on five syntactic variables of the kind described above, and this was correlated with a number of variables in the mothers' speech at the first observation, based on a segment of approximately 100 utterances.

Influenced by the controversy surrounding the claims made for innate knowledge of linguistic universals, which were discussed in the first section of this chapter, Newport et al. (1977) focused mainly on formal features of mothers' speech, asking whether this particular register constituted 'a very carefully circumscribed kind of data, presented to the child selectively in correspondence with his language growth' (p. 111). The features coded fell into four categories: degree of well-formedness; sentence complexity (calculated as MLU and sentence nodes per utterance); sentence type (declarative, imperative, etc.); and the two discourse features of expansion and self-repetition. The frequency of utterances in each of these categories was expressed as a percentage of total utterances. As Newport et al. were aware, however, the results of simple correlational analysis of the mothers' speech variables with the measures of the children's progress were misleading, as they were the result of two distinct kinds of variation: the general 'tuning' of maternal speech to the child's level of development, and the individual variation between mothers in the way in which they realized their tuning. Accordingly, a further partial correlational analysis was carried out to control for the child's age and level of development at the time of the first observation. The main results of this second analysis are shown in table 1.

As can be seen, variation on those parameters of mothers' speech that were investigated were not found, in general, to be significantly related to the children's progress, with the exception of the increased frequency of auxiliaries per verb phrase, which was positively associated with the proportional frequency of polar interrogatives in mothers' speech ($p < 0.001$) and negatively associated with the frequency of imperatives ($p < 0.05$) and maternal self-repetitions ($p < 0.05$). On the basis of these results, the authors conclude that there is little evidence that mothers' speech is a well-designed teaching language, finely tuned in its syntactic complexity to the developing competence of their children. On the contrary, they find that the broad range of children's linguistic skills develop under 'diffuse environmental conditions', progress being largely attributable to the 'universal properties of human communication systems'. Only those structures 'that are uniquely rendered in the surface forms of English (elements of the auxiliary, the inflection of noun-phrases) are sensitive to delicate variations in mothers' style' (Newport et al. 1977: 135).

Such a sweeping conclusion may, however, be unwarranted, for at least two reasons: first, the use of the statistical technique of double partial correlation to overcome an inappropriate research design reduces the likelihood of finding significant relationships even when they exist. Secondly, and more importantly, the range of variables in mothers' speech that was investigated may have failed to include those that are most strongly associated with the children's progress. Such was the view of the second group of investigators, who also focused on syntactic features in mothers' speech.

In order to control for the effect of the children's stage of development on the speech addressed to them by their mothers, Furrow et al. (1979) selected the seven children in their study so that they were all at the one-word stage and aged 18 months. The children's progress was measured after 9 months, by taking their scores on four of the same syntactic variables used by Newport et al.; mothers' speech, however, was analysed in more detail, with particular attention being given to the various types of polar interrogative (subject–auxiliary inversion; tag questions; and questions realized by rising intonation) and to such indices of syntactic complexity as the percentage frequency per utterance of main verbs, copula verbs, pronouns, contractions, etc. For both adult and child variables, the data base consisted of 100 utterances. Simple correlations were calculated between the adult and child variables and the results are shown in table 1.

The picture that emerges from this investigation is very different from that found by Newport et al. In this case, nearly half of the twenty-one mothers' speech variables originally included in the analysis were significantly associated with one or more of the measures of the children's progress. Of these, five were negative associations and four were positive. From these results they conclude that 'the role of the linguistic environment in language development is clear; it must be considered a significant contributor to all aspects of the language learning process' (Furrow et al.: 435). For children of this age and stage of development 'those aspects of motherese which reflect the use of a simpler communicative style were positively related to language growth, while the use of a more complex style was associated with relatively slower child language development' (ibid.: 436).

Taken in an absolute sense, however, this conclusion must be false: if mothers reduced their communicative style to the simplest possible form, they would not provide their children with an adequate model from which to learn. Clearly, the finding is relative to the variation existing within this particular sample of mother–child pairs, which it will be

Table 1. Comparison of published studies[a]

Adult variables[b]	MLU			Verb/Utt.			Aux/VP			NP/Utt.		Rate	
	Newport	Furrow	Wells	Newport	Furrow	Wells	Newport	Furrow	Wells	Newport	Furrow	Cross	Wells
Length and complexity													
MLU	0.14		0.29	0.38		0.16	0.34		0.19	0.22		N>A	F>S
Difference Ch.–Ad. MLU	0.37	-0.53	0.40*			0.19			0.13			N>A	F>S
Propositions/Utterance			0.11	0.05	-0.60	0.02	0.21	-0.55	0.19		-0.46	n.d.	n.d.
Utterance/Turn			0.51**			0.35*			0.46**			N>A*	F>S**
Verbs/Utterance		-0.71**	0.21		-0.78*	0.01		-0.66	-0.02		-0.55		n.d.
Copula/Utterance		-0.85**	-0.17		-0.90**	0.16		-0.58	0.15		-0.77**		S>F
Pronoun/Utterance		-0.75*			-0.81*			-0.58			-0.62		
Sentence type													
Declarative	0.10	-0.25	-0.15	-0.16	-0.28	0.02	0.25	-0.03	-0.18	0.02	-0.22	N>A	S>F
Imperative	-0.38	0.06	-0.17	-0.29	0.02	0.04	-0.55*	-0.47	-0.20	0.19	0.34	N>A	F>S
Wh-interrogative	-0.29	-0.37	-0.26	-0.02	-0.33	-0.15	-0.36	-0.30	0.07	-0.24	-0.48	A>N	S>F
Polar interrogative (Total)	0.50	0.72*	0.30	0.35	0.64	0.25	0.88***	0.85**	0.49**	0.16	0.58	A>N	F>S
Aux. inversion		0.14	0.26		0.08	0.21		0.48	0.34		-0.01	N>A	F>S
Tag question			0.03			0.21			0.27			A>N	n.d.
Other polar inter- rogatives		0.77*	0.22		0.74*	0.02		0.72*	0.26		0.69*	A>N	F>S**
Moodless	0.42	0.57	-0.05	-0.08	0.67*	-0.12	0.53	0.64	0.04	0.11	0.43	N>A	F>S
Deictic	0.13			-0.12			-0.09			-0.08			
Locus of reference[c]													
Adult & child activity			0.33			0.12			0.28				F>S**
Third party			-0.26			0.07			0.03			N>A	S>F
Non-immediate event			0.09			-0.07			-0.24			N>A	S>F

Topic incorporation[c]								
Imitation	0.23	0.40*	0.03	0.27	0.51	0.25	−0.16	A>N*	F>S
Expansion		0.30		0.38*		0.18		A>N*	F>S
Total extension		0.42*		0.37*		0.31		A>N	F>S
Extend topic NP		0.47**		0.47**		0.30		A>N	F>S**
Extend activity		0.47**		0.34		0.29			F>S*
Contrast topic		0.47**		0.47**		0.37*			F>S**
Expansion & extension		0.41*		0.39*		0.30		A>N**	F>S
Unrelated		0.31		0.40*		0.08		N>A**	F>S
Stock utterances		0.40*		0.34		0.20		N>A	F>S
Adult repetition		0.15		0.20		0.04		A>N	F>S
Adult paraphrase		0.34		0.44*		0.21		N>A	F>S**
Total adult repetition	−0.50	0.26	−0.05	0.32	−0.58*	0.18	−0.27	A>N	F>S

Significance levels:
* $p<0.05$ ** $p<0.01$ *** $p<0.001$

Rate:
N = normal
A = accelerated
F = faster
S = slower
n.d. = no difference

[a] The published studies referred to are:
Newport et al. 1977
Furrow et al. 1979
Wells 1980b
Cross 1978
Within each of the main vertical columns, the results of the individual studies are shown from left to right in the order in which they are discussed in the text. Only those child variables are included that are common to two or more of the studies being compared. All variables involve percentage frequencies except those noted in c below.

[b] Four adult variables are omitted from the table, as they were not investigated in the other studies. These were frequencies of marked tense and contractions, a noun/pronoun ratio, and an unexplained variable 'words'. All except marked tense were significantly associated with at least one of the child variables at the 5 per cent level (see Furrow column).

[c] Note that the correlations involving the Locus of reference and Topic incorporation variables are based on absolute rather than percentage frequencies in the study by Wells.

recalled, numbered only seven. When to this is added the fact that all the children were first-born children of middle-class parents, it becomes questionable how far the findings are generalizable beyond the sample investigated.

There is yet another qualification that must be added, and that concerns the method used to equate the children for initial stage of development. Although all were of the same age and producing utterances no more than one word long, this cannot be taken as firm evidence that they were all at the same developmental stage. As Bloom (1973) has shown, considerable development takes place during the one-word stage, and Nelson (1973) provides evidence of considerable growth in vocabulary during this stage, as well as of differences between children in the preferred function for which utterances are produced. Furrow et al. briefly acknowledge the existence of this problem in their discussion of the children's level of comprehension at about the time of the first observation, where they note a significant rank order correlation between the children's developmental rank order at 18 months and their 'productive developmental status' at 27 months (rho = 0.714, p = 0.05) and between the same rank order and the mother's concurrent MLU (rho = 0.714, p = 0.05). It seems possible, therefore, that some of the variation in the mother's behaviour was elicited by the children's differential comprehension ability, although it is difficult to see why the most advanced children should have received a style of speech that was syntactically simpler.

Provocative though these two studies are in their differing findings concerning the relationship between the formal properties of mothers' speech and their children's rate of progress, they are both unsatisfactory in their restricted view of the potentially facilitating function that adult speech may have for children at this stage of development. Newport et al. implicitly recognize this when they comment, 'the properties of Motherese derive largely from the fact that the mother wants her child to do as he is told right now, and very little from the fact that she wants him to become a fluent speaker in future. Whatever influences Motherese exerts on language growth have to operate within these intentional constraints' (1977: 112). And a concern with the intentions – semantic and pragmatic – of mothers' speech is precisely what is missing from the two studies considered so far.

In the study already referred to by Cross (1977) in which the extent to which mothers 'tune' their speech to their children's level of language development over the whole age range 19–32 months was investigated, the mothers' speech parameters that were found to be most consistently finely tuned to the child variables were those concerned with the semantic relatedness of the mothers' utterances to the children's preceding utterances (described as 'Topic incorporation' by Wells (1981) and Wells, Montgomery & MacLure (1979)).

Following up this study of a sample of developmentally accelerated children, Cross carried out a further study, comparing pairs of children matched for stage of development, but differing in the age at which the stage was reached (Cross 1978). Labelled 'accelerated' and 'normal' the two groups of children, again ranging in age from 19 to 33 months (with a mean age difference between the two groups of 7.1 months), were compared in terms of the same parameters in the speech addressed to them by their mothers. Some of the results are given in table 1. Additional significant differences between the two groups were found as follows: accelerated children, compared with normal children, received proportionately more partial sequential self-repetitions ($p < 0.05$), expansions and extensions ($p < 0.01$) and 'synergistic sequences' ($p < 0.01$) (glossed as 'expansions and extensions that were also repeated or paraphrased within two conversational turns of the original' (1978: 213)); on the other hand, the utterances addressed to them had less preverbal complexity ($p < 0.05$) and were less likely to be unintelligible or unanalysable ($p < 0.01$).

As will be seen, the significant differences between the two groups tend to lie in the area of topic incorporation rather than in the area of syntactic adjustment and Cross concludes that 'acceleration in linguistic acquisition is associated with an input that is substantially matched to the child's own communicative intentions . . . It was hypothesized that it is the extent to which the mother's discourse adjustments permit the child to guess accurately her meaning that is important in acquisition. By matching the child's semantic intentions and ongoing cognitions, her speech may free the child to concentrate on the formal aspects of her expressions and thus acquire syntax efficiently' (Cross 1978: 214).

Whilst our own results lend support to this conclusion (see below), the findings from this study alone are of limited significance, as Cross herself discusses in detail. The fact that, compared with normally developing children, accelerated developers receive an input that contains a greater proportion of certain types of utterance that seem intuitively to have a potentially facilitating effect has been clearly demonstrated. But, because the measures of both adult and child speech were made concurrently, the observed correlations cannot be taken as evidence that the difference in input was causally related to the difference in rate of development.

A rather confused picture thus emerges from the three studies considered so far: two claim quite important effects for the adjustments in adult speech to children, but differ as to the features that are relevant to these effects, whilst the third finds the effects to be limited and specific to particular sub-systems of the language. These discrepancies, however, may well be attributable to the differences in methodology across the three studies and to the small and homogeneous samples investigated. A further possible source of bias is the fact that the samples of conversation that were analysed in the three studies were obtained in rather similar 'play' situations with a researcher present to take notes; and in each case each mother's speech style was represented by an equal number of utterances. By controlling the natural variation in the distribution over time of different activities, and hence the differential opportunities for different types of talk (Snow 1977a) or for solitary, as opposed to social, activity, these studies may have removed one of the most substantial sources of variation in the environmental influences on language development.

The fourth study to be considered, by Wells (1980b), was designed to overcome some of these limitations. Carried out within the framework of the Bristol longitudinal study of language development (cf. Wells 1979 for details), it involved thirty-two children who were selected to be representative of the full spectrum of social background, position in family and rate of development. Observations were made of these children at three-monthly intervals from 15 to 42 months using a recording device that was programmed to record twenty-four samples of 90 seconds duration at approximately 20-minute intervals throughout the day between 9 a.m. and 6 p.m. No observer was present during the recording (contextual information being obtained in the evening on replaying the tape to the parents), and no restrictions were placed on how the day should be spent (except to avoid long absences from the home) nor on who should interact with the child being studied. Thus the speech samples recorded can be taken as an accurate representation of these children's experience of linguistic interaction during the period in question.

In order to take account of the effect of the child's stage of development on the speech addressed to him, that observation was selected for each child at which the mean length of his structured utterances[2] was as close as possible to 1.5 morphemes. The period over which progress was measured was 9 months and, for each of the linguistic variables con-

---

[2] Calculated as in Brown (1973) with the exception that unstructured utterances, such as 'yes', 'hello', 'please' were omitted.

sidered, progress was represented by the child's residual gain score (departure from the regression of the second score upon the first for the sample as a whole). All adult speech addressed to the child was coded for the variables shown in table 1 and also for the discourse function of each utterance and for the context in which it occurred. Since the absolute amount of speech addressed to the child over the same number of recorded samples varied considerably, both absolute and percentage frequencies of the different categories of utterance were calculated; all variables were then correlated with the child progress measures. Secondly, using the children's ranks on the same measures of progress, two groups of nine children at the top and bottom of the overall rank order were identified as 'faster' and 'slower' developers and the Mann–Whitney U test used to test the significance of the distribution of scores on the adult variables in relation to the two groups. The results are shown in table 1, where these can be compared with results from studies already considered.

What is interesting about these results is that they provide some degree of support for each of the other studies. Consistent with the results of Newport et al. and Cross, little effect is found for variation in the length and syntactic complexity of adult utterances. Indeed the variance on these measures of adult speech was, on the whole, quite small. The one exception was the average number of utterances per turn, where a higher ratio was associated with all the measures of child progress. This can appropriately be compared with a similar association between child progress and the frequency of 'synergistic sequences' found by Cross: typically in such turns, the adult acknowledges the child's previous utterance and goes on to make a further relevant contribution.

With respect to the proportional frequency of sentence types, the frequency of polar interrogatives is found to be associated with increase in the child's use of auxiliary verbs, with the intonationally realized sub-type ('other polar interrogatives') being one of the variables that significantly distinguishes the faster from the slower developers. This finding lends support to those of Newport et al. and Furrow et al., both of whom found the same association between polar interrogatives and auxiliary verb development, with the latter also finding an association between the intonationally realized sub-type and all measures of child progress.

As with Cross, however, whose was the only other study to include semantic parameters of adult speech, the area in which the greatest number of significant associations was found between adjustments in the adult speech addressed to them and the children's rate of progress, was that of topic incorporation. Within this group of variables, it was the frequency with which the adult's utterance took up and extended the topic of the child's previous utterance or his current activity that was associated with the greatest number of measures of the children's progress.

There were three additional adult variables significantly associated with two or more of the measures of child progress in the study by Wells (not shown in table 1). Two of these concerned the discourse functions: direct requests to control the child's behaviour and expressive utterances; the third was the total amount of adult speech addressed to the child during the recorded samples. This latter finding is of particular significance, as it indicates the need to take account of the absolute frequency of particular features of adult speech, as well as of their relative frequency, when attempting to explain the way in which such features contribute their effect to the children's rate of progress. In this case, the number of adult utterances addressed to the children over the 27 minutes analysed ranged from 12 to 286, with a mean of 105.

With a research design that is based upon multiple correlation, as are all the studies reported here, a specifiable number of significant correlations can be expected by chance. It is thus difficult to know how much confidence to place in those that do occur. In a study currently in progress, Wells et al. (in press) are attempting to overcome this problem by applying factor-analytic techniques to the full set of adult speech variables, in order to reduce the data to more manageable proportions and to discover whether there are any clusters of related variables. From work to date, it appears that there are some six identifiable clusters, of which four are significantly associated with several measures of children's progress. Of these, the most powerful predictors of progress are the factors that are best defined as extending the meaning of the child's previous utterance and directing his current activity. The other two factors are best identified by the two main types of polar interrogative: those that involve subject–auxiliary inversion and those that are signalled by rising tone. It is interesting to note that a factor identifiable as that concerned with the length and complexity of adult speech is not significantly associated with any of the measures of the children's progress.

Taking all these studies together, the weight of the evidence does seem to support an association between certain features of the adult BT register and the children's rate of language development. Whilst some of the evidence points to a specific association between the frequency of adult polar interrogatives and the children's developing mastery of the auxiliary verb, in general the relationship is of a more diffuse kind; those children who have received a greater amount, and/or a more semantically related variety, of adult speech being likely to develop more rapidly, as evidenced by a variety of measures of progress. There is also some evidence of children's progress being associated with relative simplicity in adult speech, but this is less consistent.

However, although there is not complete agreement about the precise nature of the significant associations, the arguments advanced by the authors of the four studies to explain their findings all tend to converge on an explanation in which the potentially facilitating features of BT are seen to occur in the interests of effective and mutually satisfying communication, rather than as the outcome of a deliberate intention to teach language. What is helpful about BT, it is suggested, is that it provides the child with experience of language being used to negotiate meanings and purposes in which he is directly involved, thereby providing him with the motivation and the evidence to discover the way in which the formal systems of linguistic resources are organized to realize those communicative intentions.

Such an explanation has considerable plausibility; it also provides a way of resolving some of the apparent inconsistencies between the findings of the individual investigations concerning the importance of formal simplicity, which only Furrow et al. found to be significantly associated with the children's rate of progress. Short, syntactically simple utterances do not, in themselves, account for children's progress: the range of variation between adults in this respect is not very large, and, as Newport et al. point out, many communicatively effective adult utterances (such as indirect requests) are not as syntactically simple as they might be. Wells, in fact, found that there was a significant tendency for the difference between the MLU of the child and the adult to be *greater* for the faster developing children than for the slower, and for the former group to be more likely to receive multi-utterance contributions from their adult interlocutors.

Clearly, there is an optimum upper and lower bound to the complexity of utterances which can assist the child in his learning of syntactic forms, and the ideal situation will be one in which the majority of adult utterances remain within this range. Cross has suggested that the child requires two levels of complexity: 'one level pitched very close to his own so that he can process it and comprehend the meaning, and the other slightly in advance of his own syntactic abilities. The child should then be able to comprehend the meaning and also see the relationship between his characteristic mode of expressing it and the more sophisticated version' (1977: 181). Such an ideal situation, we suggest, is most likely to occur if the adult is intent on successfully maintaining and extending communication about the situations and activities which he or she recognizes to be of interest to the child and believes him to be able to understand. Under these circumstances, syntactic simplicity most probably occurs as a realization of semantic simplicity. Without this concern for mutuality of meaning, it appears, syntactic simplicity is not particularly advantageous.

However, whilst the results of the four studies considered can be interpreted as consistent with the explanation just proffered, it is important to make a number of cautionary qualifications. First, the populations that have so far been sampled are very restricted; apart from the study by Wells, all have involved middle-class children, and only the mothers' speech to the child has been investigated. Furthermore, attention has been focused on a relatively narrow developmental span – essentially the few months in which the child first begins to produce structured utterances. If it is the case that adult speech is most facilitative when it is finely tuned to the child's developmental level, it can be expected that different features will be associated with progress at different stages of development (Cross 1978). There are already some indications that this is so in the studies by Cross (1977) and Ellis & Wells (1980).

Secondly, correlational studies, such as the four reviewed here, cannot by themselves provide evidence of a causal, facilitating, relationship between features of adult speech and children's linguistic progress; they can only suggest hypotheses to be tested by other means. In addition, the use of frequencies, whether absolute or proportional, of particular utterance types, to represent the role of adult input is far from satisfactory. As the strong associations involving the semantic variables of topic incorporation make clear, the facilitation that adult speech is hypothesized to provide does not come from individual utterances in isolation, but from their appropriateness as contributions to particular sequences of interaction. To develop satisfactory techniques for describing and measuring the part played by one participant's contribution to what is essentially a jointly negotiated undertaking is one of the most formidable tasks that has faced social psycholinguists and, as yet, no such techniques have emerged.

Finally, once the essentially reciprocal nature of conversation is recognized, it becomes necessary to reconsider the whole idea of a unidirectional influence of adult speech on children's learning. Just as research on early mothering has shown that babies 'teach' their caretakers how to interact with them (Bell & Harper 1977), so it is equally likely that young language learners 'teach' their parents how to talk to them. In a general way this has already been accepted, in the recognition that adults sequentially adjust their speech in the light of the feedback that they receive from their child interlocutors. However, what is being proposed here is that we should also be prepared to accept the possibility that there are important individual differences between children in the way in which they contribute to these same interactions. It has been a fundamental assumption of all the studies reported here that adults vary in the extent to which they provide the child with conversational experience which facilitates his language learning. It seems equally reasonable to assume that there is similar variation amongst children in the extent to which their participation elicits such facilitating adult behaviour. To investigate this possibility is another task that still awaits social psycholinguists.

7. Socio-economic status and language development

In the investigations discussed so far the questions posed have been examined under three main headings. Are there differences between adult–adult and adult–young child speech, and if so what are they? Is it possible to demonstrate linkage between characteristics of the speech addressed to children and the children's rate of language learning? Is it possible to devise experimental procedures of brief duration that can change the speech characteristics of young children? For the first question two kinds of answers have been offered: direct demonstrations of switching speech characteristics as a function of the age of the younger participant in the conversation and descriptions of BT whose overt features of lexis, grammar and prosody are perhaps sufficient for us to posit the existence of a special register. The studies of co-variation of speech of children and speech of mothers have related differential progress by children to variation in maternal behaviour, yielding results that are relatively consistent with the very few experimental manipulations of input so far conducted.

Three observations might be made:
1. The linguistic analyses have been conducted mainly in terms of the child's mastery of the lexico-grammatical component of language, especially in the individual differences work.

2. The studies of co-variation refer to mother–child pairs; the mothers have not been grouped into contrastive socially based categories such as ethnicity or socio-economic status.
3. The studies have not made explicit which theories of learning and/or instruction are underpinning their thinking, although the categories of description selected for examination and statistical procedures used might be exploited to extract some of the implicit assumptions being made.

Studies of socio-economic status differences in mother–child interaction supplement and complement the individual differences work in several ways.

1. While the linguistic analyses have included descriptions of lexico-grammar in young children, they have also posed questions of a different order, for example: Do middle and lower SES children and their mothers differ in the characteristics of speech they might use to regulate the behaviour of others?
2. Although the original point of departure has sometimes been a search for SES differences in either mothers or children studied separately, subsequent investigations have been extended both to include SES differences for mother–child pairs and further to examine within-SES differences. Such staging can investigate the extent to which the sociological patterns are realized through individual behaviour or, conversely, how individual differences combine to yield differences across socially based categorizations.
3. Many of the hypotheses examined have been derived from a sociological theory intended to explain the probabilistic but not deterministic nature of the means by which social structure reproduces itself in successive generations in a society such as Great Britain (Bernstein 1975; Bourdieu 1973), in spite of social forces acting to weaken such reproduction.
4. Although the sociological theory does not include theories of child development and learning, empirical work has made direct reference to these, as we shall see in this and the succeeding section.

While the studies so far reviewed have been academic in the best sense of the word, those associated with socio-economic status differences have been motivated by a variety of concerns and informed by a diversity of perspectives that have led to a variety of outcomes and conflicts. Generally, but not always, the concerns have had their origin in beliefs about the inequitable distribution of educational opportunities and resources in western societies. Points of departure have arisen from the disciplines of linguistics, psychology and sociology; some have been marked by atheoretical endeavours to describe the facts, others have sought to see whether the facts were consistent with the theories already constructed. Earlier studies were generally descriptive: Templin (1957) and others (see McCarthy 1954) have charted SES differences in the phonology, grammar and lexis of young children without reference to a particular discipline. Some researchers have worked from language to social variation (Baratz 1970; De Stefano 1973; Fasold & Wolfram 1973; Labov 1966, 1969, 1970, 1972). Operating from a psychological perspective, but with predominantly educational concerns, have been Bereiter & Engelmann (1966), Blank (1970), Deutsch (1966) and Hess & Shipman (1965). The models of child development and learning adopted by the psychologists have been diverse, ranging from those proposed by Rousseau through Piaget and Bruner to Skinner. The sociological perspective has been most strongly pursued out of the work of Bernstein (1961a, b, 1971, 1975). This diversity renders comprehensive review difficult, and here severe parameters are imposed.

Systematic exploration of the ways in which socially based language differences in parents may reappear in their children has been confined mainly to the dimension of SES. Some attention has been given to sex differences in children, but these have not as yet been explored systematically. Neither have they been shown to be related to differential treatment by socializing agents. Ethnic, religious, rural–urban, and other culturally significant sources of variation are likewise research problems for the future. We therefore confine this review to SES.

Before we examine the ideas and facts, we must note an important limitation that extends to all the data to be discussed here. None of the research has employed measures of 'social class' as defined by social theorists such as Marx or Weber. Families have not been classified on measures of their relationship to the means of production and distribution; neither has their economic capacity been assessed. Weber (1947) distinguished between class, status and power, 'class' referring to the economic, and 'power' to the political dimensions. 'Status' referred to influence arising from prestige. In the empirical studies to be considered, the scales used to classify families have, in fact, derived mainly from the latter, as assessed by representative or random samples of men's occupations in the society. While it is true that some work, particularly that in the Bernstein tradition, has relied on weighted combinations of the occupations and education of both parents, the most common single index has been the status of the father's occupation, as perceived by samples of the adult population at large. No investigator has used a measure of social class that has been derived from sociological theory, as such. Hence we use the term socio-economic status (SES), this being the most appropriate one for the classifications actually employed. In the main, 'middle SES' refers to the higher ranks of white-collar occupations and 'low SES' to the semi-skilled and unskilled blue-collar occupations.

Since Bernstein's explanatory framework has been the theoretical basis of a majority of the studies of SES differences in parent–child interaction in its relations to child language development, it will be used as the point of departure here, although we may wish to bear in mind that his sociological propositions were couched in terms of class not status. While the precise nature of Bernstein's thesis has eluded many who have tried to work with it (e.g. Edwards 1976; Lawton 1968; Robinson 1978), that uncertainty has not prevented the accumulation of data.

A crude summary of his thesis would focus upon the distinction between 'restricted' and 'elaborated' codes of language use. How and at what level to attempt to define the codes remains problematic (Robinson 1978), but it is helpful to remember that Bernstein (1971) wrote that in an important sense the codes can only be said to exist at the *psychological level*, in terms of verbal planning functions.

One way of posing the distinction between the codes would be in terms of the way in which a person orients to the speech of others. Is he predisposed to attend to the representational content of utterances or is he prone to decode them in terms of what they signal about the nature of the role relations between the participants? The 'restricted code' may be most constructively characterized as an orientation to attend to and interpret speech along the social dimensions, and to produce speech with a corresponding emphasis. Additionally, the kind of role relations in view are couched predominantly in terms of positional status, i.e. as expectations arising from categorization at the sociological rather than the individual level: age, sex, occupation, family relations, father, friend. The orientation is to code the affective and categorical state of these relations. Acting in this manner, the restricted code does not encourage analysis of the intentions of others as persons independent of their status; neither does it encourage a concerned assessment of the truth value of what is said. The elaborated code, on the other hand, orients the user to both of these. According to the thesis, using language to make propositional statements about the social and non-social world enters significantly into everyday life for the users of elaborated code, but not for the user of the restricted code.

In addition, it is important to observe the difference attributed to the structure of interpersonal relations as a function of the two codes. Restricted code realizes a static set of positions and statuses with externally defined obligations and rights. Elaborated code allows a more flexible analysis of roles. Moods and individual personality of participants can be invoked to temper and qualify obligations arising out of positional status.

Bernstein argued that members of families in semi-skilled and unskilled occupations would be most likely to be confined to a restricted code of language use, whereas those in higher white-collar occupations would have access to both codes. These ideas were translated into a number of hypotheses about verbal and non-verbal behaviour, and differences in speech were predicted at phonological, lexico-grammatical, semantic and pragmatic levels of analysis. In terms of the socialization of young children, the thesis was refined to contrast 'position-oriented' versus 'person-oriented' types of familial communication systems, and these were expected to be more directly linked to the speech of the children than SES itself. It was thus possible to derive predictions about SES or position- versus person-oriented family structures on the basis of this thesis.

What was missing was a theory of transmission: no model of child as learner or parent as mediator of learning was incorporated. There was, however, an assumption of intergenerational reproduction which was, as it happens, more compatible with principles of learning that rely on association, modelling, and reinforcement than with cognitive developmental self-organizing conceptions of the child – at least for children who were considered to be confined to a restricted code. Nevertheless, the work to be reviewed has generally avoided specification of the particular learning principles by asking instead about differential opportunities to learn. That is, the hypotheses to be examined have anticipated that, within the limits examined, the more frequently a child has experienced a particular event, action or object in any form in conjunction with its verbal exponents, the more likely he will be to have learned it.

If we separate the maternal role enactment into components of representing, regulating and teaching, the studies can be divided into three categories. However, the categories are not discrete. To answer an inquiry from a child may involve deliberate teaching. To instruct a child efficiently how to play a game will need to involve both representation of facts and regulation of behaviour. In the regulation of behaviour an adult may say things such as 'That will teach you.' However, other things being equal, children's questions appearing to solicit information about the world require the addressee to attend to the representational content, and discipline problems require behaviour to be regulated in some way.

The data collected relied initially on mothers' reports of what they would do or say, and on observation of mothers and/or children in contrived situations. Everyday interaction has not been collected systematically and then analysed to test Bernstein's predictions, so that we still do not know how much natural interaction is concerned with which functions, nor whether the biases of interpretation follow the suggestions of Bernstein. Whilst Wootton's (1974) radio microphone recordings of 4 year olds of different SES yielded results consistent with those obtained from reports and manipulated observations, those of Wells (1980a) are less easy to interpret in this way.

7.1. Mothers' answers to children's questions

Mothers of 5 year olds were asked how they would answer a number of 'why', 'who' and 'where from' questions as though these had been asked by their children (Robinson & Rackstraw 1972; Robinson 1973). Compared with low SES mothers, middle SES mothers were more likely to answer the questions, and to give more, and more accurate, information in a linguistic context, with fewer 'noisy' extras. They claimed to be more concerned about the truth of what they said. They made explicit more similarities and differences among objects and events. In answer to 'why' questions, they were less likely to repeat the question as a statement, e.g. 'Because they do' or to make a simple appeal to regularity, e.g. 'Because they always have done.' They were more likely to mention causes, consequences, analogues and categorizations. The overt purpose of the questions being asked was to obtain information, to fill gaps in knowledge; other things being equal, therefore, the answerer might be expected to give emphasis to the representational function of language. The middle SES mothers appeared to be competent and willing to exploit these opportunities to represent the world as a constellation of objects and events related and organized in space and time. Low SES mothers appeared not to use these opportunities to the same extent; in some respects they were containing rather than answering questions, and answering in such ways that follow-up or repeat questions would have looked like challenges to authority rather than earnest inquiries.

A number of objections have been made to the data. It has been suggested that low SES mothers would have been made more anxious by the interview situation and so their answers would have been affected.

However, if this were so, why should the increased anxiety have led to the *particular* kinds of answers given? If low SES mothers were more likely to be more anxious, then their refusal rate might have been expected to be higher; it was not, either for this or the subsequent interview. Neither did voices on tapes sound anxious. Were middle SES mothers giving what they thought were 'socially desirable' answers? But then would they not try to practise with their child what they thought was socially desirable? While these objections have logical force there is no evidence to suggest that they are empirically valid. That the answers were constructed in a make-believe situation is also a logically valid criticism, but its unspecific nature does not serve to explain why the observed differences were what they were. Objections have to be supported either with alternative explanations or with disconfirming evidence if they are to carry weight.

If it is accepted that there are SES differences in the way mothers in fact answer their children's questions, and if these constitute differential learning opportunities for their offspring, then it must be predicted that SES differences in the way children answer questions will reflect these differences, after due allowance is made for the fact that the children are children.

Two years after the mothers had been interviewed, their children were asked to answer thirty *wh*-questions; the experiments sought to encourage extended answers to the questions. Essentially, the SES differences in the children's answers reflected the maternal differences in both quality and quantity; the simplest explanation for this result is that the maternal data were valid, and that the children had learned in proportion to what had been made available to them. This interpretation is strengthened by the results of a secondary analysis of mother–daughter pairs within SES (Robinson 1973), which yielded significant predictability across the generations.

The final investigation in the series (Robinson & Arnold 1977) moved to direct observation of mothers and children interacting with each other in response to a variety of familiar and unfamiliar objects. SES differences in both mothers and children were consistent with the earlier results, but the main purpose was to examine within-SES co-variation. Two main indices of child behaviour were used: number of information-seeking questions asked of mothers and verbally mediated knowledge offered by the children about the materials presented. Scores on both variables were strongly associated with an index of 'provision of cognitive meaning' by the mother, both within and across SES groups. This index included answering questions with semantically appropriate answers, extending such answers beyond the minimal request, and setting them in a context of shared understanding. Wootton's (1974) recordings of everyday interaction of 4 year olds and their mothers corroborate the ecological validity of the interview and observational data.

How surprising these results are depends upon the initial stance of the readers. They would not be so to a psychologist who recognized the simultaneous and complementary utility of Piagetian, associationist and observational principles of learning. The units of linguistic analysis were not grammatical. They were semantic and pragmatic, but this does not render them non-linguistic.

7.2. Regulation of children's behaviour by mothers

Work on the language of control can be shown to yield comparable results at the same three levels of analysis: SES differences between mothers in relation to their children; SES differences between children; within-SES mother–child co-variation. Relying on mothers' reports of how they would handle a number of discipline problems such as spilt tea or reluctance to go to bed, and with the same population from which Robinson & Rackstraw drew their sample (1972), Cook Gumperz (1973) used a coding frame for analysis that distinguished between three main bases of appeal: imperatives, i.e. non-verbal means or threats that focused on obtaining compliance but without recourse to explanations; positional appeals, i.e. statements that located the reasons for compliance in terms of social status categories of age, sex, or family relations; personal appeals, i.e. statements that referred to the behavioural and/or emotional consequences for named persons that would result from non-compliance, e.g. 'You will be tired tomorrow.' While positional appeals were the most commonly used tactics and did not discriminate between the SES groups, the other two tactics were differentially distributed: low SES mothers more frequently employing imperatives, a result commonly reported in the literature (see Hess 1970), middle SES mothers being more likely to make personal appeals. Only middle SES mothers used appeals that referred to both the behavioural and associated emotional consequences for the child.

Turner (1973) exploited Halliday's (1974) concept of 'meaning potential' to derive a number of hypotheses about likely SES differences in children's use of language to regulate the behaviour of others. His hierarchical taxonomy first separated imperative from positional control, and then divided imperatives into commands and threats and positional controls into rule giving, disapprobation, and reparation-seeking. These could be further sub-divided into nine, twelve, eight, nine and eleven categories respectively. Each of the forty-nine categories linked specific functions to specific linguistic forms. He was additionally able to cut across and combine categories from this classification to extract options that were 'more forceful' and 'less forceful', explicit and inexplicit, more specific and less specific.

He applied the derived coding frame to the speech of the same factorial sample of the 160 5 year olds as that used by Robinson & Rackstraw (1972) and to the 127 of those children for whom similar speech was collected at age 7. The speech analysed came from stories told by the children in response to a number of questions asked in respect of a four-item picture story sequence, in which one of three boys kicks a ball through a window. A man with a shaking fist appears in the third picture and the boys move away making replies to the man.

The results are most simply summarized by asserting that middle SES children used more specific, explicit and less forceful options; they used more personal appeals referring to states of participants and fewer imperative commands, threats and verbal punishments. Two supplementary observations ought to be made. The 7-year-old low SES children were more like 5-year-old middle SES children than 5-year-old low SES children. Although significant differences associated with IQ were few in number, those which did appear indicated that high IQ children behaved more like middle SES than low SES children.

In this sample, with these materials, the regulatory speech of low SES children was significantly different from that of their middle SES peers; however, although the differences were in the direction predicted by Bernstein's thesis, they look to be more compatible with a developmental lag hypothesis.

No subsequent search was made for direct associations between the speech of children and that of their mothers either within or between SES groups; for the third phase of linkage, therefore, it is necessary to switch to data from the United States. Bearison & Cassell (1975) utilized reports of mothers as to how they would handle various child control problems in order to classify them as relatively position-oriented: position-oriented regulatory statements were those that asserted a rule, either universal ('It's wrong to steal') or restricted by time, place, situation, status, or family setting; person-oriented appeals referred to the needs, intentions, feelings, or thoughts of a specified individual who would be affected by the child's behaviour. They predicted that children of mothers who used a relatively high proportion of person-oriented appeals would be more effective and versatile communicators than those of the other mothers, in their descriptions about the procedures and rules of a simple board game. Each child offered two versions, one for a sighted and one for a blind-folded listener; in the latter condition there was no touching or pointing to pieces. (The children had a mean age of 6–7 years.) Their protocols were scored against five measures: the amount of information relayed, the incidence of inadequate referents (i.e. terms that could not be decoded by a listener), the number of words, the number of verbally explicit referents, and the number of exophoric gestural referents. The major predicted interaction was supported: the increment in verbal description scores from the sighted to the blindfolded listener condition was greater for the children of person-oriented mothers; these children additionally manifested a greater decrement in exophoric–gestural encoding, i.e. encoding that relied on the observer being able to see what the child could see and was doing.

7.3. Mothers as instructors

Hess & Shipman (1965) had mothers of different SES groups teach their 4-year-old children how to sort blocks varying on two of four possible dimensions of variation and how to co-operate in the etching of five patterns on an 'Etch-a-Sketch' machine. Frequencies of various categories of maternal activities related both back to SES and forward to variations in the behaviour of the children. For example, control strategies appealing to authority ('because I say so') were more frequently used by low SES mothers, whereas those appealing to reasoning and feeling were relatively more common among middle SES mothers (cf. Cook Gumperz 1973). The latter form of control was positively associated with successful sorting of blocks by the child. Although middle SES mothers did not give more information than low SES mothers when teaching their children how to sort the blocks, they did indulge in more attempts at motivating and orienting, they demanded a higher ratio of verbal to physical responses from their children, they required more specifically discriminatory speech and they gave more positive than negative reinforcement ('knowledge of results' should have been the term used). Four of these variables predicted success at sorting by the children.

Similar associations were found on the Etch-a-Sketch task. Use by the mothers of precise and specific verbal instructions during practice and production periods and showing the children the designs to be copied gave a multiple correlation of 0.64 (N > 140) with an assessment of success in copying the target designs. Adding SES and intelligence test scores of both mothers and children into the predictive equation increased this correlation by 0.03 only; by themselves these three correlated 0.47 with assessed success.

This study has been criticized by Ginsburg (1972) on both methodological and substantive grounds. Ginsburg points to similarities between the SES groups and the smallness of those differences which were obtained; he comments upon lack of partialling techniques to isolate what really goes with what. He neglects to note the multiple correlations on Etch-a-Sketch which seem to point to the psychological variables mediating between SES and children's behaviour, or to offer an alternative account of the significant relations between the behaviour of mothers and children. Hess & Shipman also suggest that the quantitative results reported miss essential qualities discriminating between the SES groups, of which one of the most important was the apparent 'lack of meaning in the communication system between mother and child' in the lowest SES group. While this interpretation might be contested, if there are organized meanings being transmitted and exchanged in this group, these do not appear to be directed towards teaching the child the task. Neither was the interaction warm phatic communion, since the low SES children were frequently reprimanded for not succeeding.

Haavind & Hartmann (1981) developed the design, materials and procedures of Hess & Shipman, while dropping the SES contrast. In the first place they demonstrated that mothers taught a child who was an age peer to their own using the same style as they had used with their own children. For the main study the investigators taught mothers how to play a board game and then had them teach a slightly younger child of a relative or friend how to play. The experimenters meanwhile taught the mother's child how to play the game, observing reactions during the teaching. In this way they separated possibly misleadingly high co-variations resulting from observing mother and child interacting. Informing, anticipating, demonstrating of alternatives, mentions of the competitive character of the game, emotional support, absence of ordering, absence of restriction and absence of imperative feedback by mothers correlated positively with planning, decision-making, rule-mastery, alertness, involvement, activity, and absence of task-irrelevant behaviour in their own children in the independent but identical learning situation.

While neither study makes direct tests of hypotheses derived from explicit theories of learning or instruction, both demonstrate that mothers can differ in the efficiency with which they combine verbal and non-verbal means of instruction and that these have consequences for the learning by their children.

Studies by Wood (Wood & Middleton 1975; Wood, Wood & Middleton 1978) are attempting to underpin such analyses with theories of instruction that include ideas of sequence and interdependence of action and reactions, as well as simple frequency counts of possibly relevant variables. The so-called 'contingent approach' adopted by some mothers is more successful than the other strategies observed. Further, efficient instruction is dynamic and interactive; it does not treat the child as a vessel to be filled, as a mimic to observe, or as a Skinnerian black box to be manipulated by operands. Whether middle SES mothers would be more likely to pursue the more successful strategies has yet to be investigated.

7.4. Summary and conclusions

For the verbal mediation of both representational knowledge and the regulation of behaviour, the results are remarkably similar. There are differences as well as similarities between mothers of middle and low SES children in what they report they communicate to their 5 year olds. These reported differences correspond to what has been observed directly in other studies. The reported and observed differences in the behaviour of the mothers are *reflected* in the speech of the children, once allowance has been made for the generally lower level of complexity in the children's speech. However, these differences have also been shown to occur within SES. It is thus what mothers say and do that is relevant to the children and not their SES membership per se. In summary, the children's speech is most parsimoniously explained in terms of differential opportunities to learn through observation, conceived of as an active rather than a passive process. Such an account does not explain why, generally speaking, there is a tendency for middle SES mothers to behave differently from low SES mothers, but that is beyond a frame of reference that has to account for similarities and differences among children.

Such differences as there are between the orientations and emphases of those who have worked from linguistic interests in variations in maternal input and those who began with SES differences have not precluded their arrival at mutually consistent conclusions about the identification of some of the factors likely to facilitate development of proficiency with language in young children. Perhaps the main common ground lies in the demonstrated relevance of mothers taking steps to establish and maintain effective communication in conversation with their children, whilst simultaneously taking opportunities to stretch the child's communicative competence by offering ideas and speech somewhat in advance of his understanding (cf. Cross 1978 and Wells 1980b with Robinson & Arnold 1977). Such extended conversations seem to be associated with accelerated development in both formal lexico-grammatical features and such activities as the number and structural complexity of questions asked or the range and type of meanings expressed in statements regulating the behaviour of others.

A similar parallel obtains with explanations offered in terms of enhanced opportunities for learning arising from simplification and structuring of input. Both the BT and individual differences studies point to maternal simplification of speech in terms of lexico-grammar and exaggeration of prosodic features and intonation, each of which should render discriminations easier for the child to learn. Hess & Shipman (1965) and Haavind & Hartmann (1977) in pointing to the importance of systematic structuring of instructional speech in relation to the relevant tasks are also highlighting characteristics that should render discriminations easier and materials more readily assimilable. The more linguistic and the more cognitive biases are of course simply academic abstractions of children's minds; an integration has to be achieved by academics in their thinking, just as the children's minds unite the two inside their heads.

8. Language development of young children in schools

The flow of ideas and data between pure and applied studies of language development in children has been mainly in one direction. While practitioners have sought to apply and develop ideas deriving from primarily academic activity, the academics have felt neither inclined nor obliged to integrate potential contributions from their applied peers.

What is particularly unsatisfactory about education programmes from the perspective of the theorist interested in language development is that they do not permit a detailed analysis and extraction of what leads to what. Given that a programme worked, what were its critical features? Designers and executors of programmes have been guided by theory in their conceptions of programmes, but have subsequently relied on pointing to the efficacy of their activities with an implicit or explicit suggestion that others could follow their model if they wished to enhance language development in comparable children. They have not performed detailed analyses of the procedures and materials used and offered comparative evaluations of which were successful and why.

With such important reservations in mind we can note that the evidence is amenable to some kind of assessment and that inferences can be drawn from it. Those who have worked with disadvantaged children have worked separately from those concerned with the mentally retarded, and the two resultant literatures remain separate.

8.1. Language development in disadvantaged children

Particularly in the United States and Britain, the mid 1960s witnessed a concern with 'disadvantaged' children and their educational progress. Relative to the performance of the culturally dominant upper and middle socio-economic status peers, children from other socially defined categories performed less well in primary, secondary and tertiary education. 'Disadvantage' was most commonly defined in terms of SES or ethnicity. Not using the dialect of the school as proficiently as middle SES peers was viewed as an important cause, effect and correlate of under-achievement. Theories about the reasons ranged from views which emphasized the backwardness of speech mastery per se (Bereiter & Engelmann 1966) to those that pointed to the cultural discontinuities and dialectal differences of school and home (Baratz 1970; Labov 1970). This diversity of theory was reflected in the range of educational programmes sponsored (Maccoby & Zellner 1970); what they shared with each other was an initial concern with preschool children and the inclusion of language development as part of their programme.

Although a number of such programmes were extended beyond 'Head Start' at the preschool stage to include 'Follow-Through' into primary education, the myth arose that the 'Head Start' policy had failed; that such gains as were made were subsequently lost (e.g. Coleman et al. 1966; Jencks 1972). How this myth gained credence has yet to be documented. Such conclusions ignore the differential quality of the programmes and fail to answer the important questions about the gains which were made. How were they achieved? If it is the case that these gains were not artefacts of the measurement procedures adopted, then the educational problem should be to devise means of sustaining them and the research problem that of explaining their occurrence. Advancement of our knowledge and understanding will be made, not by examining averages across the programmes (see Coleman et al. 1966), but by attending to the characteristics of individual programmes and their realization (Westinghouse Learning Corporation 1969). Once this step is taken, the myth begins to evaporate. Many programmes were successful (see Miller & Dyer 1975 and Stallings 1975 for reviews). In these, language skills were most often assessed through performances on standardized tests of attainment (e.g. Metropolitan Achievement Tests) or tests of verbal intelligence, the former sampling possible knowledge of how to use language and the latter sampling knowledge about language rather than proficiency in use. Communicative competence in conversations was not assessed; everyday speech with peers or parents was not sampled. With those very important qualifications in mind, we can observe that the language development of disadvantaged children was facilitated through training, especially when the educational programmes met the following criteria:

1. The contents and materials of the language curriculum largely matched but significantly extended the contemporary knowledge, understanding, values and motivation of the children.
2. The implementation of the curriculum used instructional techniques appropriate both to the nature of the educational topic and to the psychology of the particular children learning. For example, the formation of concepts or principles may require that the child actively construct hypotheses arising from direct or mediated experience with the topic; such understanding will require more than rote learning. The cultural and general psychology of the children is also relevant. Brophy & Evertson (1976) have shown that the kinds of teacher–child interaction most likely to promote learning in the low socio-economic status (SES) groups in their study were different from those benefiting high SES children. Crudely, the former benefited from greater *structuring* of the learning by the teacher.
3. Attention was paid to the social influence of peers and parents. Children learn better when they are with other children who are also disposed to learn. The relevance of active parental support and interest has long been established as a significant facilitator of educational achievement (Central Advisory Council for Education (Plowden Report) 1967) and the effects of integration of parents into programmes are highlighted in the work of Heber and Garber (1972).
4. Lambert & Tucker (1972) point out that their successful teaching of French to English Canadian children through a total immersion programme raises questions about the failure to equip ethnic minorities with proficiency in official or national languages. Lambert & Tucker had negotiated their programme in advance. The children were not punished for speaking their vernacular in the classroom, as for ex-

ample Welsh- and Afrikaans-speaking children have been in schools where English was the official language. To what extent was Standard American English seen as the dialect of the oppressors by speakers of Black English Vernacular or of Spanish in the United States? To learn to speak the dialect of the school could be to devalue or deny one's social identity. Programmes that have avoided this oversight have been more successful.

5. As the switch in title from Head Start to Follow Through implies, it was realized that a brief boost to achievement may represent an inadequate conceptualization of education. Programmes that were seen as priming capacity for a take-off typically revealed subsequent regression – which is what one would generally expect. Those that maintained their endeavour maintained the gains.

6. Too much return was not expected from too little investment. An analysis of the Bereiter & Engelmann programme will reveal that the children had only 10 hours of special instruction! Would it be reasonable to expect this amount of activity to increase verbal intelligence or oral achievement?

Successful programmes met more of these requirements. There is thus no doubt that very large changes can be and still could be induced in the educability of young children and in their competence with language, but such changes would require appropriate and persisting changes in the character of parent–child interaction as well as in the educational activities of schools.

8.2. Language development in the mentally retarded

We have mentioned some of the difficulties of drawing inferences from action research as two reasons why data from educational programmes have been omitted from discussions of language development. An additional reason may be cited for the mainstream neglect of work with the mentally retarded: the proportion of research workers with these children and adults who are essentially behaviourist in orientation is higher than the proportion among linguists, psycholinguists and sociolinguists generally. Words like 'reinforcement' and 'operant' commonly have multiple references in the indexes of relevant source books (e.g. Haring & Schiefelbusch 1976; McReynolds 1974; Schiefelbusch & Lloyd 1974), but this should not blind us either to the more comprehensive approaches which include applied behavioural analysis in their activity or to the diversity of programmes extant. More recent publications adopt a multiplicity of perspectives. McLean & Snyder (1977), for example, note that children have to learn to cope with the phonological, lexico-grammatical, semantic and pragmatic components of language (proficiency requires the joint mastery of all), and they ask which features and which kind of instructional procedures might be most appropriate.

Generally viewing the majority of retarded children as being delayed rather than different in the course of their language development, each of the various educational programmes for the mentally retarded is remarkable both for the detail with which the specification for activities is made and for the criterion-referenced testing (checking-up) that is built into progress through the programme.

The Brickers (Bricker & Bricker 1974; Bricker et al. 1973) have produced immensely complicated specifications of task objectives, and activities to go with these, ranging from shaping of phonemes via elicited imitations to the co-ordination of semantic structures with the actions to which they refer. Guess, Sailor & Baer (1974) treat language as instrumental in function, in the limited sense of the word used by Halliday (1975a), concentrating on children learning linguistic means of reference and control by reinforcement procedures. However, the concept of reinforcement has been extended to include social reactions from attaining joint reference with another and to maintaining friendly interaction, in addition to simple material rewards. Kent (1974) has likewise broadened the reinforcement principles deemed relevant to achieving target responses from the child. Miller & Yoder (1974) point to the limitations of a behaviour modification approach that confines itself to specific target behaviour such as sentence production. They insist on realistic functional objectives, encouraging the child to become an active participant, co-ordinating linguistic and non-linguistic experiences. However the emphasis remains upon the co-ordination of semantics with lexico-grammar and phonology; function of speech in action and discourse are less obviously highlighted. Stremel & Waryas (1974) emphasize the relations between syntax and semantics, but the behavioural-analytic techniques are applied to sequences in which the syntax is given the leading edge. Several other programmes have been developed along similar lines (Bricker, Ruder & Vincent Smith 1976; Carrier & Peak 1975; McDonald 1976; Tawney & Hipsher 1970).

Published results based on these programmes are rarer than is desirable, and faith in their efficacy derives mainly from the success of such experiments as those already referred to in an earlier section, and others which have examined more than the single units treated in those studies.

Questions have been posed about sequencing in training. Stremel (1973) asked whether to train the auxiliary or the copula use of *is* first to obtain the speedier mastery of both. Training in each case involved simultaneous presentation of visual representations of *is* and verbal models with echoic responses required from the retarded children; the verbal model was gradually and contingently faded. The copula was learned in fewer trials in either sequence, the auxiliary took almost as few trials if trained first. This is emphasized by the authors as an example of retarded children being able to exploit surface similarities in learning, but the interest here is in the level of attack and the concern for empirical checks upon efficient sequencing. More complex sequences of action had to be generated for inducing capacity with the various markers of negation (Stremel & Waryas 1974), and negation itself is treated in the last eight phases of a 43-phase programme relating comprehension through imitation to production developed out of a language programme concentrating on functional uses of objects as materials (Bricker et al. 1976).

Ruder & Bunce (1973) have exemplified two principles in their attempt to teach a retarded child to use intonation and stress via an imitation with feedback procedure. The first is that attempts to teach are more likely to be successful if the cognitive load (Shatz 1977) on the child is reduced. The second is an exemplification of the first: teach one unit at a time. Using a child with an immediate memory span of three monosyllables uttered with falling tone only, they found he could not imitate using rising tone in a sequence of this length. Once the items were reduced to two monosyllables, he could be trained to make the intonational contrast and this could than be generalized to sequences of three syllables, after approximately eighty trials. When stress on the second syllable was added as an additional contrast, performance deteriorated, but this combination achieved criterial imitation (90 per cent) within twenty trials. A fourth monosyllable was then added. After 110 trials, two values of both tone and stress had been incorporated into the child's repertoire and his immediate memory capacity increased by one monosyllable.

This attention to detail has been one of the hallmarks of behaviour analysts (see Haring & Schiefelbusch 1976), and may be contrasted with the more diffuse approach to the role of reinforcement and feedback exemplified in the work of Brown (1973), for example. The conditions of everyday activity almost certainly preclude the possibility of testing hypotheses about the learning of specific features of language; as we have already stated, however, it does not follow that principles of imitation, feedback, or reinforcement are either irrelevant or unimportant. To find out how they might apply to the learning of particular features of language by particular children would require even greater efforts of observation than those already undertaken in the longitudinal studies so far made.

What has not been examined systematically in the educational programmes for the disadvantaged or retarded and in the experiments with the retarded is the incidence of transfer and generalization of the features learned to the everyday conversation of the children. Analysis of subsequent spontaneous discourse is conspicuous by its absence and leaves the authors open to the charge that the targets they have set should have included the spontaneous application of learned units and structures to appropriate everyday contexts. Having been concerned mainly with grammar, semantics, and the relations between the two, and hence neglectful of the pragmatics of everyday speech, this outcome is perhaps not surprising. We have then still to wait upon the evidence as to whether the children so trained have gained more than competences limited to the educational and experimental situations in which these were developed.

These criticisms of work with the disadvantaged and the mentally retarded must be seen both in the context of general ideology about language development dominant in the early 1970s and in relation to the strengths of the work itself. In a climate of opinion that was generally antipathetic to the idea that language could be taught, those working with the disadvantaged and the mentally retarded were maintaining the idea that this was not so. They also kept alive and demonstrated the possible relevance of solicited imitations, feedback and reinforcement to language development. Perhaps most important, they applied these principles of learning to very thoroughly worked-out analyses of the details of the language components to be taught. Their programmes also have the merit of pointing out the complexities of the language learning task; when the learning is broken down into one step at a time (as defined by the experimenter) and the problems of discrimination, differentiation, recombination and co-ordination are set down in this degree of detail, we begin to appreciate the size of the problems facing the developing child.

9. Conclusions

In the course of this chapter evidence has been reviewed from widely differing types of research – observational and experimental, at home and in educational settings, involving normal and mentally handicapped children – all pointing to the conclusion that environmental differences in the speech addressed to the language learning child significantly affect the course and rate of learning. From this work is also beginning to emerge some indication of which characteristics of the input are associated with greater than average progress. In the experimental studies, as in the naturalistic studies, it has been found that adult utterances which are semantically related to the child's previous utterance provide the most satisfactory material from which to learn, with syntactic recastings and expansions and semantic extensions all being associated with measurable gains on one or another measure of linguistic development. In the studies utilizing mothers' reports also, provision of informative (i.e. relevantly semantically related) and extended answers to children's real and hypothetical questions has been found to be associated with similar answering strategies by the children at a later age.

Taken together, these results point to a very important characteristic of input which facilitates linguistic development, and that is that it is contingently related to the child's own behaviour – either to his preceding utterance or utterances, to his current activity, or to his (presumed) focus of attention. To be useful as linguistic evidence from which to discover more about the way in which meanings and purposes are linguistically realized, utterances that are addressed to the child, it appears, should be based on an already established intersubjective agreement about what is under discussion.

At the same time, it is clear that the lexico-grammatical and prosodic form of such utterances is not unimportant. Utterances should not be so long or complex or so full of unfamiliar words that they are too far beyond the child's processing ability. On the other hand, they should not be consistently so simple that they provide no opportunity or challenge to the child to extend his command of the various systems of linguistic form. However, as we saw from the quoted examples of parent–child interaction, there is likely to be quite considerable variation from utterance to utterance over the course of any particular sequence of conversation with respect to most of these formal parameters.

Ultimately, therefore, it is not sufficient to attend to the form and content of the individual utterances that are addressed to children, nor even, beyond a certain and as yet unspecified threshold level, to the actual frequency of such utterance types. In seeking to discover whether particular utterances provide an opportunity for further learning we must, above all, consider their tactical relationship to the context of the ongoing conversation and to the situation in which it occurs.

Although some of the more recent studies of Baby Talk (e.g. Cross 1977;

Wells 1980a) have made a move in this direction with their categorization of adult utterances in terms of Locus of reference and Incorporation, none of the research reviewed in this chapter is fully satisfactory from this point of view, for no study has yet fully come to grips with the sequential and tactical organization of the conversations of which individual utterances are constitutive parts. To find an appropriate methodology for investigating conversation remains a high priority, therefore, for anyone who wishes to gain a fuller understanding of the way in which the speech addressed to children facilitates their linguistic development.

We have also to integrate language learning into satisfactory models of child development and specify the principles of learning responsible. In respect of children's learning of language we have to find out what they learn, how they learn and why they learn. It might be argued that we have made much progress in the pursuit of the answers to the first question, particularly in relation to the mastery of phonological discriminations, morphology, basic syntax, and the meanings of words and syntactic structures. Charting the development of communicative competence is a task for the 1980s.

So far, approaches to the second problem have been mainly indirect. The studies reviewed here have focused upon the peculiar features of the primary linguistic data addressed to the child and the co-variation of linguistic features in the speech of mothers and their children. In both types of study, however, there are implicit principles of learning. In stressing the simplicity, exaggeration, and repetition of BT, investigators are indexing characteristics that should facilitate discrimination of features to be learned and render their associations more obvious. Where frequency of maternal use of a feature is associated with its early appearance in the child's repertoire, associative principles are again the simplest to invoke. However, other maternal variables, while described in grammatical terms, are perhaps better conceived in terms of function in either discourse or behaviour. The frequent use of certain kinds of interrogative by mothers, for example, is not associated so much with the early appearance of corresponding interrogatives in their children as with a generally faster rate of linguistic development. That is, the mother is soliciting speech in conversation. Even if, by definition, she is eliciting only what is already available, this means the child is practising speaking and that the facility for production or range of application of units and structures is being enhanced. Elicited imitations may be a special case of this more general phenomenon, but we can observe that this procedure has been shown to be a useful component in the training of complex skills

(Bilodeau & Bilodeau 1969; Poulton 1974). Solicited imitations have also been shown to function successfully for language learning both in the laboratory and in the naturalistic studies. Some measure of corrective feedback is also an integral part of training of skills, and its efficacy for language learning has likewise appeared in both artificial and natural contexts.

While models of the development of skills can begin to account for both the initial learning and the refinement of actions, associative principles of learning are in themselves only weakly predictive of which particular associations will be learned and retained. That is, of the infinite array of possible associations, we have to explain which ones are selected in learning and performance. Ideas of ease of discrimination can be invoked as one source of variation that can facilitate associations.

Generally in animal and human behaviour, it has been common to invoke the value of rewards and punishments when received in contiguity with particular associations as facilitators of learning. However, without stretching the concepts of reward and punishment beyond their commonly accepted denotation, they do not emerge as significant determinants either of the rate or quality of natural language learning by children. Conversation is simply not the kind of activity in which the participants generally reward or punish each other for the use of particular linguistic features; there are exceptions of course, particularly in respect of definitions of what is rude and polite.

However, the manner in which these principles actually operate in detail has yet to be determined. Which principles of associative learning operate to facilitate or inhibit the learning of which language features under what conditions for which children? To begin to answer this question will require much greater attention to the precise details of the child's experienced environment than has so far been customary. Such research calls for video-recordings over extended periods of time if we are to trace the conditions of the natural learning of any feature or system rather than simply chart its initial entry and course of development. Such recordings will not necessarily provide answers. Once we concede that 'imitations' do not have to be fair copies of an utterance close in space and time to its emission, delays between learning and appearance in performance could well extend beyond periods of several months.

Perhaps such work will become necessary. Just as research workers have already found it necessary to chart development longitudinally with infrequent recordings of speech, so in the future, if we are to explain how this development occurs, we will need much richer filming of more extended samples of behaviour.

While it is likely that associative and the related observational principles of learning will be reintegrated into explanations of some aspects of
language development, Chomsky's (1959) original objection to Skinner
retains its force – such principles cannot explain how speakers become
capable of generating an infinite number of grammatically acceptable
sentences. Neither do they explain the frequently occurring 'transitional
forms'. They cannot explain the appearance of late syntactic errors
(Bowerman 1980). They cannot explain how invented forms can emerge.
In short they cannot adequately explain the creative character of speech;
they are potentially more useful for explaining reactive learning.

However, the cognitive-development orientation of Piaget (Piaget
1952; Piaget 1954; Piaget & Inhelder 1966) or Bruner (Bruner, Olver &
Greenfield 1966) has long recognized the child as an active organism,
whose initial design characteristics equip and motivate him to develop his
adaptive capabilities through the joint operation of assimilation and
accommodation. The child accumulates schemes – rules for action –
which are progressively co-ordinated and reorganized to represent
knowledge in successively sensori-motor, symbolic and sign systems
(enactive, ikonic and symbolic in Bruner's terms). For Piaget, this learning, which he calls 'equilibration' (Piaget 1970), has its own dynamic
arising out of interactions with the physical and social environment. This
kind of conception of the child's learning and development complements
the idea of a child as a reactive learner of associations, and the articulation
of the two conceptions yields a picture of the developing child that
corresponds to apparent reality in a way which neither story offers by
itself. It would be too crude to suggest that associative principles determine which data are assimilated and that cognitive-developmental principles account for active selection and processing of those data, but such a
proportion may be a useful first approximation. This suggestion offers
two points of departure for answering why children learn language: the
associative principles being relevant to involuntary corrections being
stamped in by prominent attention-demanding stimuli in the external or
internal environment of the child; the cognitive developmental principles
making direct appeal to the design characteristics of human children – a
view not inconsistent with Chomsky's contentions.

While this dual approach provides a frame of reference within which to
answer the deeper 'why' questions, there are lower levels of possible
explanation as well. One view is that very young children learn language
in order to communicate; they wish to communicate with other people.
Halliday's (1975b) analysis of the proto-language of his son Nigel empha-

sizes the utility of language as a means of communication, while simultaneously observing that engagement in social interaction with adults can be in itself a sufficient reason for children to talk. This idea is more strongly emphasized by Trevarthen in his explanations of infant communication (Trevarthen & Hubley 1978). There are no grounds for denying this possibility, and while some research workers might claim that this explanation only serves to locate the problem more precisely, we have also to recognize that eventually in regressive ontogenetic explanations we inevitably reach a stage which invokes design characteristics of human beings. To assert that communicative functions are the sole motivating force for all language development is however not consistent with the evidence. Halliday (1975b) claims that at a later stage his child Nigel deliberately tried to discover the characteristics of language. The reappearance of 'errors' after systems have been mastered (Bowerman 1980) are not obviously explained by appeals to the child's intentions to communicate more effectively; they look more like hypothesis-testing explorations, motivated perhaps by no more (or less) than a wish to find out about language. The general case for efficiency of communication is also weakened by the observation that it implies that once communication is successful there will be no impetus for further development. We have shown how strongly mothers adjust their speech to that of their young children. Why do the child–mother systems develop? Similarly, since transitional syntactic forms are communicatively effective, why do they change and come into line with acceptable adult usage?

Although earlier work neglected the importance of communicative functions both as reasons for talking and reasons for developing greater skill, we have yet to discover when they can be used to explain why children begin and continue to develop their command of language and when other, as yet unknown, factors may be important.

Appendix: Bristol Language Development Study conventions and layout for transcription

The speech of the child being studied is set out in the left-hand column. The speech of all other participants is set out in the centre column, with identifying initials where necessary. Each new utterance starts on a new line.

Contextual information is enclosed in square brackets [ ] and set out in the right hand column.

Interpretations of utterances and descriptions of tone of voice, where applicable, are enclosed in round brackets ( ) and included immediately after the utterance to which they apply.

Utterances, or parts of utterances, about which there is doubt are enclosed in angular brackets < >; where two interpretations are possible they are both given, separated by an oblique stroke.

Symbols of the International Phonetic Alphabet are used for utterances, or parts of utterances, which cannot be interpreted with certainty. Phonetic symbols are always enclosed by oblique strokes. Except where there is doubt about the speaker's intended meaning, the speech is transcribed in Standard English Orthography.

The following is a list of additional symbols used, with an explanation of their significance. (Stops and commas are not used as in normal punctuation.)

? used at end of any utterance where an interrogative meaning is considered to have been intended

! used at the end of an utterance considered to have exclamatory intention

' apostrophe: used as normal for contractions and elision of syllables

* used to indicate unintelligibility, for whatever reason. The number of asterisks corresponds as nearly as possible to the number of words judged to have been uttered

. . . stops are used to indicate pauses. One stop is used for a very short pause. Thereafter, the number of stops used corresponds to the estimated length of the pause in seconds. Pauses over 5 seconds in length are shown with the figure for the length of the pause, e.g. . . 8 . .

___ underlining. Where utterances overlap because both speakers speak at once, the overlapping portions are underlined

" " inverted commas are used to enclose utterances considered to be 'speech for self'

+ plus mark indicates unbroken intonation contour where a pause or clause boundary might otherwise indicate the end of an utterance

− indicates a hiatus, either because the utterance is incomplete or because the speaker makes a fresh start at the word or utterance

(v) used to indicate that the preceding word was used as a vocative, to call or hold the attention of the addressee

Intonation

Some of the transcripts include a representation of intonation, in which case the following additional conventions apply:

/ tone unit boundary: where an utterance consists of only one tone unit, no boundaries are marked

' this symbol immediately precedes both prominent and tonic syllables

prominent syllables[3] take a single digit before the symbol to indicate their relative pitch height

---

[3] Prominent syllables are salient with respect to combinations of pitch, duration and intensity.

tonic syllables[4] take two or more digits before the symbol to indicate the onset level, range and direction of significant pitch movement (see 'Pitch height' below)

↑↓   shift of pitch range relatively higher or lower than that normal for the speaker

⇈ ⇊ shift to extra high or extra low pitch

:   lengthened syllable. The symbol follows the syllable to which it applies

Pitch height. The height, direction and range of significant pitch movement is represented by a set of digits corresponding to points on a scale. The pitch range of a speaker is divided into five notional bands, numbered 1–5 from high to low, thus:

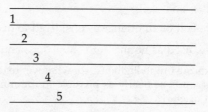

The following information is retrievable from this coding:

Direction of movement	Halliday (1967) tones
Falling (e.g. 13, 25)	Tone 1
Rising (e.g. 31, 43)	Tone 2
Level (e.g. 33)	Tone 3
Fall–rise (e.g. 343) or (e.g. 342)	Tone 4 or Tone 2[5]
Rise–fall (e.g. 324)	Tone 5

References

Anderson, E. S. & Johnson, C. E. 1973. Modifications in the speech of an eight-year-old to younger children. *Stanford Occasional Papers in Linguistics, 3*, 149–60.

Baer, D. M. & Guess, D. 1973. Teaching productive noun suffixes to severely retarded children. *American Journal of Mental Deficiency, 77*, 498–505.

Baer, D. M., Peterson, R. F. & Sherman, J. 1967. The development of imitation by reinforcing behavioral similarity to a model. *Journal of Experimental Analysis of Behavior, 10*, 405–16.

Baratz, J. C. 1970. Teaching reading in an urban Negro school system. In F. W. Williams (eds) *Language and poverty*. Chicago: Markham.

Bates, E. 1976. *Language and context: the acquisition of pragmatics*. London: Academic Press.

[4] Tonic syllables carry at least the onset of significant pitch movement. Significant pitch movement in its entirety may, of course, occur on a single syllable or be spread over a number of syllables.

[5] Fall–rise movements may be of two types, corresponding to Halliday's Tone 2 and Tone 4. They are conventionally denoted in the transcripts as follows: Tone 2 is represented with a higher terminal pitch than its onset (e.g. 342), whereas Tone 4 is represented as having a terminal pitch no higher than its onset (e.g. 232, 354).

Bearison, D. J. & Cassel, T. Z. 1975. Cognitive decentration and social codes: communication effectiveness in young children from differing family contexts. *Developmental Psychology, 11,* 29–36.

Bell, R. Q. & Harper, L. V. 1977. *Child effects on adults.* Hillsdale, NJ: Erlbaum.

Bereiter, C. & Engelmann, S. 1966. *Teaching disadvantaged children in the pre-school.* Englewood Cliffs, NJ: Prentice Hall.

Berko Gleason, J. 1977. Talking to children: some notes on feedback. In C. E. Snow & C. A. Ferguson (eds.) *Talking to children: language input and acquisition.* Cambridge: Cambridge University Press.

Berko Gleason, J. & Weintraub, S. 1978. Input language and the acquisition of communicative competence. In K. Nelson (ed.) *Children's language,* vol. i. New York: Gardner Press.

Bernstein, B. 1961a. Social class and linguistic development: a theory of social learning. In A. H. Halsey, J. Floud & C. A. Anderson (eds.) *Education, economy and society.* New York: Free Press.

1961b. Social structure, language and learning. *Educational Research, 3,* 163–76.

1971. *Class, codes and control,* vol. i: *Theoretical studies towards a sociology of language.* London: Routledge.

1975. *Class, codes and control,* vol. iii: London: Routledge.

Bilodeau, E. A. & Bilodeau, I. McD. (eds.) 1969. *Principles of skill acquisition.* New York: Academic Press.

Bingham, N. E. 1971. Maternal speech to prelinguistic infants: differences related to maternal judgments of infant language competence. Unpublished paper, Cornell University. Mimeo.

Blank, M. 1970. Some philosophical influences underlying preschool intervention for disadvantaged children. In F. W. Williams (ed.) *Language and poverty.* Chicago: Markham.

Bloom, L. 1973. *One word at a time.* The Hague: Mouton.

Blount, B. G. 1972. Parental speech and language acquisition: some Luo and Samoan examples. *Anthropological Linguistics. 14,* 119–30.

1977a. Ethnography and caretaker–child interaction. In C. E. Snow and C. A. Ferguson (eds.) *Talking to children: language input and acquisition.* Cambridge: Cambridge University Press.

1977b. Parental speech to children: cultural patterns. Paper presented at the 1977 Georgetown University Round Table on Languages and Linguistics.

Bourdieu, P. 1973. Cultural reproduction and social reproduction. In R. Brown (ed.) *Knowledge, education and cultural change.* London: Tavistock.

Bowerman, M. 1980. The role of meaning in language acquisition. Paper presented at Annual Child Language Seminar, Manchester.

Bricker, D. D., Dennison, L., Watson, L. & Vincent Smith, L. 1973. *Language training for young developmentally delayed children,* vol. ii. IMRID Behavioral Science Monograph No. 22. Nashville: Peabody College.

Bricker, D. D., Ruder, K. F. & Vincent Smith, L. 1976. An intervention strategy for language-deficient children. In N. Haring & R. L. Schiefelbusch (eds.) *Teaching special children.* New York: McGraw-Hill.

Bricker, W. A. & Bricker, D. D. 1974. An early language training strategy. In R. L. Schiefelbusch & L. L. Lloyd (eds.) *Language perspectives: acquisition, retardation and intervention.* Baltimore: University Park Press.

Broen, P. 1972. *The verbal environment of the language-learning child*. Monograph of American Speech and Hearing Association, 17, December.

Brophy, J. E. & Evertson, C. M. 1976. *Learning from teaching*. Boston: Allyn and Bacon.

Brown, R. 1958. *Words and things*. Glencoe: Free Press.
  1973. *A first language: the early stages*. London: Allen and Unwin.

Brown, R., Cazden, C. B. & Bellugi, U. 1969. The child's grammar from I to III. In J. P. Hill (ed.) *Minnesota Symposium on Child Psychology*, vol. II. Minneapolis: University of Minnesota Press.

Bruner, J. S. 1975. The ontogenesis of speech acts. *Journal of Child Language*, 2. 1: 1–20.
  1978. Learning how to do things with words. In J. S. Bruner & A. Garton (eds.) *Human growth and development*. Oxford: Oxford University Press.

Bruner, J. S., Olver, R. R. & Greenfield, P. M. 1966. *Studies in cognitive growth*. New York: Wiley.

Bynon, J. 1977. The derivational processes relating Berber nursery words to their counterparts in normal inter-adult speech. In C. E. Snow and C. A. Ferguson (eds.) *Talking to children: language input and acquisition*. Cambridge: Cambridge University Press.

Carrier, J. K. & Peak, T. J. 1975. *Non-speech language initiation program*. Lawrence, Kansas: H. & H. Enterprises.

Carter, A. 1974. The development of communication in the sensori-motor period: a case study. Unpublished PhD dissertation, University of California, Berkeley.

Cazden, C. B. 1972. *Child language and education*. New York: Holt.

Central Advisory Council for Education (England). 1967. *Children and their primary schools* [Plowden Report]. London: Her Majesty's Stationery Office.

Cherry, L. & Lewis, M. 1978. Differential socialization of girls and boys: implication for sex differences in language development. In N. Waterson & C. Snow (eds.) *The devlopment of communication*. Chichester: Wiley.

Chomsky, N. A. 1957. *Syntactic structures*. The Hague: Mouton.
  1959. Review of B. F. Skinner, *Verbal Behavior*. *Language*, 35, 26–58.
  1964. Discussion of Miller and Ervin's paper. In U. Bellugi & R. Brown (eds.) *The acquisition of language*. Monographs of the Society for Research in Child Development, 29, no. 1.
  1965. *Aspects of the theory of syntax*. Cambridge, Mass.: MIT Press.
  1976. *Reflections on language*. London: Fontana Books.

Clark, H. H. & Clark, E. V. 1977. *Psychology and language*. New York: Harcourt, Brace Jovanovich.

Coleman, J. S., Campbell, E. Q., Hobson, D. J., McPartland, J., Mood, A. N., Weinfeld, F. D. and York, R. L. 1966. *Equality of educational opportunity*. Washington, DC: Government Printing Office.

Cook Gumperz, J. 1973. *Social control and socialization*. London: Routledge.

Cross, T. G. 1977. Mothers' speech adjustments: the contribution of selected child listener variables. In C. E. Snow & C. A. Ferguson (eds.) *Talking to children: language imput and acquisition*. Cambridge: Cambridge University Press.
  1978. Mothers' speech and its association with rate of linguistic development in young children. In N. Waterson & C. Snow (eds.) *The development of communication*. Chichester: Wiley.

De Stefano, J. S. (ed.) 1973. *Language, society and education*. Worthington, Ohio: Charles A. Jones.

Deutsch, M. 1966. *The disadvantaged child*. New York: Basic Books.

Donaldson, M. 1966. Discussion of McNeill, 'The creation of language by children'. In J. Lyons & R. J. Wales (eds.) *Psycholinguistics Papers*. Edinburgh: Edinburgh University Press.

Dore, J. 1975. Holophrases, speech acts and language universals. *Journal of Child Language*, 2, 21–40.

Dore, J., Gearhart, M. & Newman, D. 1978. The structure of nursery school conversation. In K. Nelson (ed.) *Children's Language*, vol. i. New York: Gardner Press.

Drach, K. 1969. The language of the parent: a pilot study. *Working Paper 14*. Language Behavior Research Laboratory, University of California, Berkeley.

Edwards, A. D. 1976. *Language in culture and class*. London: Heinemann.

Ellis, R. & Wells, C. G. 1980. Enabling factors in adult–child discourse. *First Language*, 1, 46–62.

Engle, M. 1980. Do fathers speak motherese? In H. Giles, W. P. Robinson & P. M. Smith (eds.) *Language: social psychological perspectives*. Oxford: Pergamon.

Erber, N. P. 1979. Optimising speech communication in the classroom. In A. Simmons-Martin & D. R. Calvert (eds.) *Parent–child intervention*. New York: Grune-Stratton.

Ervin-Tripp, S. M. 1973. *Language acquisition and communicative choice*. Stanford, California: Stanford University Press.

  1980. Speech acts, social meaning and social learning. In H. Giles, W. P. Robinson & P. M. Smith (eds.) *Language: social psychological perspectives*. Oxford: Pergamon.

Fasold, R. W. & Wolfram, W. 1973. Some linguistic features of negro dialect. In J. S. de Stefano (ed.) *Language, society and education*. Worthington, Ohio: Charles A. Jones.

Ferguson, C. A. 1964. Baby talk in six languages. *American Anthropologist, 66*, 103–14.

  1977. Baby talk as a simplified register. In C. E. Snow & C. A. Ferguson (eds.) *Talking to children: language input and acquisition*. Cambridge: Cambridge University Press.

Ferrier, L. 1978. Some observations of error in context. In N. Waterson & C. Snow (eds.) *The development of communication*. Chichester: Wiley.

Fraser, C. & Roberts, N. 1975. Mothers' speech to children of four different ages. *Journal of Psycholinguistic Research*, 4. 1, 9–16.

Friedlander, B. Z., Jacobs, A. C., Davis, B. B. & Wetstone, H. S. 1972. Time-sampling analysis of infants' natural language environments in the home. *Child Development*, 43, 730–40.

Furrow, D., Nelson, K. & Benedict, H. 1979. Mothers' speech to children and syntactic development: some simple relationships. *Journal of Child Language*, 6, 432–42.

Garnica, O. K. 1977. Some prosodic and paralinguistic features of speech to young children. In C. E. Snow & C. A. Ferguson (eds.) *Talking to children: language input and acquisition*. Cambridge: Cambridge University Press.

Garvey, C. 1977. The contingent query: a dependent act in conversation. In M. Lewis & L. A. Rosenblum (eds.) *Interaction, conversation and the development of language.* New York: Wiley.

Ginsberg, H. 1972. *The myth of the deprived child.* Englewood Cliffs, NJ: Prentice Hall.

Grimshaw, A. D. 1977. A sociologist's point of view. In C. E. Snow & C. A. Ferguson (eds.) *Talking to children: language input and acquisition.* Cambridge: Cambridge University Press.

Guess, D., Sailor, W. & Baer, D. M. 1974. To teach language to retarded children. In R. L. Schiefelbusch & L. L. Lloyd (eds.) *Language perspectives: acquisition, retardation and intervention.* Baltimore: University Park Press.

Guess, D., Sailor, W., Rutherford, G. & Baer, D. 1968. An experimental analysis of linguistic development: the productive use of the plural morpheme. *Journal of Applied Behavioral Analysis, 1,* 297–306.

Haavind, H. & Hartmann, E. 1981. Mothers as teachers and their children as learners. In W. P. Robinson (ed.) *Communication in development.* London: Academic Press.

Halliday, M. A. K. 1967. *Intonation and grammar in British English.* The Hague: Mouton.

1974. *Language and social man.* London: Longman.

1975a. Talking one's way in: a sociolinguistic perspective of language and learning. In A. Davies (ed.) *Problems of language and learning.* London: Heinemann.

1975b. *Learning how to mean.* London: Arnold.

1977. Language as code and language as behaviour: a systemic–functional interpretation of the nature and ontogenesis of dialogue. To appear in S. M. Lamb & A. Makkai (eds.) *Semiotics of culture and language.*

Haring, N. G. & Schiefelbusch, R. L. 1976. *Teaching special children.* New York: McGraw Hill.

Heber, R. & Garber, H. 1972. *Rehabilitation of families at risk for mental retardation.* University of Wisconsin, Madison, Progress Report.

Heider, E. R. 1971. Style and accuracy of verbal communications within and between social classes. *Journal of Personality and Social Psychology, 18,* 33–47.

Hess, R. D. 1970. Social class and ethnic influences on socialization. In P. H. Mussen (ed.) *Carmichael's Manual of Child Psychology.* New York: Wiley.

Hess, R. D. & Shipman, V. C. 1965. Early experience and the socialisation of cognitive modes in children. *Child Development, 36,* 869–86.

Hymes, D. 1972. On communicative competence. In J. B. Pride & J. Holmes (eds.) *Sociolinguistics.* Harmondsworth: Penguin Books.

Jencks, C. 1972. *Inequality, a reassessment of the effect of family and schooling in America.* New York: Basic Books.

Kent, L. R. 1974. *Language acquisition program for the severely retarded.* Champaign: Research Press.

Kobashigawa, B. 1969. Repetitions in a mother's speech to her child. *Working Paper 14.* Language Behavior Research Laboratory, University of Calfornia, Berkeley.

Labov, W. 1966. *The social stratification of speech in New York City.* Washington, DC: Center for Applied Linguistics.

1969. The logic of non-standard English. *Georgetown Monographs in Language and Linguistics, 22,* 1–31.

1970. The study of language in its social context. *Studium Generale*, *23*, 39–87.

1972. *Sociolinguistic patterns*. Philadelphia: University of Pennsylvania Press.

Lambert, W. E. & Tucker, G. R. 1972. *Bilingual education of children*. Rowley, Mass.: Newbury House.

Lawton, D. 1968. *Social class, language and education*. London: Routledge.

Lenneberg, E. H. 1967. *Biological foundations of language*. New York: Wiley.

Lovitt, T. C., Guppy, T. C. & Blattner, J. E. 1965. The use of a free-time contingency with fourth graders to increase spelling accuracy. *Behavior Research and Therapy*, *7*, 151–69.

Lovitt, T. C. & Hurlbut, M. 1974. Using behavioral analysis techniques to assess the relationship between phonics instruction and reading. *Journal of Special Education*, *8*, 57–72.

Luria, A. R. 1961. *The role of speech in the regulation of normal and abnormal behaviour*. Oxford: Pergamon.

McCarthy, D. 1954. Language development in children. In L. Carmichael (ed.) *Manual of child psychology*, 2nd ed. New York: Wiley.

Maccoby, E. E. & Zellner, M. 1970. *Experiments in primary education*. New York: Harcourt, Brace.

McDonald, J. D. 1976. Environment language intervention. In F. Withrow & C. Nygren (eds.) *Language and the handicapped learner*. Columbus, Ohio: Merrill.

McLean, J. E. & Snyder, L. K. 1977. A transactional approach to early language learning. Nashville: George Peabody College, Project no. R0077FP B.

Macnamara, J. 1972. Cognitive basis of language learning in infants. *Psychological Review*, *79*. 1: 1–13.

McNeill, D. 1966. The creation of language by children. In J. Lyons & R. Wales (eds.) *Psycholinguistics Papers*. Edinburgh: Edinburgh University Press.

1970. *The acquisition of language*. New York: Harper, Row.

McReynolds, L. V. (ed.) 1974. *Developing systematic procedures for training children's language*. Monograph of American Speech and Hearing Association, 18.

Malouf, R. & Dodd, D. 1972. Role of exposure, imitation and expansion in the acquisition of an artificial grammatical rule. *Developmental Psychology*, *7*, 195–203.

Miller, G. A. 1977. *Spontaneous apprentices*. New York: Seabury Press.

Miller, J. & Yoder, D. 1974. *A syntax teaching program*. In R. L. Schiefelbusch & L. L. Lloyd (eds.) *Language perspectives: acquisition, retardation and intervention*. Baltimore: University Park Press.

Miller, L. B. & Dyer, J. L. 1975. *Four preschool programs: their dimensions and effects*. Monographs of Society for Research in Child Development, 40, no. 162.

Moerk, E. 1972. Principles of interaction in language learning. *Merrill-Palmer Quarterly*, *18*, 229–57.

Mowrer, O. H. 1960. *Learning theory and the symbolic processes*. New York: Wiley.

Nelson, K. E. 1973. *Structure and strategy in learning to talk*. Monographs of the Society for Research in Child Development, 38, no. 149.

Nelson, K. E. 1977. Facilitating children's syntax acquisition. *Developmental Psychology*, *13*, 101–7.

Nelson, K. E. & Bonvillian, J. D. 1978. Early language development: conceptual growth and related processes between 2 and 4½ years of age. In K. E. Nelson (ed.) *Children's language*, vol. I. New York: Gardner Press.

Nelson, K. E., Carskaddon, G. & Bonvillian, J. D. 1973. Syntax acquisition: impact of experimental variation in adult verbal interaction with the child. *Child Development*, 44, 497–504.

Newport, E. L., Gleitman, H. & Gleitman, L. R. 1977. Mother, I'd rather do it myself: some effects and non-effects of maternal speech style. In C. E. Snow and C. A. Ferguson (eds.) *Talking to children: language input and acquisition*. Cambridge: Cambridge University Press.

Ninio, A. & Bruner, J. S. 1978. The achievement and antecedents of labelling. *Journal of Child Language*, 5, 1–16.

Phillips, J. 1970. Formal characteristics of speech which mothers address to their young children. Unpublished doctoral dissertation, John Hopkins University.

  1973. Syntax and vocabulary of mothers' speech to young children: age and sex comparisons. *Child Development*, 44, 182–5.

Piaget, J. 1952. *The origins of intelligence in children*. New York: International Universities Press.

  1954. Language and thought from the genetic point of view. *Acta Psychologica*, 10, 88–98.

  1970. Piaget's theory. In P. H. Mussen (ed.) *Carmichael's manual of child psychology*. New York: Wiley.

Piaget, J. & Inhelder, B. 1966. *The psychology of the child*. London: Routledge.

Poulton, E. C. 1974. *Tracking skill and manual control*. New York: Academic Press.

Ratner, N. & Bruner, J. S. 1978. Games, social exchange and the acquisition of language. *Journal of Child Language*, 5, 391–402.

Remick, H. 1976. Maternal speech to children during language acquisition. In W. von Raffler-Engel, and Y. Lebrun, (eds.) *Baby talk and infant speech*. Lisse, Netherlands: Swets and Zeitlinger.

Robinson, W. P. 1973. Where do children's answers come from? In B. Bernstein (ed.) *Class, codes and control*, vol. II. London: Routledge.

  1978. *Language management in education: the Australian context*. Sydney: Allen and Unwin.

Robinson, W. P. & Arnold, J. 1977. The question–answer exchange between mother and child. *European Journal of Social Psychology*, 7.

Robinson, W. P. & Rackstraw, S. J. 1972. *A question of answers*. London: Routledge.

Ruder, K. & Bunce, B. 1973. Training suprasegmental features of speech-effects of memory load. Unpublished MS. Bureau of Child Research Laboratories, Working Paper, University of Kansas, Lawrence.

Ruder, K., Smith, M. & Hermann, P. 1974. Effects of verbal imitation and comprehension training on verbal production of lexical items. In L. V. McReynolds (ed.) *Developing systematic procedures for training children's language*. Monographs of American Speech and Hearing Association.

Rūķe-Draviņa, V. 1977. Modifications of speech addressed to young children in Latvian. In C. E. Snow and C. A. Ferguson (eds.) *Talking to children: language input and acquisition*. Cambridge: Cambridge University Press.

Sachs, J. S., Brown, R. & Salerno, R. 1976. Adults' speech to children. In W. von Raffler-Engel, and Y. Lebrun (eds.) *Baby talk and infant speech*. Lisse, Netherlands: Swets and Zeitlinger.

Schiefelbusch, R. L. & Lloyd, L. L. (eds.) 1974. *Language perspectives: acquisition, retardation, intervention*. New York: Macmillan.

Schumaker, J. & Sherman, J. 1970. Training generative verb usage by imitation and reinforcement principles. *Journal of Applied Behavioral Analysis, 3,* 273–87.

Searle, J. R. 1969. *Speech acts: an essay in the philosophy of language.* Cambridge: Cambridge University Press.

1975. Indirect speech acts. In P. Cole & J. L. Morgan (eds.) *Syntax and semantics,* vol. 3: *Speech acts.* New York: Academic Press.

Shatz, M. 1977. The relationship between cognitive processes and the development of communication skills. *Nebraska Symposium on Motivation.* Lincoln: University of Nebraska Press.

Shatz, M. & Gelman, R. 1973. *Development of communication skills.* Monographs of the Society for Research in Child Development, 152.

Skinner, B. F. 1957. *Verbal behavior.* New York: Appleton-Century-Crofts.

Slobin, D. I. 1973. Cognitive prerequisites for the development of grammar. In C. A. Ferguson & D. I. Slobin (eds.) *Studies in child language development.* London: Holt Rinehart.

Smith, D. D. & Lovitt, T. C. 1973. The educational diagnosis and remediation of written *b* and *d* reversal problem: a case study. *Journal of Learning Disabilities, 6,* 356–63.

Snow, C. E. 1972. Mothers' speech to children learning language. *Child Development, 43,* 549–65.

1977a. Mothers' speech research: from input to acquisition. In C. E. Snow & C. A. Ferguson (eds.) *Talking to children: language input and acquisition.* Cambridge: Cambridge University Press.

1977b. The development of conversation between mothers and babies. *Journal of Child Language, 4,* 1–22.

Stallings, J. 1975. *Implementation and child effects of teaching practices in follow through classrooms.* Monographs of the Society for Research in Child Development, 40, no. 163.

Stern, D. N. 1974. Mother and infant at play: the dyadic interaction involving facial, vocal and gaze behaviors. In M. Lewis & L. A. Rosenblum (eds.) *The effect of the infant on its caregiver.* New York: Wiley.

1977. *The first relationship: infant and mother.* London: Open Books.

Stremel, K. 1972. Language training: a program for retarded children. *Mental Retardation, 10,* 47–9.

1973. Personal communication, 1973. Data given in K. F. Ruder & M. D. Smith, *Issues in language training* (page 571). In R. L. Schiefelbusch & L. L. Lloyd (eds.) *Language acquisition.* New York: Macmillan, 1974.

Stremel, K. & Waryas, C. 1974. A behavioral–psycholinguistic approach to language training. In L. McReynolds (ed.) *Developing systematic procedures for training children's language.* Monographs of American Speech and Hearing Association, 18.

Tawney, J. W. & Hipsher, L. W. 1970. Systematic instruction for retarded children. Part II: systematic language instruction. (Project 7 1205) U.S. Department of Health, Education and Welfare Grant. University of Illinois.

Templin, M. C. 1957. *Certain language skills in children.* Minneapolis: University of Minnesota Press.

Trevarthen, C. 1974. Conversations with a two-month-old. *New Scientist,* 2 May, p. 230.

Trevarthen, C. & Hubley, P. 1978. Secondary intersubjectivity: confidence, confiding and acts of meaning in the first year. In A. Lock (ed.) *Action, gesture and symbol: the emergence of language*. London: Academic Press.

Turner, G. J. 1973. Social class and children's language of control at ages five and seven. In B. Bernstein (ed.) *Class, codes and control*, vol. II. London: Routledge.

Weber, M. 1947. *The theory of social and economic organization*, trans. T. Parsons & A. M. Henderson. New York: Oxford University Press.

Wells, C. G. 1975. The contexts of children's early language experience. *Educational Review*, 27. 2, 114–25.

1979. Describing children's linguistic development at home and at school. *British Educational Research Journal*, 5, 75–98.

1980a. Apprenticeship in meaning. In K. Nelson (ed.) *Children's language*, vol. II. New York: Gardner Press.

1980b. Adjustments in adult–child conversation: some effects of interaction. In H. Giles, W. P. Robinson & P. M. Smith (eds.) *Language: social psychological perspectives*. Oxford: Pergamon.

1981. *Learning through interaction: the study of language development*. Cambridge: Cambridge University Press.

in preparation. *Language development in the pre-school years*. To be published by Cambridge University Press.

Wells, C. G., Barnes, S., Gutfreund, M. & Satterly, D. in press. Characteristics of adult speech which predict children's language development. *Journal of Child Language*.

Wells, C. G., MacLure, M. & Montgomery, M. 1981. Some strategies for sustaining conversation. In P. Werth (ed.) *Conversation, speech and discourse*. London: Croom Helm.

Wells, C. G., Montgomery, M. & MacLure, M. 1979. Adult–child discourse: outline of a model of analysis. *Journal of Pragmatics*, 3, 337–80.

Westinghouse Learning Corporation, Ohio University. 1969. *The impact of Head Start, an evaluation of the effects of Head Start on children's cognitive and affective development*, vol. I. Washington, DC: Clearinghouse for Federal Scientific and Technical Information, Department of Commerce, National Bureau of Standards.

Whitehurst, G. J. 1974. The role of comprehension in the generative production of direct–indirect object sentences by pre-school children. Unpublished paper. State University of New York at Stony Brook.

Wood, D. & Middleton, D. 1975. A study of assisted problem-solving. *British Journal of Psychology*, 66, 181–91.

Wood, D., Wood, H. & Middleton, D. 1978. An experimental evaluation of four face-to-face teaching strategies. *International Journal of Behavioral Development*, 1, 131–47.

Wootton, A. J. 1974. Talk in the homes of young children. *Sociology*, 8, 277–95.

1981. Children's use of address terms. In P. French & M. MacLure (eds.) *Adult–child conversation: studies in structure and process*. London: Croom Helm.

3. A social psychological approach to the study of stuttering*

RAINER KRAUSE

1. Introduction

Looking at the history of stutterer treatment is like visiting a chamber of horrors. In 1841, a surgeon named Dieffenbach published a paper with the title: 'The cure of stuttering by a new surgical operation' (Dieffenbach 1841). What he actually did was to cut out little wedge-shaped pieces from the roots of the tongues of stutterers. He 'treated' a lot of people in this way and some of them died. He was convinced that by doing so, he could weaken or prevent the muscular spasms which he thought to be the cause of the disturbance. Strangely enough the cure worked for a while, so Dieffenbach had followers all over the world, cutting out pieces of stutterers' tongues. Dieffenbach was not the first to hold the tongue responsible for stuttering. Aristotle thought that the tongue was too sluggish to keep track of the flow of thoughts. Others thought the tongue was too weak or too wet, and Francis Bacon treated stutterers' tongues with hot wine, to make the tongue mobile and flexible. Of course a modified version of this cure, namely drinking alcohol, is used even today and quite a few of my patients claimed to be fluent after consuming alcohol or marijuana (Krause 1981). The causes of stuttering are no longer attributed to any efferent motor organ – at least in the scientific community of researchers of stuttering – despite the fact that abnormal muscular innervation patterns of the face, the larynx (Freeman & Ushijima 1976), and sometimes the whole body, can of course be found during a stuttering spell (Krause 1981).

Very few people claim that these abnormal innervation patterns are the reason for stuttering; it seems more likely that they accompany the

* This research is part of a project on stuttering and non-verbal interactive behaviour sponsored by the Swiss National Fund for the Advancement of Science, grant number 810.329.75, awarded to the author.

stuttering spell and are a rather complex result of expecting to stutter and trying very hard not to, plus some general physiological and motoric correlates of high arousal, stress and anxiety, as well as the specific techniques stutterers use to cope with these phenomena (Hill 1944a, b; Perkins 1970).

Many theories about stuttering are still asocial in so far as they do not take into consideration the social background of speech.

2. The frequency of stuttering and the question of hereditability

Stuttering is fairly common in the industrialized countries, and estimates range from 1 to 4 per cent of the total population (American Speech and Hearing Association 1957; Van Riper 1971). Most estimates are around 1 per cent, but this rises to nearer 4 per cent if all children who had a temporary stuttering problem are included (Bloodstein 1975).

There are great differences in the incidence of stuttering between different cultures. In a cross-cultural investigation, Bullen (1945) came to the conclusion that within the Navajo, Polar Eskimo and New Guinea tribes stuttering was rare or non-existent. More recent observations shed some doubts on Bullen's claims. Johnson (1944) and Snidecor (1947) stated that there was no stuttering among the Bannock and Shoshone Indians, and from their observations generalized that there was no stuttering among the North American Indians. This position cannot be held anymore.

Lemert in a 1970 overview comes to the conclusion that 'Stuttering does occur in preliterate societies and . . . it occurs apart from the influence of acculturation. It is also reasonably certain that stuttering varies in its incidence from culture to culture' (p. 175). The same author lists three possible ways whereby culture asserts its influence in inducing stuttering.

1. Stuttering is a pattern directly learned from others.
2. Culture exerts stress upon the individual either through competion or conflicting demands, in such a way as to disrupt speech co-ordinations.
3. Culture operates through values or themes as part of a socio-psychological process which produces stuttering.

One might think that points 2 and 3 are nearly the same, since there could be cultural systems which produce a great amount of stress simply in enforcing values. The first hypothesis is rather unlikely since stuttering occurs in children who had no stuttering models.

Since, as I will show later, stuttering is a childhood disturbance in that it nearly always starts in childhood, the nature of stress and conflicting demands must be centred around the transmission of values and expectations from parents to children. Some of the differences which can be found in different North American Indian societies might have to do with the expectation on children to compete like little adults. Lemert (1970), in fact, comes to the conclusion that primitive societies with structures most nearly resembling our own are most likely to generate a high incidence of stuttering.

In a more recent survey of the incidence of stuttering, Bloodstein (1975) comes to a rather similar conclusion:

> Reflecting upon all these observations we may perhaps conclude that even though a great many questions about stuttering remain unanswered, research appears to have shown the disorder to be a significant comment on the culture that produces it. To say that there are many stutterers in a given society is apparently to say that it is a rather competitive society that tends to impose high standards of achievement on the individual and to regard status and prestige as unusually desirable goals, that it is sternly intolerant of inadequacy or abnormality, and that, as a by-product of its distinctive set of cultural values, it in all likelihood places a high premium on competence of speech. (pp. 97f.)

The question of what kind of adult standards the child is expected to live up to is not addressed in these conclusions.

We have reason to assume that it is not the status of the social class to which the adults actually belong that creates these kinds of expectations, but rather the strong desire on the part of the parents to be members of a higher status group. Morgenstern (1956), in a careful study in Scotland, found that families with very intensive upward-mobility aspirations had significantly more stutterers. The fact that male children may be more affected than female is then not too surprising, since the expectations of an upwardly mobile family are mostly centred around male children. A different interpretation of this fact is given by Kidd et al. (1978). They assume, on the basis of genealogical data, that the threshold for the development of stuttering may be genetically lower for males than for females. The question of the hereditability of stuttering is not yet completely solved. Clearly some families have more stutterers than others (Andrews & Harris 1964). On the other hand, some of the data on family history are suspect; it is not easy to arrive at reliable diagnoses of 'stuttering' on the basis of a stutterer's reports about the supposed stuttering of distant ancestors. There is a lot of hearsay involved and stutterers seem to have a strong tendency to find other stutterers among their ancestors (Sheehan & Martyn 1967). The mathematical analysis of the distribution of stuttering within the families of stutterers and non-stutterers shows that two different models of gene-trait interactions can be fitted to the data (Kidd 1978). It is obvious from the same data that non-genetic factors play an important role too. Gray (1940) was able to demonstrate, by analysing the incidence of stuttering within two separate branches of one family, that the frequency distribution of stuttering differed considerably between the two. He thought that there might be distinctive features in the 'climate' of the family which fosters stuttering. Among other things, the belief that stuttering is inherited creates an anxiety-laden, over-watchful behaviour pattern on the part of parents, making disturbance in the offspring more likely (Johnson & Associates 1959).

It is apparent, however, that there are more stutterers among the ancestors of stutterers than among those of non-stutterers, but it is still not clear why. Some researchers claim that stuttering is passed down the generations by certain social strategies, while others think of a gene–environment interaction. Few think of a strictly hereditary causation. It seems that this genetic component can, at most, be some sort of readiness to develop the speech disturbance under specific social influences. It is certain that the severity of stuttering is not related to genetic factors (Kidd et al. 1978).

3. Childrearing practices fostering stuttering

Given that cultural and familial backgrounds can be unfavourable, it is not surprising that cultures as well as families hold the tongue or the genes, instead of themselves, solely responsible for stuttering. In our investigations, for example, the parents of the stutterers we were study-ing either believed that stuttering was a result of shock experience – usually a dog, cow or other animals acting in a threatening way – or that it was inherited. But 40 per cent of the parents never spoke to the child about possible reasons. Very few of them ever mentioned that something might have been wrong in their childrearing practices.

Our stutterers sharply disagreed with these parental hypotheses. More than two-thirds of them thought that the main reason for their stuttering was parental errors in their upbringing. This of course might be a result of psychotherapeutic indoctrination, but very few of them had experienced insight-oriented psychotherapy.

It is true that very often shock experiences can be found in the life histories of stutterers (Ierodiakonou 1970), but this is true for most chil-dren. A big dog barking at the 4-year-old boy, or getting lost in his uncle's garden, may well be an apparent starting point for stuttering, but the ground for being so vulnerable to these kinds of experiences was laid long before. In other cases, the shock theory clearly serves as some kind of family mythology. For example, one such myth was that the stuttering originated from an intra-uterine shock, experienced by the unborn boy in a basement of a German city, during heavy bombing. The latency for the appearance of the stuttering was about four years!

Of course, asking stutterers retrospectively about the childrearing practices of their parents can introduce serious distortion, but the little data we have, based on observations of interactive behaviour of parents with their stuttering children, seems to give an even worse picture than the stutterer remembers (Motsch et al. 1976). In my experience and in that of other clinicians, stutterers tend to rely strongly on the defence mechanism of idealization, especially of the mother (Barbara 1954; Murphy & Fitzsimons 1960). In our own investigations (Krause 1981), we found that stutterers described their fathers as being significantly more authoritarian, undemocratic, unpredictable, and especially more distant than did same-aged, same-status controls. There were no significant differences regarding the descriptions of mothers, but stutterers' reports still tended to be less favourable than those of the control group.

Glasner (1970: 252) describes the familial setting stuttering children come from: 'In the first place, most of the mothers described themselves as highstrung, nervous and lacking in patience. They are found to be rigid, domineering, perfectionistic and overprotective, and are the dominant of the two parents.' We found a very rigid separation of sex-specific roles for parental activities. The mother is thus only dominant inside the house, but very submissive and shy outside.

Johnson (1959), in one of his many investigations of the onset of stuttering, found that mothers of stutterers are generally more dissatisfied with their children, their husbands, their general life circumstances and themselves. This might be the psychological side of the 'strong upward mobility' referred to above. Bloodstein, Jaeger & Tureen (1952) found that parents of stutterers placed stronger emphasis on fluent speech and were more ready to diagnose 'stuttering' on the basis of audiotaped speech than were parents of fluent speakers. One concrete finding was the use of more punitive techniques in toilet training (Johnson 1959: 54, 226).

One result we found, which I will return to later in connection with our theory of stuttering, was that the stutterers' parents, according to the stutterers, showed significantly less affective and expressive behaviour than the parents of the control group. Additionally these parents tried to suppress affective and expressive behaviour on the part of the children. So, the whole family of the stutterer, in general, seems to be unexpressive and not very affective. We have good reason to believe that this kind of affect-suppression takes place long before speech development proper. Ierodiakonou (1970) found an impressive list of psychological problems in stuttering children, most of which centred around eating, before stuttering developed. Giffin & Heider (1967) claim that what we refer to at a later age as 'speech anxiety', which is a prominent part of stutterers' pathology, grows on the basis of communication suppression. This occurs 'when a child who desires to express himself obtains negative reactions from his parents' (p. 314).

This is true for preverbal communication even more than for verbal communication. So we have reason to believe that the personality of the child who subsequently stutters is already insecure, shy, sensitive, polite to adults, but at the same time unhappy and full of resentment, before the appearance of the speech disturbance proper (Ierodiakanou 1970: 170).

Of course the psychological and behavioural problems to be found after the appearance or diagnosis of stuttering might be a consequence of that diagnosis, and Ierodiakonou's data, for example, were gathered retrospectively after the children had already been labelled 'stutterers'. I do not know any investigation which describes the behaviour patterns and the psychological make up of children who *later* become stutterers.

In addition, these kinds of listings of unfavourable childhood experiences do not provide an adequate explanation for the stuttering. They are usually so non-specific that it is not clear why a child with such a background ends up as a stutterer and not as a compulsive neurotic or a depressed person. In order to make sense of the term 'social', we need much more detailed knowledge of the everyday routine of parent–child interactions than these global lists can give us.

I will try to comment on this when discussing the development of the disturbance. I have already proposed that the basis for vulnerability to this disturbance is laid in the preverbal stage. Let us now consider the subsequent phases.

4. The development and stabilization of the disturbance through parental and therapeutic coping strategies

Stuttering is a childhood disturbance; it starts and develops in childhood, usually at the same time as speech is acquired. The probability that stuttering might subsequently show up follows a negatively accelerating growth curve with increasing age. In rare cases, I have heard of stuttering beginning after puberty. One of my own patients lost a very severe psychogenic childhood asthma at age 15, but simultaneously acquired a severe stuttering problem.

The number of spontaneous remissions is very high during childhood, whereas adults who still stutter rarely ever lose their problem. Estimates of the incidence of spontaneous remissions in childhood vary between 42 and 79 per cent (Milisen & Johnson 1936; Andrews and Harris 1964). The latter figure seems more reliable since it is based on a developmental study involving the total population of children in an English town. Around 10 per cent of all children seem to have a stuttering problem at least for a while (Dickson 1971). This usually cannot be remembered in adulthood. Childhood stuttering is, therefore, a relatively common occurrence in our society, but it is very different from adulthood stuttering in its phenomenology and in the way it is experienced by the stutterer. In addition, the labelling by parents of childhood language as stuttering seems to be heavily determined by specific expectations or standards on the part of the parents.

The stuttering of an adult can be a very impressive chain of actions, for the listener or spectator, as well as for the stutterer himself. One of our patients funnelled his lips intensively, raised his eyebrows and opened his eyes maximally. At the same time his pupils disappeared upwards, so that only the white part of the sclera could be seen. His upper trunk moved quickly forward and his head upwards. These kinds of pictures are not encountered every day, and so listeners react very markedly even if they try to follow the social rules that this is a 'normal' conversation. And, in a sense, the stutterer himself is very impressed too. It is a well-known clinical phenomenon that adult stutterers overestimate the benefits of fluent speech and very often think all their problems would vanish if they could only talk fluently. This hampers a realistic perception of the self. Adult stutterers are so intensively preoccupied with the expectation, avoidance and fight against stuttering, that it interferes with nearly every action (Barbara 1954; Murphy & Fitzsimons 1960). Childhood stuttering does not yet have these qualities.

Bloodstein (1960a, b, 1961), for example, describes four phases in the development of stuttering, which must be understood not solely on the basis of the audible stutter response, but also by taking into consideration the cognitive and affective coping strategies the stutterer is using. These include the evaluation of the disturbance by the stutterer and his 'significant others'.

So between 3 and 6 years, according to Bloodstein (1975), many stutterers can be found with the following characteristics:

In the *first* phase:

1. The difficulty has a distinct tendency to be episodic.
2. The child stutters most when excited or upset, when he seems to have a great deal to say, or under conditions of communicative pressure.
3. The dominant symptom is repetition.
4. There is a marked tendency for stuttering to occur at the beginning of the sentence, clause or phrase.
5. In contrast to more advanced stuttering, the interruptions occur not only on content words, but also on the function words of speech – the pronouns, conjunctions, articles and prepositions.
6. Most of the time children in the first phase of stuttering show little evidence of concern about the interruptions in their speech. (Bloodstein 1975: 24f.)

In the *second* phase:

1. The disorder is essentially chronic.
2. The child regards himself as a stutterer.
3. The stuttering occurs chiefly on the major parts of speech – nouns, verbs, adjectives, and adverbs.
4. Despite his self-concept as a stutterer, the child usually evinces little or no concern about his speech difficulty.
5. The stuttering is said to increase chiefly under conditions of excitement or when the child is speaking rapidly. (Bloodstein 1975: 25)

In the *third* phase:

1. The stuttering comes and goes largely in response to specific situations.
2. Certain words and sounds are regarded as more difficult than others.
3. In varying degrees, use is made of word substitutions and circumlocutions.
4. There is essentially no avoidance of speech situations and little or no evidence of fear and embarrassment. (Bloodstein 1975: 26)

Characteristics of the *fourth* phase (the apex of its development) are:

1. Vivid fearful anticipations of stuttering.
2. Feared words, sounds, and situations.
3. Very frequent word substitutions and circumlocutions.
4. Avoidance of speech situations, and other evidence of fear and embarrassment. (Bloodstein 1975: 26)

These kinds of phases are naturally problematic in many ways, and Bloodstein himself calls them abstractions. Van Riper (1971) arrived at a somewhat different developmental typology. However, all of these descriptions clearly show the increasing impact of anticipatory control attempts which the stutterer uses more and more during his career, together with the very clear connection between early stuttering and the affective state of the young speaker. If we bear in mind that the spontaneous remission rate in the early phases of development is very high, and that there is virtually no remission after phase 4, then the key to treatment and understanding of the disturbance might be found in the process of becoming a phase 4 stutterer. I will deal with this question in detail later, since we first need a clearer understanding of the stuttering response proper and how it is part of the process of communication.

One of the reasons why behaviour therapeutic techniques are considered appropriate for the treatment of stuttering lies in the mistaken perception that the disturbed behaviour – namely the stuttering – is clearly segmented in time and is clearly audible and visible. So the therapist does not have to fight with the usual problems of how to define the disturbed behaviour and the goal behaviour, since both seem well defined. The only problem seems to be to find techniques for changing the one into the other. This is a fatal error, made repeatedly by generations of therapists. Defining fluent speech as the absence of audible stuttering is very problematic, since, as I will show later, something in the general communication process of the phase 4 stutterer is disturbed which goes far beyond stuttering per se. In many ways, stuttered speech is more natural than controlled stuttering, during which the stutterer successfully avoids the audible manifestation of the disturbance, and the interaction partner does not realize that he is talking to a stutterer (Freund, 1966; Krause 1978, 1981).

If we take as examples speech accompanied by a metronome or by delayed auditory feedback, or even reading in chorus, it can easily be shown that such speech is in many respects more unnatural than stuttered speech. This kind of speech is asocial in that synchronization phenomena, which usually accompany social speech in dyads, cannot be found. It is 'non-human' in that the affective parts, which are usually carried by differences in segmentation, temporal organization, variation in pitch and breathing patterns, etc. are 'filtered out' by these techniques. It is interesting to note that in movies in which computers are able to talk, they usually adopt speech patterns which are very similar to the patterns that some therapists of stuttering try to teach their patients. It is considered typical for computers that they do not show affect. The usefulness of these techniques usually disappears as soon as the stutterer masters them so well that his natural speech breaks through again (McCabe & McCollum 1972). Additionally this kind of speech has no reinforcement value, either for the speaker or for the listener (Tunner 1974).

One of the great problems is that very few therapists appear to have ever thought deeply about what it is that makes for 'natural speech', and by 'natural speech' I do not mean necessarily fluent speech. Therapists have been as impressed by the stuttering spell as have the stutterers themselves and their speaking partners, and so have defined fluency as the ultimate goal of therapy, and fluency means the absence of audible 'disturbances'. This goal is certainly not too difficult to obtain for a while (Van Riper 1973). Nearly every device or therapy leads to short-term improvements of fluency. This phenomenon is so clearly recognizable that it was called the distraction effect (Sheehan 1970a), indicating that the stutterer is 'distracted' from his stuttering by new stimuli and strange speaking techniques and his speech defect thereby diminishes. As I will show below, the process the stutterer is distracted from is not the speech planning per se, but the moderation of his affective arousal.

In our own investigations, the intensity of the disturbance as measured by ratings of tape recordings and as assessed in a speech clinic did not correlate with the subjectively felt degree of suffering (Krause 1981). Stutterers who control their disturbance by techniques which lead to long phases of 'fluency', are very often under more pressure than others who stutter openly. Expectation anxiety, their permanent control attempts, and the fear that in the most important moments they cannot rely on their control techniques, create more uncertainties than the stuttering behaviour itself. Given that as yet we do not know how natural speech is produced, it seems questionable whether we do the stutterer a great favour by attempting to make him fluent whatever the cost.

This narrow conception of stuttering and its treatment is based on ideas about the disturbance which come from popular psychology, according to which repetitions of syllables are considered as one of the major symptoms. Interjections, postponements and prolongations are experienced as 'normal' disfluencies (Johnson 1959, 1961). This perception of stuttering is used by the adult stutterer, to hide his difficulties. He tries to change into 'normal' disfluencies the anticipated difficult parts, with their anticipated word and syllable repetitions and blocks. This technique is often successful in so far as the interactive partner does not realize that he is talking to a stutterer, although something odd remains about the communication process, and the stutterer himself knows that he has avoided stuttering (Few & Lingwall 1972; Wendahl & Cole 1961).

Van Riper (1973), a stutterer himself, drew up an ordinal fivefold classification system, which is of interest in this respect. The first technique by which the stutterer may prevent stuttering is by *substituting for feared words and by circumlocution*. These techniques may be used very effectively, but they frequently produce strange statements. One of my patients reported intense feelings of disappointment and shame when, in the course of a fluent statement during a public discussion, he actually said something very different from what he had intended. My interpretation of these kinds of phenomena (which I elaborate below) is that the stutterer decides not only to choose different words in a step by step fashion, but also to avoid a forceful presentation, and thus he talks in an unduly calm manner that does not reflect his real affective state.

A second category of techniques consists of *postponement strategies*, used in the hope that, by waiting, the block may pass. Some stutterers can place their postponements in normal speech pauses, or they may interject expressions like 'well', 'you see'. With either or both of these techniques used efficiently, the partner will not realize that he is talking to a stutterer, but speech is disturbed nevertheless; for example, pauses are unnaturally long.

A third category is called '*starting tricks*', enabling the stutterer to say a feared word by helping him to produce the first difficult sound of the word (Bloodstein 1975: 12). This technique may consist of movements, grimacing or of first saying some easy thing like 'mmh', 'ah', 'uh'.

The fourth category consists of *escape trials*, enabling the stutterer to come out of the block. The behaviour I described above (p. 83) partly demonstrates this technique, but there are other forms of facial or gestural behaviour patterns. They can be rich, distinctive and idiosyncratic. Every stutterer may develop patterns that are at least partially distinctive. It is not clear why and how these seemingly bizarre chains of behaviour develop, although Luper (1968) developed an interesting but not wholly satisfactory (since he does not deal at all with the expressive side of these facial phenomena) theory, offering an explanation based on operant conditioning procedures (see also below).

The fifth category, *symptoms of anti-expectancy*, includes expedients the stutterer uses for preventing the anticipation of difficulty from arising, by adopting monotonous speech patterns, for example, so that no particular word stands out to be feared. This category could subsume self-instructions not to think about stuttering and to be completely calm and relaxed. As I have already mentioned I would interpret these kinds of behaviours differently, namely as an attempt to keep affect below a critical threshold.

It should now be evident that all adult avoidance techniques are triggered by anticipated stutter events; but for the partners in the interactions only some of them can be easily decoded as stuttering. It is therefore erroneous to restrict stuttering treatment to audible defects like sentence, word and syllable repetitions, or to prolonged vocalizations.

Many researchers in the field of stuttering who stutter themselves (I know of twenty-four in the USA) recommend their fellow sufferers to talk openly and naturally and to forget about avoiding stuttering (Hood 1978).

If your experiences as a stutterer are similar to mine at all, you spend a good part of your life listening to advice like relax, think what you have to say, trust yourself, breathe deeply or even talk with pebbles in your mouth. By now you have realized that it does not help at all; if anything it aggravates the problems. There is a good reason why these legendary remedies fail, because they all have something artificial as a basis, namely the suppression of stuttering, the covering up. The more you cover up, and the more you try to avoid stuttering, the more you stutter. (Sheehan 1978: 17; translated from German)

You must overcome your avoidance behaviour radically. Whenever you replace a word by another one, or use a vocal trick to start speaking, or postpone or give up the intention to speak, you will aggravate your suffering. If you evade your anxieties they develop anew and grow, instead of disappearing. So the avoider has to be on guard permanently and is forced to find new ways to avoid situations all the time. (Emerick 1978: 6; translated from German)

These self-therapeutic recommendations can be interpreted as an attempt to change phase 4 stuttering back into the phase 1 of childhood stuttering. Obviously stutterers experience great subjective gain by reconnecting the disturbance to affective arousal and by simultaneously giving up the tormenting anticipatory avoidance strategies. But this process is extremely laborious and is accompanied by intense feelings of shame and anxiety.

5. Some speculations on the nature of the communication process and its relation to stuttering

Many of the problems with stuttering therapies, especially current behaviouristic techniques, are a consequence of shallow or inadequate conceptions concerning the process of 'natural' social speech and the onto- and phylogenetic development it is based on.

By the time the child starts to talk, a non-verbal communication system governing the relations between the child and his parents has already been relatively fully developed. This non-verbal system does of course make use of vocal parameters of all kinds as well as non-vocal expressive behaviour patterns. This communicative system is centred around the mutual induction and communication of affect (Krause 1979a; Tomkins 1962–3). The spoken symbolic language is superimposed only very gradually on these normally well-functioning affect communication systems. Even the organization of the adult's spoken language still varies in relation to his different affective states. Reading identical texts, for example, in states of high anxiety and in states of joy produces differences in pitch, temporal segmentation, loudness and many other parameters (Feldstein 1964; Scherer 1979).

Ekman & Friesen (1969) and Ekman (1977) tried to classify acts of non-verbal communication on the basis of their phylo- and ontogenetic origin and their function. I will briefly present their descriptions because we shall need them later for our model of the stuttering process and its empirical verification.

Emblems are:

symbolic actions where the movement has a very specific verbal meaning, known to most subscribers to a sub-culture of a culture, and typically employed with the intention of sending a message. (Ekman 1977: 40)

The head nodding 'yes' or head shaking 'no' are examples of emblems. According to Ekman, emblems are also used in conversation by the person listening and serve as what Dittman (1972) has called 'listener responses' (Ekman 1977: 41). Other authors would subsume these kinds of behaviour under the term 'regulators'.

Body-manipulators are:

movements in which one part of the body does something to another part. Scratching the head, picking the nose, wringing the hands, licking the lips are examples. Also included would be the use of a prop in other than an instrumental act; for example, playing with a pencil, twisting a book of matches, using a paper clip to scratch an ear. (Ekman 1977: 47)

They are considered to be signs of discomfort, and people producing a lot of such behaviour are perceived as awkward, tense and untrustworthy. Body manipulators have no direct relationship to the flow of speech as emblems might have, but Ekman states that brief body manipulators of less than two seconds often occur in phonemic clauses, where there are many speech disruptions. Theoretically these kinds of movements are considered to develop first as a part 'of adaptive efforts to satisfy self- or bodily needs, or to perform bodily actions, or to manage emotions, or to develop or maintain prototypic interpersonal contacts, or to learn instrumental activities' (Ekman & Friesen 1969: 84).

Illustrators are:

movements which are intimately tied to the content and/or flow of speech. We distinguish a number of different types of illustrators in terms of how they relate to the simultaneous speech:

Batons:	Movements which accent a particular word;
Underliners:	Movements which emphasize a phrase, clause, sentence or group of sentences;
Ideographs:	Movements which sketch the path or direction of thought;
Kinetographs:	Movements which depict a bodily action or a non-human action;
Pictographs:	Movements which draw the shape of the referent in the air;
Rhythmics:	Movements which depict the rhythm or pacing of an event;
Spatials:	Movements which depict a spatial relationship;
Deictics:	Movements which point to the referent.

(Ekman 1977: 49)

Regulators are those kinds of non-verbal behaviour systems which 'maintain and regulate' the back and forth nature of speaking and listening between two or more interactants (Duncan 1974). Duncan & Fiske (1977) who have studied the turn system in great detail, describe for example 'back-channel actions' consisting of head nods, and short back-channel statements like 'mhm' and smiles. These are actions performed by the auditor in order to keep the speaker talking.

Emotional expressions are distinctive innervation patterns of the facial muscles which are specific for seven genetically preprogrammed primary affects in humans and in non-human primates. These primary affects are happiness, anger, surprise, fear, disgust, sadness and interest. There is good evidence that they are culturally universal, which does not mean that socialization would have no influence on the experiencing and the expression of affect. On the one hand, the relation between the 'affect antecedents' like social events and the affect itself is partly defined by social conditions. There is no reason to assume that the same events produce the affect anger in all cultures. On the other hand, culture asserts heavy influence on the management of the affect expression. This means that members of a given society have to learn which affect can be expressed to what degree without social sanctions.

Figure 1 depicts a simple model using Ekman's terms. It is based on Brunswik's lens-model and some ideas from Scherer (1974) and from my own work (Krause 1977). A's intentions and expectations in relation to B (the receiver) as well as A's affective reactions and moods influence organized systems of his body boundaries. These organized systems are sometimes called 'channels' using the morphology of the body as a classification system. In the German research tradition on the psychology

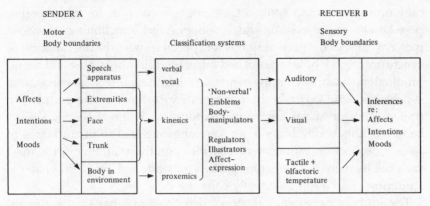

Figure 1. An extended model of communication

of expression these systems were called 'fields of expression' and every one had a corresponding science. 'Physiognomie', for example, was the science of inferring meaning from the static properties of the face. This limitation on one channel makes sense only in relation to the technology needed to measure the expressive phenomena. The process of social perception in humans relies on simultaneous processing of the information coming in on all channels. Ekman's classification, as depicted, in the middle of figure 1, is not centred around channels but functional properties of the behaviour described. So it is closer to the decoding procedure in the receiver.

B perceives with the corresponding sense organs the alterations of A's body boundaries and of his motor behaviour. B infers on the bases of some built-in or learned decoding rules the 'true' intentions, expectations and affects of A, and reacts with what from his point of view is appropriate action. This process of inferring, which means that subjectively the receiver *perceives* the intentions and affects of the sender, does not need conscious decision-making.

The same types of processes take place simultaneously in both interactants. The separation between sender and receiver makes sense only in relation to spoken language. The process of talking to one another requires ordered succession of speaker and listener states, since a listener trying to talk at the same time cannot succeed in processing both activities. Non-verbal communication can be sent and received simultaneously.

Affect displays, body manipulators and probably some forms of regulators and emblems are ontogenetically and, in some respects, phylogenetically much older than spoken language, which is, so to say, superimposed on these pre-existing and, one hopes, well-functioning behaviour patterns. One of the preconditions for speech seems to be the capacity for synchronizing a whole series of body processes, like breathing and sound production, illustrative movements and loudness, etc. The capacity to synchronize one's own body movements with those of the partner is a prerequisite for social language according to Bullowa (1975). Disturbances of this bodily basis of spoken language lead to disturbances of speech production proper, whereby the cognitive planning of the message, at least in the semantic part, is not affected. This is what the stuttering of an adult essentially consists of.

The study of psychological speech defects shows that a patient might regress in the usage of the speech organs to prespeech and precommunicative stages.

Before speech became a practical means of communication, the activities of the organs of speech had a purely libidinal and discharging function. The development goes from the level of autoerotic babbling or screaming, through the levels of magically influencing the environment by means of the vocal apparatus, to the gradual acquisition of the understanding of words, to the final attainment of the level at which speech is used as a purposive means of communication, this development is a highly complex process subject to disturbances at various points . . . In more severe cases of stuttering the function of communication has been given up entirely, the organs of speech are again intended to be used autoerotically. (Fenichel 1946: 315).

There is evidence now more and more that the skill in interpersonal matching of communication rhythms is a prerequisite to speech learning. Jaffe & Anderson make the point based on studies of mother–child interaction (Beebe, Stern & Jaffe 1979), that conversation 'grows ontogenetically out of rhythmic co-action between a mother and her baby' (Jaffe & Anderson 1979: 2), whereby in the early years of development the modality in which the rhythmic co-action takes place – acoustic, visual, tactile kinesthetic – is less crucial than the temporal patterning of that stimulation.

Psychoanalytic clinicians have known for some time, and have described in clinical terms, that the 'unempathetic mother' is the one unable to synchronize her affective behaviour and states with that of her child (Miller 1979). Constant mismatching in this area is extremely detrimental to mental health, since later on the capacity for matching communication rhythms – sometimes called congruence – is the behavioural correlate of interpersonal attraction and even assortative mating (Welkowitz, Cariffe & Feldstein 1976). The clinical symptoms of autism and so called narcissistic personality frequently consist of these subtle, barely perceivable but functionally very powerful deviations of rhythmic synchronization (Krause 1979a).

Using these ideas and the model in figure 1, we can return to the subject of stuttering.

5.1. Distortion of the speech process through treatment procedures applied by parents, therapists and the stutterer himself

As I have already mentioned, the first childhood stuttering consists of speech disfluencies and repetitions, which show up if the child is in a state of affective arousal, very often a conflict situation with high communicative pressure. To a certain extent this holds true for adult stutterers also. Thus most stutterers report that affects like anger, shame, etc. seem to foster the disturbance, but in relation to anger at least we found that there is an upper threshold above which the speech disturbance disappears. Thus the very rare fits of rage are usually completely fluent, that is, as long as the stutterer does not try to control it.

The necessity for controlling even mild forms of hostility and other affects arises from the coupling of pairs of conflicting emotions, for example anger and anxiety, through the childrearing procedures mentioned above. The affective basis of the stuttering spell is not therefore 'arousal' per se, but the presence of two relatively intense antagonistic states of affect. The two most important for stuttering, as we know from psychoanalytic treatment of stutterers are anger–fear conflicts and conflicts around exhibitionistic wishes versus shame. I do not mean that exhibitionism is an affect, but it requires for its realization in a social group specific forms of non-verbal behaviour which are in many ways antagonistic to the ones accompanying shame.

Some stuttering spells I have analysed in detail, at least where facial activities are concerned, can be considered as a very rapid oscillation between attempts to produce an angry message and a fearful one; a consequence of these antagonistic states is that *nothing* comes out.

The majority of the stutterers – I would guess about 70 per cent of our male stutterers – have permanent anger–fear conflicts. I have also seen and treated some woman stutterers and have found a very clear conflict pattern in one of the patients between distress and shame. Common to all stutterers is the intense coupling of antagonistic states of affect. So anger *always* activates fear at the same time. Non-stutterers may suffer temporarily from the same problem, as for example in stage fright where, as a consequence of antagonistic states, the speech process is interrupted. But here it is only a temporary phenomenon.

We have to assume an automatic affect activation system which triggers both affects simultaneously. That is the affective side of what is called 'ambivalence' in decision-making. Introspectively, the summation of anger and fear, especially when frequently triggered, is not the experience of feelings of anger plus feelings of fear, but, following the 'over-summativity rule' of Gestalt psychology, something amorphous described as 'excitement' or arousal. In my view, therefore, arousal is a relatively uninformative term for simultaneous antagonistic primary affects, which cannot be experienced as such.

It is only in the very rare cases, when one affect becomes clearly predominant over the other, that speech becomes fluent. These are usually situations of real emergency where self-defence is absolutely vital. In these situations, people temporarily 'forget' their neurotic structures. It is biologically senseless to remain chronically in antagonistic states, since affects have the function of facilitating behavioural programmes which are also antagonistic; the obvious examples in this case are aggression and attacking versus flight. On the other hand, somebody continually triggering both states might end-up glued to the middle like the famous donkey between the two trusses of hay.

5.2. The affect display rule of de-emphasizing any emotion and its relation to stuttering

Instead of tying his speech production to affective flow, the stutterer tries to keep his whole affective system below the lower threshold of arousal, knowing that in states of extreme relaxation speech is possible. This kind of self-instruction has a long history, since the disfluent child, being disfluent in states of affective 'arousal', is constantly encouraged to adopt behavioural strategies which ignore or suppress his affective 'arousal' – an integral part of expressive behaviour – from the speech production proper. In our investigations we found that, to prevent disturbances, parents used the following strategies (listed in order of frequency of usage):
1. talk slowly
2. general relaxation
3. repeat message but slowly
4. breathing techniques

5. silence
6. threats
7. correction of body posture
8. punishment

One of the consequences of all these strategies is that body correlates of affect are changed and reduced. Usually nobody worries about such long-standing consequences, since the behaviour strategies are thought to enable fluent speech.

All of us know that 'calm' children are easier to handle than excited children. Calm in this respect means children without negative affects like anger. We have reason to assume that the strategies mentioned above are used by parents on an unconscious level to control and suppress hostile affect. Unconsciously, these are not meant to handle the speech disturbance per se, which is anyway a widespread phenomenon at this age and for many parents a subject of little concern. (It is, by the way, inappropriate at the age when speech disturbances begin to expect children to control their affects. In our culture at least, the capacity for affect control in normal circumstances is not acquired before puberty.) These strategies can only continue to be harmful, and markedly so, because of the fact that they are based on interactive strategies from preverbal stages when the control of affect is a dominant goal of parental education.

This idea is not altogether new, since most clinicians have been forced to single out the parent–child relationship as the dominant, if not sole, factor in the origin of stuttering. But such specific forms of maladaptive interactions have not been proposed before.

The roots of stuttering originate in interpersonal relationships, most specifically around verbal or nonverbal tasks during early socialization experiences with important elders. (Murphy and Fitzsimons 1960: 145)

Children in early years actually communicate only verbally when they are calm and their attention is directed. Under emotional influence they revert to mimical expression . . . Lack of responsiveness to this nonverbal, pregestural behaviour may, through negative conditioning, serve as a basis for later communicative disorders. (Ibid.: 54)

A striking feature of many therapeutic approaches to stuttering is that they incorporate instructions to be calm and relaxed in all 'important' communication situations. This, of course, is nonsense, especially with children. It is part of being a child to be flooded with affect in important situations, and even as an adult to be calm and peaceful in such situations could, for example, do harm to your career: if you want to get your ideas across, it is often wise to be openly aroused. Yet generations of stutterers report that they went through all kinds of more or less sophisticated techniques and tricks designed to make them peaceful and calm. I have come to the conclusion that people in western cultures, including therapists, operate along the same defence lines as stutterers' parents and later on stutterers themselves. There is a very high premium placed on control of affect and many sanctions on 'uncontrolled' emotional behaviour, especially for males. This affect control could well be the psychological correlate of intense desires for upward mobility and of strong ambition of parents in relation to the careers of their (male) children.

On a subconscious level, one of the concomitants of this kind of socialization is an intense respect for intellectuality and a strong aversion for affective behaviour, an attitudinal pattern regularly to be found in stutterers. (On an unconscious level it is just the reverse.) This manifests itself in the belief system that with a strong will and a sharp intellect, everything is possible. Stutterers treat themselves as *Willensathleten*, 'athletes of the will', and they are very susceptible to therapeutic techniques suggesting that they could control everything, including the stuttering, if they really wanted to. 'In each of these institutions we chanted slogans full of suggestions, such as the following: "I will, I will, I WILL. I shall be strong, I'll not be weak, I shall not stutter, Hear me speak . . ."' (Van Riper 1973: 21).

The control of affect is basically a control of the skeletal muscle system of the body. Not only is speech affected, therefore, but it is also well known that the handwriting of stutterers is 'untidy, clumsy, obstructed in fluence and continuity, and marked by interruptions and repetitions' (Roman 1960). All these activities are based on complex subconscious integrations of bodily affective processes with cognitive planning activities.

There is now evidence that the functional lateralization of the two hemispheres of the brain is of great importance for the process of speech production and listening. The right hemisphere is specialized to a certain degree for the processing of non-verbal modes of representation and the processing of emotional information and music (Geschwind 1979; Sperry & Peilkowski 1972), whereas the left hemisphere is more specialized for verbal thinking, speaking, arithmetic and sequential activities. Jaffe (1978) argues persuasively that the processes of listening, including the production of monosyllabic interjections like 'hmm', have a melodic, emotional quality and are perfectly synchronized with non-verbal listener responses like head nods. He argues that cerebral hemispheric specialization in man has evolved under the selective pressure of efficient face-to-face conversation. The right hemisphere is more sensitive to biologically preprogrammed sounds like coughing, laughing and crying, and the left to the production and comprehension of rapid rhythms of spoken syllables, particularly to stop consonants like *b*, *d*, *g*, *p*. Now, in face-to-face interaction the right hemisphere of the *listener* also processes the right hand of the speaker who gesticulates. This happens because most of the time the listener is looking at the face of the speaker and the speaker is gesticulating with the right hand. Jaffe therefore postulates that hemispheric specialization might have to do with the constraints of dyadic interaction.

The speaker role imposes an output bias on the linguistic system such that speech input is jammed. Phrases are fluently generated by the motor apparatus of the left brain under continuous control of the receptive apparatus of that same hemisphere. Occasional pauses between phrases anticipate paralinguistic interjections by the listener, the quality of which may be processed by the speaker's idling right brain. Finally, the left hemispheric activation during speaking entails a rhythmic gesture of the right hand which is synchronized with the phrase rhythm. (Jaffe 1978: 65)

In contrast, the normal listener's role biases the linguistic system toward reception, with output confined to brief vocal interjections accompanied by head nods. The motor apparatus is subordinate to the perceptual process and its output is suppressed. When left-brain damage produces a disorder of the listening role, the patient seems to be locked in the speaking role of conversation. (Ibid.: 64)

As I show below, stutterers are not only bad speakers, but even worse listeners, and moreover the switching between speaking and listening in dyads in which stutterers are involved, is seriously disturbed. This can mean that if the stutterer speaks, he often finds it difficult to stop. We had cases where fluent speakers unsuccessfully tried more than seven times to take over the floor using signals which would work immediately with other fluent speakers. It is possible that in such cases the stutterer jams his listening capacity to such a degree that he is unable to grasp the emotional message of his own speech and that of the listener's back-channel behaviour. The permanent control or suppression of affect therefore hampers the listening process. If we bear in mind that the most important defence mechanism of compulsive personalities is the technique of isolating ideational content from its emotional cathexis, so that they appear cold, abstract and emotionless (Fenichel 1946: 289), we can speculate that, as a result of certain longstanding and profound learning experiences, serious problems arise in the process of integrating the bodily non-verbal affective processes of the right hemisphere with the activities of the left hemisphere which have to do with speech, language production, verbal thinking and arithmetic. Stutterers, it might be noted, are usually excellent in abstract thinking and arithmetic. Most of our patients had professions where they had to deal with figures.

We think that this process of integration is hampered by strategies of continually attempting control of the body with regard to affect. In western culture, male children have more intensive training in regard to affect control. Van Riper's slogans could have come out of training camps for soldiers and other male heroes, and there is every reason to believe that western culture produces countless male compulsive personalities, in whom the leading symptom is the above mentioned isolation of the ideational content from its emotional cathexis. Ekman & Friesen (1975: 20) mention the US display rule that 'little men do not cry or look afraid'. There are numerous examples of this attitude in our patients, which resemble the example, mentioned by Fenichel, of the patient who made a note 'that he should not forget that he was angry'.

One of my stuttering patients was plagued by the fantasy that he should twist the beautiful necks of swans around whenever he saw such a bird. This fantasy was never accompanied by the slightest sign of aggression, either introspectively or behaviourally. His mother had taught him to hold his hands up in the air when he was in their beautiful living room, in order to prevent the child leaving fingerprints on the shining furniture.

6. Some testable hypotheses derived from our model concerning the communicative behaviour of stutterers

Arising from these speculations, and from sustained observation of stutterers in group therapy, was my proposal in a theoretical paper (Krause 1976) that adult stutterers have internalized these behaviour strategies as more or less conscious affect display rules. Affect display rules are cultural or family-specific rules defined and learned for the expression of affect. They monitor which affects might be expressed with what intensity and under which social conditions (Ekman & Friesen 1975).

These rules are generally overlearned and do not need any conscious control for their activation. The display rules the stutterers are using are based on the typically male display rule of western culture, which we may call the rule of de-emphasizing any emotion (Ekman & Friesen 1979; Krause 1981). My 30-month-old son gave me a striking lesson in this male affect display rule. One day he insisted that I should go back to school in order to learn 'crying' since it was obvious to him that he and his mother were very able to do this, whereas I was very poor at it. He never actually saw me crying and assumed that I had never learned how to do it; only with difficulty did I explain that it was something I had done in the past.

Based on such learning histories, stuttering is, as Johnson said after long investigation of the onset of stuttering, probably a diognosogenic disturbance 'not in the child's mouth, but in the parent's ear' (Johnson 1944). To the best of my knowledge, Johnson did not answer – nor even ask – the question whether false diagnoses by the parents are randomly distributed or alternatively systematic errors based on their selective perceptual tendencies and unconscious expectations. I believe the latter; there are a lot of clinical hints supporting my opinion (Murphy & Fitzsimons 1960). The child, who later turns out to be a stutterer, grows up, even before speech development, in a setting in which fully expressive and affective behaviour is neither used, practised, nor welcomed by the parents.

Therefore, I would expect stutterers not only to stutter but also to use a communicative style which follows a display rule of general but incomplete affect inhibition. In particular, I would expect a reduction in the variability and intensity of affect expression in the face, as well as a suppression of illustrators and regulators, which are the behavioural events especially closely connected to affect expression and speech.

This is the 'motoric' or 'efferent' side of the affect control programmes. But since the affective states of other people are very powerful releasers of affect in oneself (Tomkins 1962–3), there must be a sensory correlate of affect control techniques. I mentioned the poor decoding ability of male subjects, and we can assume that stutterers also immunize themselves against the emotional parts of the messages of their speaking partners as well as their own messages. There are several strategies for doing that; the first and by far the most powerful one is to avoid contact at all. This holds true for most stutterers, but they ascribe their loneliness, falsely I believe, to the stuttering per se.

A less extreme strategy is for the stutterer to accept contact, but at the same time hinder his partner from communicating. Thus, if the stutterer cannot rely on his usual strategy of 'leaving the field', he is likely to take up more floortime than his partner. He can do this either by talking, or vocalizing in some way, himself, or by causing his partner to 'dry up' as a result of his, the stutterer's, poor listening behaviour.

A third strategy, which can involve both sensory and motoric control, consists of preventing affect from 'spilling over' and having a contagious effect on behaviour. A motoric technique that I have already mentioned is the pretence that one's body is turned to stone, with consequent immobility. A more sensory technique is the closing of one's eyes to prevent all sensory input. Another would consist of preventing the synchronization of rhythms of non-verbal behaviour which I mentioned earlier under the term 'congruence'.

The phenomenon of 'congruence' (Feldstein & Welkowitz 1978), 'symmetry' (Meltzer, Morris & Hayes 1971) or 'pattern matching' (Cassotta, Felstein & Jaffe 1964) is well documented in both psychotherapeutic sessions and normal dyadic conversational situations. These terms imply that the paralinguistic speech characteristics – loudness, latency before speaking, pause length, etc. – of the two interactants become more similar over time (Natale 1975).

As I have already mentioned, Jaffe & Anderson (1979) claim that the interpersonal matching of communication rhythms (sometimes called conversational coupling, synchrony, convergence, or congruence) is an important phenomenon of interpersonal attraction and assortive mating.

It has been shown that field dependent women are particularly adept to modify their endogenously generated speech rhythms to match those of the dialogic partners . . . and, that the degree of this rhythmic entrainment to an exogeneous speech is associated with positive social evaluation and interpersonal attraction. (Jaffe & Anderson 1979)

The ability of communication partners to synchronize the paralinguistic aspects of their speech is the basis of what clinicians call 'eroticized speech', whereby people talking about politics, for example, find out whether they want to have sex with one another or not. Somebody unable to synchronize may well be considered a bad lover, on the assumption that the person will be unable to tolerate the experience of affect synchronization necessary for the experience of mutual orgasms. The capacity of the man to synchronize affective behaviour may even have a selective advantage from the woman's point of view, since she can readily assume that this man will react affectively to the affects of the future child, and by doing so help her to handle and raise it, whereas somebody unable to stand affect will avoid children as potential releasers of unbearable states. Of course, all this is pure speculation going far beyond my prediction that stutterers will prevent synchronization phenomena, but it is in line with the arguments of the sociobiologists on the selective advantages of 'altruistic behaviour' (Dawkins 1976; Wilson 1975).

7. Some empirical results

The investigations to be described took place over a period of six years and are not yet finished. We are currently investigating the success of a therapeutic technique based on our model. Since we are concerned here with the social psychology of language, we will concentrate on the epidemiological and preventive aspects of our investigation rather than the therapeutic consequences.

The analysis of the non-verbal and linguistic behaviour which I now describe was conducted with twenty-eight male stutterers, who volunteered after we announced a research project on stuttering in some Zürich periodicals (the volunteers were paid for their participation). In a subsequent investigation of twenty of the original volunteers, conducted by Dr C. Schwartz, head of the Speech Clinic at the Zürich hospital, to whom I am greatly indebted, they were all confirmed as stutterers.

The control group consisted of fifty male speakers, who had no speech problems. They were matched so that every stutterer had a speaking partner who was roughly equivalent in age and occupational status. In addition, there were eleven dyads of fluent speakers. No partners knew each other in advance. Each pair was led into a comfortable group therapy room which was equipped with three remote control video cameras. The experimenter left the room with the remark that he would be busy adjusting the cameras for about four more minutes, so people should get acquainted with one another. In fact this initial part of the interaction was being filmed. After four minutes the experimenter came back and explained to the subjects that the research concerned problem-solving behaviour; we were especially curious about how people solved political problems. The task for the subjects would be to come to an agreement, within twenty minutes, on the three most important political and social problems to be resolved during the next year in Switzerland.

It was never mentioned that the subjects were taking part in an observational study of stuttering, and some of the fluent speakers who were partnering non-manifest stutterers did not realize that they were talking to a stutterer.[1] Instructions and observational methods for the twenty-

[1] I have already mentioned the very efficient hiding techniques used by some stutterers and, in addition, that the disturbance is episodic in nature, so that the non-manifestation of the speech problem proper might have been a consequence of 'successful' control attempts or of being genuinely stutter-free for the twenty-minute period of our investigation. In using the term 'successful', I do not mean that the communication process is identical to that of non-stutterers.

two fluent speakers talking to one another were identical to the above. The experimental situation is shown diagrammatically in figure 2.

In addition, a one-hour clinical interview with each stutterer, which had taken place three months before the main study, was stored on a stereo-audiotape. Throat microphones had been used in order to separate interviewee from interviewer clearly on the tape. Questionnaires on childrearing practices were also administered to the stutterers and to the control group.

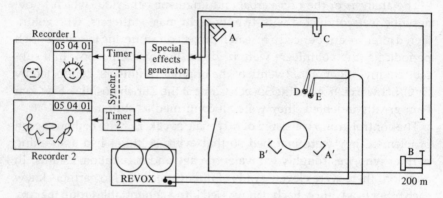

Figure 2. Data-recording set-up in the experiment
Cameras A and B are equipped with remote-control zoom lenses. The faces of persons A' and B' are filmed for 5 minutes using these cameras. Then a 5-minute film of subject torsos is made, then the faces again, etc. The recordings of the two interactants are fed into recorder 1, using a special effects generator, together with a digital clock with 1/100 sec. precision. Camera C, with a wide angle lens, records both interactants in full size on recorder 2. A second timer, synchronized with the first is fed into this recording. Sound is recorded separately on a 4-track Revox recorder using the two gun microphones D and E fixed to the ceiling

Later, two independent raters decided, on the basis of listening to the audiotapes, whether stuttering was audible or not. Reliability of these judgments was 0.95 (phi-coefficient). Sixteen of the twenty-six stutterers did stutter audibly, with different degrees of intensity. Ten of them either used hiding techniques or really did not stutter in this social situation.

We used a variety of tools for the analysis of these data:

1. Facial behaviour, head movements and head positions were analysed on the basis of FACS (Facial Action Coding System; Ekman & Friesen 1979), a coding system allowing an exhaustive description of all facial events or actions. It is based on a functional anatomy and allows coding of the temporal duration and the intensity of some actions. Reliability is satisfactory in relation to the determination of beginning and

ending of events. Reliability testing based on our own data was high (0.79).

Since the coding of facial expression using FACS is extremely time-consuming, the samples were reduced to 20 seconds speaking time and 20 seconds listening time. We usually started coding after 5 minutes of talking, so the first 3 minutes called 'greeting' were not analysed in relation to facial expression. The same time period was used in coding the speaking partner. So measures of synchronization could be developed.

2. Paralinguistic data were analysed using the Automatic Vocal Transaction Analyzer (AVTA). This is an automatic computerized system for the statistical analysis of sound-silence segments, or on–of patterns, of two speakers simultaneously, which was developed by Feldstein and others at the University of Maryland (Feldstein & Welkowitz 1978). AVTA is a computerized analog digital converter which computes automatically the following measures for defined time samples: speaker-switches, pauses, switching pauses, vocalizations and simultaneous speech (figure 3 graphically illustrates the five temporal measures). The validity and usefulness of these speech parameters, as well as their characteristics within different groups of conversationalists and different social situations, have been described by Feldstein & Welkowitz (1978).

The time samples which were used for these analyses were: three 10-minute samples within the clinical interview, at the beginning, middle and end of the interview; one 3-minute sample in the greeting situation; one 10-minute sample within the political discussion.

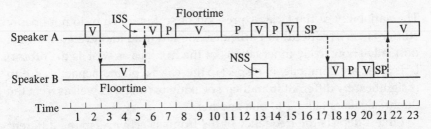

Figure 3. Parameters of the AVTA system (V = vocalization; ISS = interruptive simultaneous speech; P = pause; NSS = non-interruptive simultaneous speech; SP = switching pause = latency time)

3. For body movements and positions, we used an extensive coding system developed at the University of Bern (Frei et al. 1978). The system is based on coding the position of specific parts of the body at a given moment of time in relation to a special reference-system. Based on these highly reliable descriptive data, complex measures of body behaviour in

space and time are computed. For technical reasons – specifically the bad quality of some films – the sample was smaller for this part of the investigation than for the others (seven stutterers and seven non-stutterers). The time sampling was based on 0.5-second intervals within a total of 2 minutes sampling time. This meant 240 measurements on each part of the body.

4. The semantic content of the discussions was analysed using a computerized content-analytic method developed by Drewek (1978). This method allows context-free statistical analysis of single words. In addition, using the Harvard *Third Psychology Dictionary*, seventy-four psychologically relevant semantic categories were analysed in relation to their frequency distribution. The time sample consisted of 9 minutes of the 15-minute political discussion (3 minutes at the beginning, middle and end). Seventy-four discussants were included in the analysis.

The very complex methodology of these different data reduction and analysis techniques will be published elsewhere (Krause 1981),[2] and readers interested in methodological problems are asked to contact the author directly. Here, I will concentrate on the results and their implications for a social psychology of language. Before relating the results to our hypothesis and before I try to integrate them in our model, and thereby refine it, I will list them in a rather unsystematic way based on the data analysis techniques we used.

7.1. Facial activities, head positions and movements

The variability of the facial expression of stutterers who do not openly stutter is very reduced. In particular, the forehead and eye area, which normally show lively innervations of the frontalis as well as the orbicularis oculi, are immobile. In respect to these facial phenomena, this group is significantly different from their speaking partners, as well as from the fluent speakers talking to one another.

Table 1 depicts the frequency of the frontalis activities in the different groups, separated according to speaking and listening positions. This innervation pattern can be considered as an 'illustrator' in the sense above; it is used to emphasize the things actually said or the listening process. It is evident that the group of stutterers produces significantly

[2] For some of these analysis techniques, students working on their final theses in clinical psychology at the University of Zürich did a great part of this work. I am deeply indebted to them. The corresponding publications are Frei et al. 1978, for body motions and the general part of the study, and Steiner 1980, for the content analysis of the political discussion.

Table 1. *Frequency of brow raising activities (action units 1 and 2) in the listener and speaker positions*

No. of subjects		Stutterers	Fluent speakers
with zero activities	listening	20	29
	speaking	14	7
with 1 or more activities	listening	2	11
	speaking	8	32

Listening position:
x^2 = 2.90
df = 1
p = 0.09

Speaking position:
x^2 = 13.00
df = 1
p = 0.0003

less upper face innervations, especially during speaking. The results are clearly in the same direction for listening. If we bear in mind that the upper face innervations very often are part of the stuttering spell, we can talk of a syndrome of upper face restraint in stuttering.

The speaking partners of manifest stutterers smile during 22 per cent of their speaking and listening time, compared to only 4 per cent of the time for speaking partners of stutterers who keep control of the disturbance. The differences are highly significant. Figure 4 shows the total duration of smiling in speaker position in the following dyads: first, manifest stutterers and their fluent partners; secondly, non-manifest stutterers and their partners; and thirdly fluent speakers talking to one another. Figure 5 shows the same data for the listening position. In dyads where stutterers are involved you find a relatively one-sided frozen smiling, whereas the situation of smiling in the control group of fluent speakers talking to one another is more balanced between speakers. The accuracy and frequency of synchronization of facial activities was also analysed. As table 2 shows,

Table 2. *Average frequency of synchronizing of zygomaticus major (action unit 12; smiling) and frontalis innervations (action unit 1; brow raising)*

Manifest stutterers and their partners (N = 11 dyads)		Non-manifest stutterers and their partners (N = 11 dyads)	Fluent speakers and their partners (N = 9 dyads)
Mean	0.73	1.18	1.77
Standard deviation	1.29	2.87	1.72

t-values:
$t_{1,3}$ = 3.628 $p < 1\%$
$t_{2,3}$ = 0.880

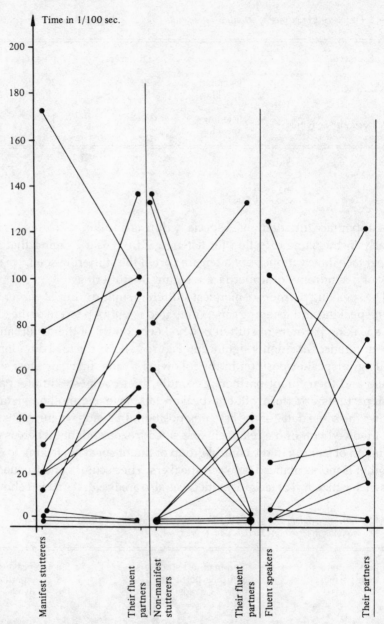

Figure 4. Total innervation time of zygomaticus major (smiling) during speaking within the time sample of 20 seconds. The dyads are connected by lines

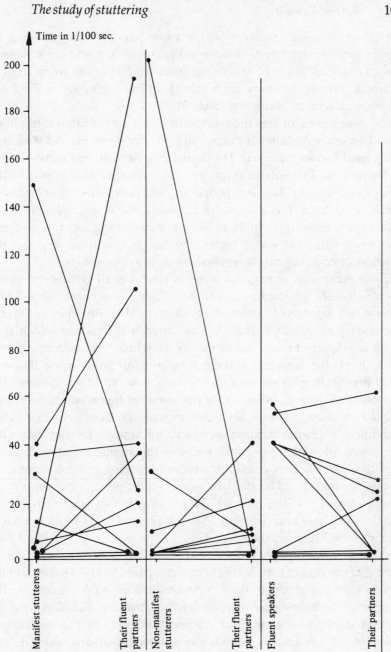

Time in 1/100 sec.

200

180

160

140

120

100

80

60

40

20

0

Manifest stutterers

Their fluent partners

Non-manifest stutterers

Their fluent partners

Fluent speakers

Their partners

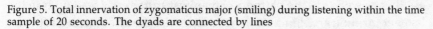

Figure 5. Total innervation of zygomaticus major (smiling) during listening within the time sample of 20 seconds. The dyads are connected by lines

the group of fluent speakers talking to one another has significantly greater synchronization between speakers of smiling and brow raising. The accuracy of timing of synchronization is significantly worse in both groups in which stutterers are involved, at the beginning of the facial activities as well as at the end (table 3).

The poor timing of synchronization in dyads with stutterers implies a lack of spontaneous affective expression of happiness; instead smiling is being used as a social signal. This signal may have many functions. One of them is the intensification of 'pseudo-listening'. This is part of the usual behaviour of 'healthy' people in confrontation with stigmatized speaking partners. It is also part of a pattern of over-engagement which adults use to encourage children. Some nurses dealing with their patients also rely on this behaviour pattern, which, in the same way, has the function of covering up the expression of negative affects.

Facial expression of negative affect is absent in all groups except the fluent speakers talking to one another. They show very clear full face innervation patterns of contempt, of extremely short duration, i.e. micro-momentary expressions. It should be noted that dyads in which stutterers are involved show immobility of the whole face, with two exceptions. First, the manifest stutterers have significantly more lip-press behaviour during listening and speaking than all other groups. The non-manifest group, however, is immobile in this respect. Secondly, manifest stutterers show significant increase of facial activities (other than micro-momentary expressions) which I consider as relevant for the expression of contempt. Table 4 shows the frequency of such facial activities. Usually they consist of a blend of smiling and contempt combining innervations of levator labii superioris (upper lip raiser) and zygomaticus major (smiling muscle). This is functionally a combination of social friendliness and contempt. The general results in relation to facial activities are listed in tables 5 and 6.

Stutterers who openly stutter hold their eyes partly or totally closed during 22 per cent of their listener time, compared to 11–13 per cent of the time within the group of fluent speakers talking to one another. The number of head movements accompanying speech production is significantly reduced in the group of stutterers, whether or not stuttering is manifest. This is true in comparison to fluent speakers talking to one another as well as to the partners of manifest stutterers. Head nods in the listener position are significantly reduced in the group of manifest stutterers, in comparison to fluent speakers talking to one another, as well as in comparison to their partners. The range or angle of the head position is

Table 3. *Precision of synchronizing of brow raising and smiling (action units 1, 2 and 12) within the three groups of dyads*

	1. Manifest stutterers and their partners (14 events)		2. Non-manifest stutterers and their partners (13 events)		3. Fluent speakers and their partners (12 events)	
	start	end	start	end	start	end
Average synchronizing time	2.38	2.26	1.60	1.70	0.66	0.58
Variance	8.04	2.78	1.37	1.76	0.86	0.59
Standard deviation	2.94	1.73	1.21	1.38	0.96	0.32

Action units:
1 = brow raising
2 = brow raising
12 = smiling

F-values of variance testing:
$F_{1,3, start}$ = 9.348 p < 1%
$F_{1,3, end}$ = 8.687 p < 1%
$F_{2,3, start}$ = 2.04 —
$F_{2,3, end}$ = 4.28 p < 1%

t-values of differences of means:
(Estimate of Σ Diff. for heterogeneous variance)
$t_{1,3, start}$ = 2.13 p < 5%
$t_{1,3, end}$ = 7.44 p < 1%
$t_{2,3, start}$ = 2.27 p < 5%
$t_{2,3, end}$ = 7.72 p < 1%

Table 4. *Combination of action units relevant for the facial expression of contempt*

	L14 S	L14 L	10+15 S	10+15 L	L10 S	L10 L	12+15 S	12+15 L	10+12 S	10+12 L	Σ S	Σ L	Σ L+S
Manifest stutterers N = 12	1	0	0	0	4	0	0	0	6	5	11	5	16
Partners N = 12	0	0	0	0	0	2	0	0	2	0	2	2	4
Non-manifest stutterers N = 11	0	0	0	0	1	0	0	0	5	3	6	3	9
Partners N = 11	1	0	2	2	1	0	1	1	0	0	5	3	8
Fluent speakers N = 16	0	1	0	0	3	0	0	0	2	4	5	5	10

Action units:
L = unilateral innervations
10 = upper lip raiser
12 = lip corner puller
14 = dimpler
15 = lip corner depressor

The following differences are significant:
Manifest stutterers against their partners: S, Σ(S+L)
Manifest stutterers against fluent speakers: S

Table 5. *Frequency of all facial activities except miscellaneous actions*

	Speaking$_1$	Listening$_2$	Σ$_3$
1. Manifest stutterers N = 12	197	91	288
2. Fluent partners N = 12	130	80	210
3. Non-manifest stutterers N = 11	49	22	71
4. Fluent partners N = 11	61	40	101
5. Fluent speakers N = 16	135	78	213

Table 5 *contd*

Significant z-values:
z = 2.63 p<1%
z = 1.96 p<5%

Manifest stutterers against partners:
All facial activities speaking:
$z_1 = -3.70$
All facial activities listening
$z_2 = -0.84$
Σ all activities
$z_3 = -3.49$

Non-manifest stutterers against partners:
$z_1 = 1.14$
$z_2 = 2.28$
$z_3 = 2.28$

Manifest stutterers against fluent speakers:
$z_1 = -6.01$
$z_2 = -2.84$
$z_3 = -6.54$

Fluent partners of manifest stutterers against fluent speaker talking to fluent speakers:
$z_1 = -1.99$
$z_2 = -1.93$
$z_3 = -2.76$

Non-manifest stutterers against fluent speakers:
$z_1 = 3.70$
$z_2 = 3.67$
$z_3 = 5.15$

Partners of non-manifest stutterers against fluent speakers:
$z_1 = 2.53$
$z_2 = 1.35$
$z_3 = 2.83$

Fluent partners of manifest stutterers against fluent partners of non-manifest stutterers:
$z_1 = -4.4$
$z_2 = -3.21$
$z_3 = -5.47$

Table 6. *Scheme of the results of facial activities in the different groups*

I Manifest stutterers	II Partners	III Non-manifest stutterers	IV Partners	V Fluent speakers
Significant increase against III, IV and V	Significant increase against III, IV and V	Significant decrease against I, II and V	Significant decrease against I, II and V	Significant decrease against I and II; increase against III and IV

significantly reduced, especially in stutterers who keep control over their disturbance. Turning of the head towards the partner as well as head downwards positions are significantly reduced with regard to frequency and duration. Partners of manifest stutterers react with a prominent intensification of head movements towards the stutterer.

There are the following significant differences in body behaviour be-tween stutterers and fluent speakers. Stutterers turn their trunks more to their speaking partners while, at the same time, the head positions are turned away from them. The average openness of hands and arms is defined as the average position of hands and arms away from the trunk. Stutterers are less open in this respect. Symmetric positions of the legs are rare in stutterers. Complexity of movements is defined as the number of all body parts simultaneously involved in one movement. Stutterers' movements are significantly less complex. Nominal differentiation of movements was defined as the relation between the empirically found number of different positions and the maximal possible number of different positions. This nominal differentiation is significantly reduced in stutterers (Frei et al. 1978).

7.2. Paralinguistic data

In relation to the paralinguistic data produced by the AVTA system we found the following results:

1. The manifest stutterers occupy significantly more *floortime* than their partners in both the greeting and the discussion situations.[3] The non-manifest stutterers occupy significantly more floortime in the discussion and significantly less in the greeting situation. Speakers, in dyads of fluent speakers, were randomly divided into two half-groups. The two half-groups each take up approximately half the total time, i.e. 90 seconds in the greeting situation and 300 seconds in the discussion.

The average duration of *floortime* is significantly longer, compared to their partners, for the manifest stutterers (6.19 versus 4.54 seconds) and significantly shorter for the non-manifest stutterers (3.91 versus 4.34 seconds) in the greeting situation. Fluent speakers talking to other fluent speakers have even shorter average floortimes in that situation, namely 3.42 seconds. Their average floortime is prolonged in talking to a stutterer, whether he is manifestly stuttering or not. In the discussion there is no significant difference, but the tendencies are in the same direction

---

[3] Some of this effect may be due to the fact that the manifest stutterer actually takes longer to deliver a message, although that delay is probably not very sizeable.

(12.44 seconds for the manifest stutterers, 8.77 seconds for their partners; 10.54 seconds for non-manifest stutterers, 8.80 for their partners; 9.47 seconds for the fluent speakers talking to fluent speakers).

In the discussion, the interactors have a strong tendency to adjust the average floortime, which is revealed by correlation coefficients of 0.52 for the non-manifest stutterers and their partners, 0.54 for the fluent speakers and their partners. *There is no convergence of this speech parameter in dyads in which a manifest stutterer is involved.*

2. In conjunction with this asymmetry of floortime, the number of turns or speaker switches is significantly less in dyads in which a stutterer is involved. The results are highly significant for the greeting situation; they are not for the discussion, although they are in the same direction. It is important to bear in mind that it is not relevant whether the stutterer talks much more or less than his partner; in either case the vivacity of the dialogue breaks down.

3. The amount of *simultaneous vocalization* is significantly different amongst the groups in the greeting situation. The fluent speakers talking to one another initiate much more simultaneous speech. Since simultaneous speech is highly correlated with the amount of speaker switches we computed several multiple regressions, with the speech parameters and speech disturbance group as independent variables and simultaneous speech as the dependent variable. The average duration of switching pauses, duration of pauses, duration of floortimes and the amount of speaker switches together account for 76 per cent of the variance of the dependent measure. The classification according to the speech problems has no additional predictive validity. The high amount of simultaneous speech in the dyads of fluent speakers is associated with the high amount of speaker switches and the short duration of mutual silences or latency times. In the dyads involving non-manifest stutterers a significant divergence phenomenon can be found. The more simultaneous speech one partner initiates the less the other does ($r = -0.55$).

4. The *average latency* is not significantly different amongst the five groups, in any of the social situations. The number of latency times is significantly different in the greeting situation. There are very strong convergence phenomena within the group of fluent speakers ($r = 0.90$), and moderate ones in dyads involving manifest stutterers ($r = 0.58$). *The non-manifest stutterers show no significant synchronization with their partners.* Again the differences regarding latency times disappear in a multiple regression accounting for the other speech characteristics, especially speaker switches, duration of latency times and average duration of

latency time. These three parameters account for 87 per cent of the variance of the dependent variable latency.

5. In relation to congruence the following results hold. For stutterers, average floortime duration is very stablé between the clinical interview and the political discussion which took place, with different partners, several months later; the correlation coefficient is 0.74. This amount of stability is very unusual, at least with different partners, as a study done by Feldstein seems to indicate (Feldstein & Welkowitz 1978). If somebody shows such stability, it implies that his partners are being forced to adapt their own speech characteristics to those of the person. This marked stability is true of both manifest and non-manifest stutterers.

In the group of fluent speakers talking to fluent speakers, the most stable measure over different situations is the latency time. This stability disappears for the fluent speaker if he is talking to a stutterer. The most stable measures of stutterers are not the silence parameters but the duration of vocalization and floortime. Now if vocalization is a stable personality trait, it seems logical that the partner has to give in. To test this assumption empirically, we computed the amount of mutual congruence at the beginning, the middle and the end of the clinical interview. Each sample was 10 minutes long. Analyses of variance with repeated measurements showed significant changes in the direction of more congruence for pauses and latency times, but not for vocalizations. Congruence is most strikingly to be observed for latency times, a result which was found elsewhere. The work of adapting the period of silence to that of the partner is completely done by the therapist, so again congruence is a consequence of the partner giving in to the speaking style of the stutterer, whether he stutters or not, and not the other way round.

7.3. Content-analytic methods

Comparisons of the words being uttered during the 9 minutes sampled from each political discussion show the distributional characteristics given in table 7. This is a confirmation of the AVTA data, which showed that stutterers occupy floortime longer than their partners. It is also a confirmation of our congruence statements based on AVTA and facial activities. The dyads in which stutterers are involved not only function asymmetrically in certain quantitative respects discussed above, but also in relation to certain content aspects. Seven of the fourteen dyads of stutterers have differences of word frequency of more than 20 per cent. Only three of the twelve fluent dyads have differences of this size. As the

Table 7. *Distributional characteristics of word frequencies*

	Types	Tokens	Type–token ratio
Manifest stutterer	242.9	772.3	0.315
Fluent partner	250.1	631.6	0.396
Non-manifest stutterer	273.0	717.8	0.380
Partner	256.0	638.5	0.401
Fluent speaker	285.0	740.0	0.385

type–token ratios in table 7 show, the manifest stutterers have the most restricted repertoire in talking. They talk a good deal, but very often repeat the same words. This might be a consequence of a coping strategy which involves using familiar words.

Using the Harvard *Third Psychological Dictionary*, seventy-four categories covering psychological processes were analysed in relation to the frequency distribution within the different groups (for the detailed methodology, see Steiner 1980). In general, few of the seventy-four categories significantly discriminate between the groups, but the few differences which are found are relevant for our model of the disturbance. Manifest stutterers use the pronoun *we* significantly less frequently than fluent speakers and non-manifest stutterers and their partners. Partners of stutterers use the pronoun *I* significantly more often than stutterers. In both groups of stutterers, categories indicating direct emotional involvement are significantly under-represented. Stutterers are extremely reluctant to use words indicating even a rather moderate emotional engagement, for example: *to hope, to feel, to be touched*, etc. Words indicating anger are significantly less frequent in the speech of partners of stutterers. This can be considered as the verbal correlate of the compulsive friendliness we found in the smiling behaviour.

Fluent speakers and their partners use the conditional form significantly more often. This can be interpreted as implying that they do not make firm statements but introduce topics with the expectation that their partners may possibly hold a different opinion. This is not to be found in stutterer dyads. All synonyms for the term *bad* are less frequent in both stutterer groups. A marked contrast between stutterers and fluent speakers can be found in relation to the frequency of words expressing an approach behaviour. In stutterer dyads, there is significantly less talk about politics, planning and other political problems, whereas talk relating to catastrophies, danger, anxiety and misfortune is markedly over-represented in stutterers. Moreover, words covering health, sickness and medicine are significantly *less frequent* in the stutterer dyads. Within the manifest stutterers, these frequencies approach zero. Fluent speakers use more overstatements and superlatives than the other groups.

8. Conclusions

Let me try to summarize our investigations and our model. On a macro-social level, I assume that societies with great status differences, and the expectation that their members should compete without being overtly aggressive, provide a suitable environment for the stutterer to develop. Cultures whose members are forced to compete through compulsive ritualization and politeness are especially likely to produce stutterers. On a social psychological level, situations producing great communicative pressure can be considered as stimuli for eliciting the disturbed behaviour in an adult stutterer, who might be fluent in other situations. Status differences between the stutterer and his partner, unfamiliarity of the interactors, and audience size are some of the well-known social releasers of stutterer spells.

These social situations are related to certain affective releasers, which become chronic in stutterers through the coping strategies they adopt. The affect pattern corresponding to the social situations mentioned above is mainly a fear–anger conflict of a certain intensity. This chronic, conflict-laden affect-pattern is *causal* in hampering the speech production process. The social conditions mentioned above cause the affective conflicts, but they are not responsible for the speech disturbance and for the chronic nature of the disturbance. Disruption of speech is a consequence of intense antagonistic affects. Everybody can suffer for a while from this problem. Stutterers, aided by parents, therapists and other well-meaning societal agents, try to deal with these affect conflicts in the specific way sanctioned by the macro-societal cultural rules for dealing with affect, specifically anger.

Our investigation of non-verbal behaviours deals mostly with the chronic defensive coping strategies the adult stutterer uses. They can be subsumed under the general rule: *'Avoid affect'*. Every behaviour pattern we found empirically and described above, can be subsumed under this meta-regulatory principle. Figure 6 is an attempt to depict these coping strategies in the form of a problem-solving tree. Alternatively we can transform the problem-solving tree into the instructions a stutterer might unconsciously give to himself in 'dangerous' situations: 'Try to avoid physical and social contact completely, then you do not run any risks.' (Most stutterers do this anyway, and are very lonely people, but at least

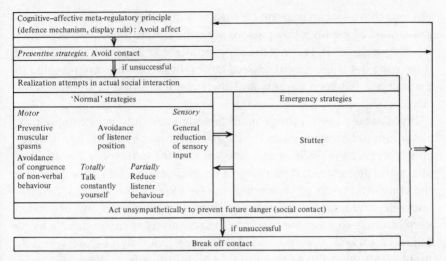

Figure 6. Social strategies among stutterers for avoiding 'affect'

they are secure from being overwhelmed by affect.) 'If you cannot avoid making contact, try to stay in the background and say nothing. If you cannot avoid talking, like in this experiment Dr Krause is conducting, avoid being influenced affectively. This can be done by trying very hard not to take over the listener role, which in turn can be done by either talking constantly and by keeping the floor through stuttering or by trying hard to listen as poorly as possible. Attentive listening is very dangerous, since it is hard to know, in advance, what might come in through the sensory systems of your body. If you do not listen, this fits well into a general sensory coping strategy of trying not to perceive the speaking partner, so that there is no risk of become aroused by perceiving the partner's behaviour.

'In addition, try to control affect on the motoric side by permanent contractions of the skeletal system. Thus you cannot be influenced by the behaviour of your partner. In particular, rhythmic congruence of body behaviour is potentially dangerous. By being unexpressive (inhibited) and over-contracted, you thereby indirectly discourage your partner from producing any affect either. In the face of all these coping strategies it is very unlikely that this person, your current speaking partner, will ever try to talk to you again. He will avoid you from now on and then you will be secure.'

I hope that this anecdotal version of unconscious stutterer self-instruction may help as an integrative account of our research. It is obvious that a lot can be done for the prevention of stuttering and for the prevention of the unhappy personality structure stutterers usually suffer from. As a clinician, I cannot make proposals at a macro-societal level, but if we consider these macro-societal cultural rules as they are revealed in interactions between parents and their children, then I can offer some advice.

If you, as a parent, cannot avoid making your child very competitive, allow him to be angry, nasty or the like at the same time. It is unreasonable to expect the child to compete without the corresponding affect of anger and aggression. If you cannot stand an angry child, stop fostering the competitiveness of your child, or else look for professional help for yourself. You might need it. If you think that your child stutters, listen very carefully to what the child has to say, and try to understand why he might be excited or afraid. Try not to calm him down before you fully understand what it was that brought about the affect. When it is over, then you may comfort and calm the child, but do not comfort the child for your own comfort. Do not trust practitioners who recommend speech control and relaxation techniques for the child. They are harmful in the long run.

As a clinician, most of my work consists of developing a new treatment programme for the unfortunate people who are suffering from the coping strategies they learned in order to deal with their stuttering and their affect. This is not the place to consider at length such issues, which I have discussed elsewhere (Krause 1981). Let me just conclude with three brief general assertions on the treatment of stutterers.

1. Adult stutterers should not be treated with affect control techniques like systematic desensitization, hypnosis, self-suggestion techniques, autogenic training, etc. They appear to be useless (but they are continually used nevertheless). In my opinion, they may result in a methodologically refined augmentation of the debilitating control techniques the stutterer is already using himself. Instead of these techniques, techniques which sensitize the stutterer to affective states and arousal should be learned.

2. Observation of the stutterer's own behaviour must play a central role in every treatment. This happens best in groups of stutterers. The secondary gain of the disturbance disappears when they talk to other stutterers.

3. Techniques which rely too heavily on speech are probably inadequate since, in my opinion, the problem is not one of speech mechanisms per se. Group techniques relying on non-verbal processes and

exercises seem to me more adequate. I am thinking of certain strategies of Gestalt therapy, body work and psycho-drama.

References

American Speech and Hearing Association. 1957. White House conference report on speech disorders and speech correction. *Journal of speech and hearing disorders*, *17*, 129–37.

Andrews, G. & Harris, M. 1964. *The syndrome of stuttering*. Clinics in developmental medicine, *17*. London: Spastics Society Medical Education and Information Unit.

Barbara, D. A. 1954. *Stuttering: a psychodynamic approach to its understanding and treatment*. New York: Julian Press.

Beebe, B., Stern, D. & Jaffe, J. 1979. The kinetic rhythm of mother–infant interactions. In Siegman, A. W. & Feldstein, S. (eds.) *Of speech and time*. Hillsdale, NJ: Erlbaum.

Bloodstein, O. 1960a. The development of stuttering: I. Change in nine basic features. *Journal of Speech and Hearing Disorders*, *25*, 219–37.

1960b. The development of stuttering: II. Developmental phases. *Journal of Speech and Hearing Disorders*, *25*, 366–76.

1961. The development of stuttering: III. Theoretical and clinical implications. *Journal of Speech and Hearing Disorders*, *26*.

1975. *A handbook on stuttering*. Chicago: National Easter Seal Society.

Bloodstein, O., Jaeger, W. & Tureen, J. 1952. Diagnoses of stuttering by parents of stutterers and nonstutterers. *Journal of Speech and Hearing Disorders*, *17*, 308–15.

Bullen, A. K. 1945. A crosscultural approach to the problem of stuttering. *Child Development*, *16*, 1–88.

Bullowa, M. 1975. When infant and adult communicate how do they synchronize their behaviours? In: Kendon, A., Harris, R. M. & Key, M. R. (eds.): *Organization of behaviour in face to face interaction*. The Hague: Mouton.

Cassotta, L., Feldstein, S. & Jaffe, J. 1964. AVTA: a device for automatic vocal transaction analysis. *Journal of Experimental Analysis of Behaviour*, *7*, 99–104.

Dawkins, R. 1976. *The selfish gene*. Oxford: Oxford University Press.

Dickson, S. 1971. Incipient stuttering and spontaneous remission of stuttered speech. *Journal of Communication Disorders*, *4*, 99–110.

Dieffenbach, J. 1841. *Die Heilung des Stotterns durch eine neue chirurgische Operation*. Berlin: Förster.

Dittmann, A. T. 1972. Developmental factors in conversational behaviour. *Journal of Communication*, *22*, 404–23.

Drewek, R. 1978. *LDVLIB, Dokumentation des Rechenzentrums der Universität Zürich*. Zürich.

Duncan, S. Jr. 1974. On signalling that it's your turn to speak. *Journal of Experimental Social Psychology*, *10*, 234–47.

Duncan, S. Jr & Fiske, D. W. 1977. *Face-to-face interaction: research, methods and theory*. Hillsdale, NJ: Erlbaum.

Ekman, P. 1977. Biological and cultural contributions to body and facial movement. In: Blacking, J. (ed.) *Anthropology of the body*. San Francisco: Academic Press.

Ekman, P. & Friesen, W. V. 1969. The repertoire of non-verbal behaviour: categories, origins, usage and coding. *Semiotica*, *1*, 49–98.

1975. *Unmasking the face*. Englewood Cliffs, NJ: Prentice-Hall.

1979. *Manual for the facial action code*. Palo Alto: Consulting Psychologists Press.

Emerick, L. L. 1978. Sag was oder fahr als Frachtgut. In Hood, S. (ed.) *An einen Stotterer. Stottererselbsthilfe*. Düsseldorf.

Feldstein, S. 1964. Vocal patterning of emotional expression. *Science and Psychoanalysis*, *7*, 193–210.

Feldstein, S. & Welkowitz, J. 1978. A chronography of conversation. In defense of an objective approach. In: Siegman, A. W. & Feldstein, S. (eds.) *Nonverbal behavior and communication*. Hillsdale, NJ: Erlbaum.

Fenichel, O. 1946. *The psychoanalytic theory of neurosis*. London: Routledge.

Few, L. R. & Lingwall, J. B. 1972. A further analysis of fluency within stuttered speech. *Journal of Speech and Hearing Research*, *15*, 356–63.

Freeman, F. J. & Ushijima, T. 1976. Laryngal muscle activity in stuttering. *Haskings Laboratory, Status Report on Speech Research*, 45–6.

Freund, H. 1966. *Psychopathology and the problems of stuttering*. Springfield: Thomas.

Frei, R., Hofmann, J., Huber, E., Limacher, B. & Ritzmann, M. 1978. *Vergleichende Untersuchung zum körperlichen Verhalten von Stotterern und Nichtstotterern in einer sozialen Interaktion*. Lizentiatsarbeit an der Philosophischen Fakultät I der Universität Zürich.

Geschwind, N. 1979. Die Grosshirnrinde. *Spektrum der Wissenschaft*, *11*, 126–35.

Giffin, K. & Heider, M. 1967. The relationship between speech anxiety and the suppression of communication in childhood. *Psychiatry*, Quarterly Supplement *41*, 311–22.

Glasner, P. J. 1970. Developmental view. In. Sheehan, J. G. (ed.) *Stuttering: research and therapy*. New York: Harper.

Gray, M. 1940. The X family: a clinical and laboratory study of a 'stuttering' family. *Journal of Speech Disorders*, *5*, 343–8.

Hill, H. E. 1944a. Stuttering 1. A critical review and evaluation of biochemical investigations. *Journal of Speech Disorders*, *9*, 245–61.

1944b. Stuttering 2. A review and integration of physiological data. *Journal of Speech Disorders*, *9*, 289–324.

Hood, S. 1978. *An einen Stotterer. Stottererselbsthilfe*. Düsseldorf. (First published as *To a stutterer*. Memphis: Speech Foundation, 1972.)

Ierodiakonou, C. S. 1970. Psychological problems and precipitation factors in the stuttering of children. *Acta Paedopsychiatrica*, *37* (6), 166–74.

Jaffe, J. 1978. Parliamentary procedure and the brain. In Siegman, A. W. & Feldstein, S. (eds.) *Nonverbal behavior and communication*. Hillsdale, NJ: Erlbaum.

Jaffe, J. & Anderson, S. W. 1979. Communication rhythms and the evolution of language. In Siegman, A. W. & Feldstein, S. (eds.) *Of speech and time*. Hillsdale, NJ: Erlbaum.

Johnson, W. 1944. The Indians have no word for it. I. Stuttering in children. *Quarterly Journal of Speech*, *30*, 330–7.

1961. *Stuttering and what you can do about it*. Minneapolis: University of Minnesota Press.

Johnson, W. & Associates 1959. *The onset of stuttering.* Minneapolis: University of Minnesota Press.

Kidd, K. K. 1978. A genetic perspective on stuttering. MS. (To appear in *Journal of Fluency Disorders.*)

Kidd, K. K., Oehlert, H., Heimbuch, R. C., Records, M. A. & Webster, R. L. 1978. Familial stuttering patterns are not related to one measure of severity. MS. Department of Human Genetics, Yale University.

Krause, R. 1976. Probleme der psychologischen Stottererforschung und Behandlung. *Zeitschrift für klinische Psychologie and Psychotherapie, 24,* 20–37.

1977. *Produktives Denken bei Kindern.* Weinheim: Beltz.

1978. Nonverbales interaktives Verhalten von Stotterern und ihren Gesprächspartnern. *Schweiz. Zeitschrift für Psychologie und ihre Anwendungen, 23,* 16–31.

1979a. Affekte und nonverbale Kommunikation. *Berichte aus der Abteilung für klinische Psychologie, 8,* 1–14. Zürich.

1979b. Stottern und nonverbale Kommunikation: Untersuchungen über den Zusammenhang zwischen Affektinhibition und Stottern. In *Kongressbericht der Deutschen Gesellschaft für Verhaltenstherapie, Hamburg, 1978,* Sonderheft II.

1981. *Affekt und Sprache: Untersuchungen über das Stottern und seine Behandlung.* Stuttgart: Kohlhammer.

Lemert, E. M. 1970. Sociological perspective. In Sheehan, J. G. (ed.) *Stuttering: research and therapy.* New York: Harper.

Luper, H. L. 1968. An appraisal of learning theory concepts in understanding and treating stuttering in children. In Gregory, H. (ed.) *Learning theory and stuttering therapy.* Evanston, Ill.: Northwestern University Press.

McCabe, R. B. & McCollum, J. D. 1972. The personal reactions of a stuttering adult to delayed auditory feedback. *Journal of Speech and Hearing Disorders, 37,* 536–41.

Meltzer, L., Morris, W. & Hayes, D. 1971. Interruption outcomes and vocal amplitude: explorations in social-psychophysics. *Journal of Personality and Social Psychology, 18,* 392–402.

Milisen, R. & Johnson, W. 1936. A comparative study of stutterers, former stutterers and normal speakers whose handedness has been changed. *Archives of Speech, 1,* 61–86.

Miller, A. 1979. *Das Drama des begabten Kindes.* Frankfurt: Suhrkamp.

Morgenstern, J. J. 1956. Socio-economic factors in stuttering. *Journal of Speech and Hearing Disorders, 21,* 25–33.

Motsch, M., Affeld-Niemeyer, P., Beder, L. & Hoefert, H. 1976. Zur Analyse der Interaktion von stotternden Kindern und ihren Eltern. In *Mitteilungen der Deutschen Gesellschaft für Verhaltenstherapie, Kongressbericht Berlin, 1976,* Sonderheft II.

Murphy, A. T. & Fitzsimons, R. M. 1960. *Stuttering and personality dynamics.* New York: Ronald.

Natale, M. 1975. Convergence of mean vocal intensity in dyadic communication as a function of social desirability. *Journal of Personality and Social Psychology, 32,* 790–804.

Perkins, W. H. 1970. Physiological studies. In Sheehan, J. G. (ed.) *Stuttering: research and therapy.* New York: Harper.

Roman, H. G. 1960. Handwriting and speech. In Barbara, D. A. (ed.) *Psychological aspects of speech and hearing.* Springfield: Thomas.

Scherer, K. R. 1974. Persönlichkeit, Stimmqualität und Persönlichkeitsattribu-
tion: pfadanalytische Untersuchungen zu nonverbalen Kommunikations-
prozessen. In Eckensberger, L. H. & Eckensberger, U. S. (eds.) *Bericht über
den 28. Kongress der Deutschen Gesellschaft für Psychologie in Saarbrücken*, vol. 3.
Göttingen: Hogrefe.

  1979. Non-linguistic vocal indicators of emotion and psychopathology. In
  Izard, C. E. (ed.) *Emotions and Psychopathology*. New York: Plenum Press.

Sheehan, J. G. 1970a. Personality approaches. In Sheehan, J. G. (ed.) *Stuttering:
research and therapy*. New York: Harper.

  1970b. Role conflict theory. In Sheehan, J. G. (ed.) *Stuttering: research and
  therapy*. New York: Harper.

  1978. Botschaft an einen Stotterer. In Hood, S. (ed.) *An einen Stotterer*. Düsseldorf.

Sheehan, J. G. & Martyn, M. M. 1967. Methodology in studies of recovery from
stuttering. *Journal of Speech and Hearing Research, 10*, 396–400.

Snidecor, J. C. 1947. Why the Indian does not stutter. *Quarterly Journal of Speech,
33*, 493–5.

Sperry, R. W. & Peilkowski, B. 1972. Die beiden Gehirne des Menschen. *Bild der
Wissenschaften, 9*, 921–7.

Steiner, F. 1980. Inhaltsanalytische Untersuchungen politischer Diskussionen
zwischen Stotterern und flüssigen Sprechern. Lizentiatsarbeit an der Philosophischen Fakultät, Zürich.

Tomkins, S. S. 1962–3. *Affect, cognition, consciousness*, vols. 1 and 2. New York:
Springer.

Tunner, W. A. 1974. Analyse und Modifikation des Stotterns. In Kraiker (ed.)
Handbuch der Verhaltenstherapie. Munich: Kindler.

Van Riper, C. 1971. *The nature of stuttering*. Englewood Cliffs, NJ: Prentice-Hall.

  1973. *The treatment of stuttering*. Englewood Cliffs, NJ: Prentice-Hall.

Welkowitz, J., Cariffe, G. & Feldstein, S. 1976. Conversational congruence as a
criterion of socialization in children. *Child Development, 47*, 269–72.

Wendahl, R. W. & Cole, J. 1961. Identification of stuttering during relatively
fluent speech. *Journal of Speech and Hearing Research, 4*, 281–6.

Wilson, E. O. 1975. *Sociobiology*. London: Harvard University Press.

4. Language and situation: the *pars pro toto* principle

THEO HERRMANN

1. Preliminary remarks

In this chapter the theoretical discussion and the empirical studies reported are concerned with the problem of how specific features of verbal behaviour depend upon specific features of the situations in which people speak. The *pars pro toto* principle serves as the major theoretical notion upon which our work is based. Speech is the result of the selection and verbal encoding of parts or components of mental data. These mental data can be described in terms of propositional structures. Situational cues determine in each case which components of such propositional structures are selected for encoding.

We discuss variations in the *naming of objects* and the influences which distinguishing features of objects, object distances and learned dimensional preferences have upon variations in naming. Furthermore, we are interested in specific variants of *requesting* and the determination of such request variants in terms of the way in which the speaker recognizes his partner's understanding of the situation, the latter's willingness to perform the desired action and the legitimation of his request. In addition, we are concerned with the choice of quasi-synonyms for the naming of objects, assuming that these quasi-synonyms belong to disparate *sublanguages*. We consider the social distance between the communicative partners and the speaker's emotional–cognitive distance with regard to the topic of conversation to be essential determining factors in the choice of words.

Our considerations lead to the formulation of eight theoretical postulates concerning the connection between situational cues and specific characteristics of verbal behaviour. In this chapter we report some empirical investigations which we have carried out in order to test these postulates.

A well-known sociolinguistic question is 'Who speaks what language to whom and when?' (Fishman 1965). In this chapter we are concerned with an even more general question: 'What do people say in what situation?' Or somewhat more precisely and more psychologically: 'How can specific characteristics of verbal behaviour be predicted and explained from specific situational conditions?' Or: 'In what ways is speech dependent upon situation?' Obviously these questions must in each case be made more concrete, if they are to be the object of scientific investigation. It is also clear that only relatively modest partial answers to these questions can be obtained within a single research programme. The state of psychological research regarding the dependency of speech upon situation is far from satisfactory. It seems to us that research into verbal behaviour is particularly unsatisfactory with regard to situations that, unlike greetings, leave-taking, telling stories or describing one's flat (cf. e.g. Clark & Clark 1977: 223ff.), are not highly standardized or ritualized; and it is with such less ritualized situations that our own research is concerned.

Nomological psychology studies human behaviour and its conditions and consequences. Accordingly, as a branch of psychology, the psychology of language is concerned with verbal behaviour and with its conditions and consequences. In accordance with traditional psychological methods, it is possible to test experimentally how specific characteristics of speech co-vary with specific situational features. Theories of speech production are employed in order to conceptualize these characteristics of speech and of situation, to explicate rules for the empirical identification of these features and to make hypothetical statements about the relationship between verbal behaviour and situation.

The problem of what people say in certain situations can be dealt with using the classical repertoire of methods in experimental psychology. This does not necessarily mean that this research strategy is the only one possible, or the most likely to produce success. Other sciences concerned with language have other methods and develop other types of theories. Even within psychology, experimentation is not the only legitimate research method. Furthermore there is no single psychological theoretical concept by means of which the dependency of language upon situation might be described and explained.

Language is such a difficult problem with such widespread ramifications that it should not be dealt with in terms of any single science, any single scientific 'school' or even any one source of references to relevant work. We still know so little about language that a pluralism of scientific approaches and avoidance of premature reduction to *one* **science,** *one* method or *one* theory appear to be advantageous. Every research prog-ramme which takes linguistic phenomena as its problem area, should make free use of its own methodological and theoretical potential in order to increase our knowledge of language. This can only occur if there is no 'Supreme Court' of the sciences of language which decrees what methods and theories are to be applied.

Research work in the domain of language should not, for example, be discredited simply because the authors do not base their work on the conceptual framework of the philosophy of speech acts (cf. Searle 1969), or on the semantic features theory (cf. Herrmann & Deutsch 1976: 174ff.), or because the approach – *horribile dictu!* – might be considered to be behaviouristic. It cannot be ultimately decided in Oxford, in California or elsewhere which psychological or non-psychological research strategy is to be permitted in the examination of linguistic data.

Given the present state of knowledge, research on language and speech should retain its multidisciplinary character. Thus linguistic theories cannot be given the role of proto- or meta-theories, in the light of which all other theories pertaining to linguistic phenomena should be evaluated. (Psychology of language is psychology and not (psycho-) linguistics.)[1]

2. The research problem

2.1. The level of analysis

Patterns of behaviour such as speech can be analysed in many different ways. One can distinguish very different, variable features in them. The speech of two people or one person at different points in time can, for example, vary in the following ways: according to volume, intonation pattern, accompanying mimicry and gesture, the way in which certain phonemes are realized acoustically, dialectal colouring, specific choice of words, the syntactic structure of sentences, semantic differences of ex-pression, speech acts (e.g. warning vs. threatening), general speech

[1] The investigations and theoretical considerations regarding the situational dependency of language, which are the subject of the following report, orginated at the Universities of Marburg and Mannheim (FRG). A large number of psychology students and in particular my colleagues, Werner Deutsch, Siegfried Hoppe-Graff, Manfred Laucht, Hermann Schöler, Aige Stapf and Peter Winterhoff, participated in the work. Our experimental investigations were made possible by the support which we received from the German Research Association (Deutsche Forschungsgemeinschaft).

strategies, discourse types, etc. Which variable features of speech are taken into consideration and examined depends on the particular research problem and the preliminary theoretical decisions connected with it. In psychophonetic investigations the general speech strategy of a speaker will scarcely be analysed. If we are interested in the dependency of choice of words upon situation, we will hardly base our investigation of speech upon the level of sounds and phonemes. It is obviously illusionary to wish to examine all possible features of speech at one and the same time.

In our research programme we analyse speech and its dependency upon situational features at the level of the *meaning* of words, clauses, sentences and texts, and also give limited consideration to syntactic variables. Phonetic and paraverbal features of speech, such as the nonverbal behaviour which accompanies speech, have not been a topic in our research. We are primarily concerned with the *semantic input*, which constitutes the basis for the production of natural language strings (utterances) (cf. Rosenberg 1977). More simply, what we are interested in is not so much *how* something is said as *what* is said and how this *What* is dependent upon specific situational features.

2.2. An introductory example

Professor H and his assistant L are jointly revising a manuscript on the psychology of language. They are sitting opposite each other in H's study. L suddenly discovers a spelling error. He wants to erase it. He notices that he has no rubber within reach and sees that there is one in H's reach. L says to H:

(1) Can you, please, give me the rubber?

L does *not* say to H:

(2) Can you, please, give me the rubber-wubber?

(3) I command you to give me the rubber.

(4) I would be pleased if I now had the rubber.

(5) Can you, please, give me the thingumabob?

(6) Can you, please, give it to me?

Why does L say sentence (1) and not sentences (2)–(6)? L's utterance occurs after the communicative situation, in which L and H find themselves, has already been in existence for some time. The utterance does not open a *dialogue*. Dialogues can be specified by means of the invariance of those communicating (e.g. L and H), the invariance of the topic (e.g. joint revision of a manuscript) and the invariance of further features of the total, interpersonal situation (e.g. no audience). L's utterance occurs, however, at the beginning of a (speech) *episode*. Episodes are parts of dialogues which can be specified by, among other things, the specific behaviours and goals of the participants. Such partial goals and the behaviour leading up to their achievement can result *endogenously* within the dialogue as a consequence of the previous course of conversation (e.g. the elucidation of a misunderstanding which has arisen; the presentation of a counter-offer; the conclusion of the dialogue through leave-taking). They can also be *exogenously* determined (e.g. it turns out that there is a draught and this situation must be settled by a request to the partner to close the window; pointing out to one's partner that his tea is getting cold). The rubber-episode came into being exogenously.

L utters sentence (1) and not sentences (5) or (6), because utterances (5) and (6) do not contain the information which would allow H to identify the desired object. If H is unable to identify the desired object, L does not achieve the goal of his verbal action i.e. getting hold of the rubber. The fact that (1) and not (5) or (6) is uttered can be discussed in terms of the *avoidance of confusion* (cf. Herrmann & Deutsch 1976; Olson 1970).

But why does L utter sentence (1) and not sentences (2)–(4)? One can assume that H would adequately understand the utterances (2)–(4) and even the expression 'rubber-wubber'. Explanations according to the principle of avoidance of confusion are not applicable in the case of utterance (2), which L does not produce because he is using a form of communication which is invariant within the dialogue with H. Such invariant forms of communication can be explained by the following postulate: by means of the nature of his utterances a speaker signals to his partner in what sort of social–emotional relationship he stands towards him or would wish to stand. This is true not only for constellations of roles, social distance, status relationships, but also for quite personal and idiosyncratic relationships between people. As a rule the speaker says only what is compatible with this established or intended social–emotional relationship and he says it in an appropriate way. Thus, for example, in German and French the use of 'Du' and 'Tu' is not compatible with social distance between the partners. Certain word choices, turns of phrase, etc. are incompatible with certain dialogue-invariant communication forms.

Words have connotative features (implicit additional meanings), which in certain circumstances may not be appropriate to the established or intended relationship between the speaker and his partner. Such words are generally avoided and replaced by quasi-synonyms which do not possess the undesirable connotations but fulfil the same referential purpose, e.g. *wash-room* or *bathroom* instead of *lavatory*. Consequently L utters sentence (1) and not (2). *Rubber-wubber* belongs to a level of speech which L finds inappropriate for communication with H.

Why does L utter sentence (1) and not sentences (3) or (4)? It is primarily a question of the directness of requests (cf. Gordon & Lakoff 1971; Searle 1975; Wunderlich 1972). Utterance (3) can be considered an extremely direct request and utterance (4) an extremely indirect request. The actual sentence used, (1), lies somewhere between these two extremes. What specific situational markers decide which of several possible request variants a speaker chooses will be discussed further in 3.2.

2.3. The *pars pro toto* principle

In our example L says: 'Can you, please, give me the rubber?' We have asked why L made this utterance rather than utterances (2)–(6). We can easily imagine other situations in which L, or some other person, could have made utterances (2)–(6). Therefore, it seems appropriate to assume that L's utterance is determined by specific situational features. For example, L calls the object a 'rubber' and does not replace this word by the pronoun 'it' or by the verbal joker 'thingumabob', which in different contexts of situation would have been perfectly possible. L avoids the expression 'rubber-wubber' and says 'rubber'. In a different social relationship between L and H, L could use the word 'rubber-wubber' without question. L selects a request of average directness. In other situations L will express either very direct, or very indirect, requests.

It is part of the task of the psychology of language to conceptualize and operationalize specific features of speech and of situations in a systematic way and to predict specific features of speech on the basis of the occurrence of specific situational features. The quest for such empirically demonstrable situational and behavioural relationships may be facilitated by a number of general theoretical considerations. In a dialogue or speech-episode speakers verbalize mental data, which we can imagine to be a complex of semantic units. The mental data are embedded in larger units and have their own structure. Psychologists, linguists and researchers, concerned with artificial intelligence, tend to call such data 'schemata', 'frames' or 'scripts'. These conceptualizations cannot be discussed here (cf. e.g. Anderson & Bower 1973; Chafe 1979; Kintsch 1977; Lindsay & Norman 1972; Minsky 1975; Schank & Abelson 1977; Winograd 1977). We are also unable to discuss here how mental data are subjectively represented. It is, however, our supposition that they contain semantic ('cognitive') as well as pictorial and linguistic (e.g. lexemic, phonetic) components and that they may very well have a personal, idiosyncratic character. We can describe such mental data more simply as *structures of propositions*, whereby the propositions themselves are conceived as consisting of predicates and arguments (cf. Kintsch 1974, 1977). For our present purpose we shall adopt this type of description.

The question 'How do people encode thoughts into natural language strings?' (Schank & Abelson 1977: 7) can be expressed more concretely as: 'How do people encode mnestically actualized (i.e. retrieved from memory) or innovatively produced structures of propositions, when they recognize specific situational cues?' Speakers verbalize *components* of their 'schemata', i.e. *parts* of their propositional structures. As our 'rubber' example was intended to make clear, speakers have several alternatives at their disposal for the verbalization of one and the same propositional structure. Speakers behave as though they select among several verbal alternatives when producing utterances. This selection is obviously not arbitrary but corresponds to certain general principles (cf. Herrmann & Laucht 1977, 1979).

(i) Speech production does not mean encoding the whole propositional structure but only *components* of it. Speakers could almost always say much more about their mnestically actualized or innovatively produced propositional structure than they do in fact say. For example, L might have said to H in our example:

(7) There is a big, red rubber. It has got an ink blot. I remember that it feels soft. I have often seen it with you. You keep it in your pen case. I mean that rubber-wubber, that thingumabob, that thing for rubbing out. I would like to use the rubber. The name 'Bruner' is spelt wrongly. I have got nothing to rub it out with and I would like to have this rubber. I can only use it, however, if you give it to me and you can give it to me and are prepared to do so. So I want you to give it to me. It accords with the ruling conventions when I instruct you to give me the rubber, for which reason I herewith request you to give me the rubber. (etc.)

The speaker, L, and anyone else for that matter is very unlikely to use such a verbalization, which appears almost pathological in form. What the speaker in fact does is to verbalize only a part of what might be said with regard to mental data. The speaker verbalizes – *pars pro toto* – single components of propositional structures (cf. Herrmann & Laucht 1977). (The Latin phrase *pars pro toto* means 'the part for/instead of the whole'.)

(ii) The selection of those components of propositional structures which – *pars pro toto* – are verbalized is probably determined by two major factors: (a) *information* (for the partner) and (b) *instrumentality* (for the achievement of the goal intended by the transfer of information).

(a) *Information*. The speaker says what in his experience is informative for the listener (Grice 1975; Herrmann & Deutsch 1976; Olson 1970).

When there is a soft white, and a soft red rubber on the table, and the speaker wants to have the soft red rubber, he does not say:
(8) Please, give me the soft rubber!
Rather, he says:
(9) Please, give me the red rubber!
Even when the speaker sees and knows that the rubber needed by him is soft and red, he verbalizes – *pars pro toto* – only that feature of the object (red), the verbalization of which is informative for the receiver. (In reply to utterance (8) the listener would presumably answer: 'Which one?')

Speakers verbalize in such a way that the listener can identify those mental data intended by the speaker. The listener is thus enabled not only to understand what the immediate content of the utterance of the speaker is, but also, in the most favourable instance the listener is able to *reconstruct* on the basis of his stored knowledge the whole of the propositional structure, of which the speaker verbalizes only a part. This is possible when the understanding of the situation and the 'knowledge of the world' are sufficiently similar for the speaker and the listener. (If the listener decodes utterance (9), for example, he identifies the rubber meant by the speaker and can *also* call to mind among other things that this rubber is *soft*. This is, however, information which the speaker did not give him.) In other words, when the conditions of cognition are very nearly identical, listeners can reconstruct – *totum ex parte* – the whole propositional structure intended by the speaker on the basis of that part of a propositional structure encoded by the speaker (cf. Bransford, Barclay & Franks 1972; Hörmann 1976: 460ff.). And this possibility is known to the speaker.

To what extent our *pars pro toto* explanation is compatible with the proposal that the propositions verbalized by the speaker are intended to *modify concepts* of the listener cannot be discussed here (cf. e.g. Kintsch 1974). In any case the long-standing proposal that verbal communication merely implies the encoding of a message by the speaker and the complementary decoding of this message by the listener is too simple.

(b) *Instrumentality*: In most cases there is not one but several verbal alternatives which would enable the listener to reconstruct the propositional structure intended by the speaker. In our example H can infer what is meant just as well from utterances (2)–(4) as from utterance (1). If several verbal alternatives are informative for the listener according to the experience of the speaker, the speaker chooses alternatives which he knows to be successful as a means of accomplishing his goal in other equivalent classes of situations. (L has most certainly learned that utterances of type (3) in situations like the one in which he finds himself lead to failure and are threatened with social sanctions.) Verbal alternatives, which are thoroughly informative for the partner, may be inappropriate as a means of accomplishing a goal or even damaging. It is not enough for the speaker that the listener should understand him. The listener should also behave in the way intended by the speaker.

(iii) We shall not enter into a discussion here of how one could conceptualize the mnestic actualization or the innovatory production of propositions (cf. e.g. Bredenkamp & Wippich 1977; Dörner 1976; Klix 1971). We make the assumption that a speaker finds himself in a situation in which he intends to communicate a propositional structure to a partner. In accordance with (i) he always verbalizes (encodes) only components of such propositional structures, not, however, the whole propositional structure. He selects components and encodes them. The selection of components can be explained in the following way: There are types of variable verbal behaviour $R_a, R_b, \ldots R_j, \ldots R_n$, cf. choice of words, level of speech, directness of request . . . and so on. The occurrence of an instance of behaviour R_j is the result of the selection of specific components and their encoding. $S_a, S_b, \ldots S_i, \ldots S_n$ designate situational cues which are relevant within dialogues. R_{js} is that sub-set of verbal behaviour in the set R_j which has shown itself to be *successful* (adequate) for the speaker with regard to the presence of cues S_i from the point of view of information and instrumentality.

In the course of the speaker's learning history he constructs implicational bonds of the sort: 'If S_i, then R_{js}' ('$S_i \rightarrow R_{js}$'). If the speaker recognizes cues S_i in the course of a dialogue, this leads to the mnestic actualization of learned implicational bonds $S_i \rightarrow R_{js}$. Like a 'psychological syllogism' (cf. Bolles 1972), the result of S_i and $S_i \rightarrow R_{js}$ is the verbal behaviour R_{js}, which is realized by the speaker by means of specific selection and encoding of components: 'If S_i, then R_{js}. Now we have S_i. Therefore: R_{js}.'

One sub-class of S_i cues is dialogue-invariant. Forms of verbal behaviour R_{js}, which are associated with these cues, are retained by the speaker during the whole dialogue (e.g. 'Du' and 'Sie' in German). Other cues occur only in single or sometimes very small segments of the dia-logue and partly determine very specific features of verbal utterances R_{js} (e.g. a special form of object naming).

The points of view sketched under (i), (ii) and (iii) obviously present no empirically testable theory in the strictest sense. In our view they can, however, be understood as being something like a heuristic principle, with the help of which hypothetical assumptions about situational and behavioural relationships of the type $S_i \rightarrow R_{js}$ can be developed. These assumptions must be so constructed that they can be empirically tested.

3. Theoretical assumptions with regard to the situational determination of verbal behaviour

The theoretical assumptions which we wish to report on here have been discussed elsewhere, cf. e.g. Herrmann 1976, 1978a, b; Herrmann & Deutsch 1976; Herrmann & Laucht 1976, 1977, 1979. We refer the reader to these publications and give here only a summary overview.

3.1. The determination of object naming

Since the beginnings of modern psychology (cf. Wundt 1862), the percep-tual process has been considered to be an active, constructive and selec-tive event (e.g. Metzger 1954; Neisser 1967; Rosch 1975; Treisman 1968). The perception of objects may not be compared with the photographing or filming of objects. The person perceiving *uses* the information recorded by means of the senses in order to produce cognitive (re-)constructions of his environment on the basis of the information received and on the basis of his aims, comprehension of the situation and experiential knowledge. These cognitive constructs ('schemata') may very well be different in the same environment. Put another way: variable results derived from cog-nition may correspond to the same physical facts. The individual subjec-tive results of cognition may be described as the structures of proposi-tions, which are held to be true for particular sections of reality. Thus we may describe, for example, the cognitive construct which a perceiver produces on the basis of a physical fact as follows: 'That's a canary. It's yellow. It's singing . . .' The same physical fact may result in the follow-ing construct for another perceiver: 'That's a bright yellow bird. It's sitting near a red bird. It's tweeting. The tweeting is shrill . . .'

3.1.1. The constructive and selective character of object perception

becomes clear when we consider the following situation: a speaker is confronted with a variety of objects and intends, by means of a verbal utterance, to cause a partner to identify one of these objects (cf. Olson 1970). For example, the speaker sees among many other objects on a table a big white rubber, a big red rubber and a small white rubber. Verbally, he would like to cause his partner to identify the big red rubber. The speaker should have this intended object in the focus of his attention. At the same time he will (re-)construct it cognitively in a quite specific way.

Objects like the big red rubber can be cognized in highly different ways. For example, it might be considered as an element in a spatial pattern consisting of objects; we may notice what sort of shadow it throws; small imperfections in it may be perceived, etc. In the present case the speaker will take into consideration those characteristics of the object which *distinguish* it from the other objects. Consequently, the speaker will classify the intended object as a rubber, which already distinguishes it from many other objects in the field of perception. Its size and colour will also be a matter of interest, because these dimensions can serve to distinguish it from the two other objects which also belong to the class of rubbers. A perceptual comparison shows that the intended rubber distinguishes itself only from one of the two alternative rubbers because of its size, while the colour (red) is a feature unique to it. (Other objects on the table may be red in colour, too, although they are not rubbers.) When the speaker wishes to differentiate between the intended object and the alternative objects, he will form a cognitive construct, which among other things will contain two dominant components. Both of these components may be described in terms of the two following propositions: (a) the thing is a *rubber*; (b) the thing is *red*. From the whole range of those things which could be said about the object, the speaker selects precisely these two components. The verbal behaviour R_{js} (see 2.3), by means of which the speaker attempts to cause his partner to identify the intended object, can be understood to be the result of the verbal encoding of precisely those two components (a) and (b). The verbalization of other propositions relevant to the object (e.g.: the thing throws a shadow; the thing is relatively big) would be inadequate as far as the information for the partner is concerned (see 2.3). Thus the speaker will say something like: 'Look at the *red rubber*, will you!'

Now let us assume that the speaker again wishes to cause his partner to identify the big red rubber, but the situation is different from the one just outlined. Now there are two small red rubbers on the table instead of the small white rubber and the big white rubber. Consequently, the intended object of perception is the same as in the example above, but the *object context* has changed. We assume that the cognitive object construct produced by the speaker will be different from the one described previously in the following way: rubber is still a distinguishing feature, but it is not now the colour but the size which is the other relevant distinguishing feature. The cognitive construct which the speaker produces with regard to the intended object can now be described in terms of the following dominant propositions: (a) the thing is a *rubber*; (b) the thing is *big*. The adequate verbal behaviour R_{js} will, according to our view, contain the verbalization of precisely these two features of the object. The speaker will perhaps say: 'Look at the *big rubber*, will you!' The object, which has remained the same, will, therefore, be referred to differently.

When a speaker attempts to cause a listener to identify an object (or an event or fact), he must recognize those features of an object which it alone possesses, in comparison with other (alternative) objects. These features of an object are the *distinguishing features* of the object. The distinguishing object features serve the speaker as cues S_i which govern his verbal behaviour. His naming of the object R_{js} contains words or word groups which are the result of the verbal encoding of precisely these distinguishing features. As far as the example above is concerned we may reconstruct the naming process hypothetically in the following way: in order to achieve his goal – i.e. the identification of the intended single object by the listener – the speaker uses the following, learnt string of implications: 'When the distinguishing features S_i can be ascribed to the object intended, the corresponding verbal reaction R_{js} contains a verbal encoding of S_i.' The speaker ascribes to the object the distinguishing features (S_i), *rubber* and *big*. As a result he produces an utterance R_{js}, which contains the verbal equivalents of *rubber* and *big*.

Two problems which occur with regard to the naming of objects and the influence of specific situational features cannot be discussed fully here. First, the identification of the object by the listener may be unsuccessful if listener and speaker have different conceptions of the field of reference. This can, for example, occur when the listener has alternative objects in mind which the speaker does not take into consideration in the cognitive construction of the object to be named. (The partner can confuse the intended object with an object which the speaker has not cognized.) Deutsch & Clausing (1979) report on the psychological conditions under which the risk of such misunderstandings is minimized. Secondly, the naming of objects can be very different depending upon the aim or goal which the speaker has. A speaker can cause the listener to identify an intended object by saying to him, for example: 'The thing I mean is a red rubber.' Or he can say: 'Give me the red rubber!' Or, simply: 'That red rubber there', etc. In relation to the present discussion the adequate verbal behaviour R_{js} is determined only by the verbal encoding of *distinguishing features* whereby these words or word groups can be integrated into very different utterances.

The points set out above suffice to explain our first theoretical postulate with regard to the dependency of verbal behaviour upon situation. This postulate corresponds to assumptions made by Olson (1970), which the present author has developed from a different theoretical framework.

Postulate 1. Identical objects are variably named as follows: The naming R_{js} of an object varies in accordance with the distinguishing features of this object S_i.

3.1.2. Postulate 1 is inadequate when verbalization of *several* existing distinguishing features of an object are suitable in order to make it possible for the listener to identify the object (= multiple verbal codability). To keep to our rubber example, we can imagine, for example, that a big light-coloured and a small dark-coloured rubber are on the table and that the big light-coloured rubber is the object intended by the speaker. The listener can identify this object when the speaker says: 'Give me the big rubber!' Similarly, he can also recognize it when the speaker says: 'Give me the light-coloured rubber!' But which of the equally appropriate utterances R_{js} does the speaker actually choose?

This question can be answered quite easily when the two objects differ more obviously with regard to colour than to size. In this case both objects have a greater *object distance* with regard to the dimension of colour than with regard to the dimension of size. The speaker is likely to emphasize those features of the intended object which mark off the object most clearly in the general context. In cases of multiple codability the speaker will prefer to ascribe that particular distinguishing feature to the intended object which corresponds to the greatest object distance. Accordingly, the verbal reaction R_{js} will contain as a matter of preference the verbal encoding of just this feature. Consequently, in the example given the speaker would say: 'Give me the light coloured rubber!'

Postulate 2. In the case of multiple verbal codability the naming R_{js} of an object varies with those distinguishing features S_i of the object which offer the greatest object distance with regard to the alternative objects.

3.1.3. Given that more than one appropriate naming reaction R_{js} is possible for the identification of an object by the partner, what happens if the objects have comparable object distances with regard to their distinguishing features, i.e. the differences with regard to colour and to size are negligible? In this case, how do speakers choose their naming reactions R_{js} when there is multiple codability *and* no distinguishable object distance?

Our supposition is that, from several distinguishing features, the feature which is used as a cue for the selection of a naming reaction R_{js} is the *most conspicuous* or salient with regard to the senses (cf. Garner 1974). When the intended object has, for example, a particularly bright colour or a particularly strange shape and when these features are also distinguishing ones, they are preferred to other distinguishing features for verbalization purposes. Furthermore, we are of the opinion that people *learn* to pay special attention to specific sensory nuances of the characteristics of objects as opposed to other nuances. Such preferred nuances, which are the result of *past learning*, have the greatest chance of being verbalized in cases of multiple codability. Consequently, a person may have learnt, for example, to pay more attention to the size of elements in a class of objects than to colour (cf. Herrmann & Deutsch 1976: 35, 99ff.).

Postulate 3. In cases of multiple codability where there are no distinguishable object distances the naming R_{js} of an object varies in accordance with those distinguishing features S_i of the object which (a) are most conspicuous to the senses and/or (b) belong to distinguishing nuances which, as the result of learning experience, enjoy a privileged position.

3.1.4. Our suppositions with regard to situation-specific object naming R_{js} can be summarized briefly as follows: When the object intended by the speaker distinguishes itself from the alternative objects in terms of *one* distinguishing feature (or *one* group of distinguishing features), the naming reaction contains the verbalization of precisely that *distinguishing feature*. When the intended object distinguishes itself from the alternative object in a number of ways, the naming reaction contains the verbalization of that distinguishing feature which has the greatest *object distance*. If the object distances are not distinguishable and there is multiple codability, the naming reaction contains the verbalization of the *most conspicuous* feature and/or that feature which belongs to a featural nuance which is *privileged as the result of learning experience*. (Obviously, the situation-specific naming of objects is not *only* dependent upon these conditions.)

We have also concerned ourselves with one aspect of the problem of object naming which we cannot discuss here for reasons of space. In postulates 1, 2 and 3 we predicted which words or word groups *must* occur in naming reactions R_{js} which are appropriate in the situations we envisaged. We did not, however, take into account which *non-distinguishing* features in R_{js} *may also* be verbalized. When a speaker is confronted with a small red, and a small white rubber, as well as with other objects which are not rubbers, and when he wishes to cause the listener to identify the small red rubber, he may possibly say: 'I would like to have the small red rubber.' While the verbalized features *rubber* and *red* operate here as distinguishing features, *small* is non-distinguishing and thus, as far as the informational content for the listener is concerned (see 2.3), unnecessary. This naming reaction is *redundant*. Such redundancies in object naming are difficult to explain. Some initial discussion and findings are to be found in Deutsch 1976 and Herrmann & Deutsch 1976: 86ff.

3.2. The determination of request variants

3.2.1. We shall discuss the situation in which a speaker S requests a communication partner P by means of the verbal behaviour R_j to carry out an action A or not to do so. Such request reactions R_j can vary considerably. As we have already mentioned, requests can be distinguished with regard to their directness (cf. Clark & Lucy 1975). We assume that people learn what the conditions and the consequences of requests are. This knowledge, too, is in our opinion organized in the form of propositions. Thus the (hierarchical) structure of request conditions and their consequences can be described as a structure of propositions. At this point we shall give only a rather simplified account of our theoretical assumptions and refer the reader to the more precise presentation in Herrmann & Laucht 1979.

3.2.2. We assume the existence of a propositional structure 'To request someone to do something' consisting of the *conditions E, A and C* and the *consequence I*.

Condition E. When requesting one's partner to perform an action A, a situation or the occurrence of an event must be aimed for, which can be brought about by means of action A. This is at least true for those communicational norms usual for us (cf. Grice 1975). Thus the following components can at first be distinguished with regard to the conditions for making a request: (a) *The speaker S prefers the situation or the event E to non-E.* (b) *E is not in existence.* (c) *Hence, S wishes for the situation/event E.* This is the primary (episode-specific) aim of his action.

Condition A. When the speaker S requests his partner to perform action A, he is wishing not only for the situation/event E. A further condition for the request is that S assumes that E can be realized only, or with the minimum effort for S, if P carries out the action A. Furthermore, P must be in a position to do A and at least prepared in principle to do A. Consequently speaker S wants P to carry out the action A. This is the secondary aim in S's behaviour. Condition A can be analysed in terms of the following single propositions: (d) *If P does A, then E.* (e) *P can do A.* (f) *P is prepared to do A.* (g) *Hence, S wants P to do A.*

Condition C. When S asks P to do A, it is not enough that S wants P to do A. For one thing S must assume that P will do A only if S obliges him (by means of the request reaction R_j) to do A. Furthermore, it must be possible for S to oblige P to do A: there must be such things as social norms (orders, rules, laws, etc.) according to which a class of persons X is allowed to oblige another class of persons Y to carry out action A in the existing class of situations K. (Sometimes, of course, such obligations may not hold in the society at large, but only in certain sub-groups.) S must also assume that the situation to which such conventions apply actually exists and that he himself belongs to X and that P belongs to Y. Only when all these conditions are fulfilled can S oblige P to do A. Condition C thus consists of the following propositions: (h) *Only if S obliges P to do A, P will do A.* (i) *There is a social convention N: Y can be obliged by X to do A under the situational condition K.* (j) *Condition K exists.* (k) *S belongs to class X.* (l) *P belongs to class Y.*

Conditions E, A and C have the *consequence I*, which can be formulated in a further proposition: (m) *S obliges P to do A.* The elements E, A, C and I, which belong to the speaker's knowledge about making requests, stand in the following logical relationship to one another: consequence I only when conditions C and A; condition A only when condition E. (S obliges P to do A only when P can be obliged to do A and when S wants P to do A; S only wants P to do A when S wants E.)

Our explanatory model for the choice of request variants R_{js}, which are *adequate* with regard to information and instrumentality under the variable situational conditions S_i, is based on the following thought: observable request variants can be understood as the results of verbal encoding of the propositions (a)–(m). In order to produce *appropriate* request reactions R_{js}, the speaker must select specific propositions from the set (a)–(m) according to specific situational cues S_i and encode the selected propositions verbally.

Based on our discussion so far, propositions (a)–(m) can be classified as follows: propositions (a)–(c) represent condition E; propositions (d)–(g) represent condition A; propositions (h)–(l) represent condition C; proposition (m) represents consequence I, which is based upon conditions E, A and C. Thus observable request variants R_j can be classified as the result of the verbal encoding of propositional elements from the four categories E, A, C and I. Hence, a partner P can be requested to do A when we explicitly oblige him to do A (= I) or when single conditions for the obligation are verbalized (= E, A or C). Consequently, verbal requests can consist of the verbalization of *conditions* for an obligation (cf. Gordon & Lakoff, 1971).

We give some examples of the verbalization of categories I, C, A and E:
I: Open the window! (= proposition (m)) – I order you to open the window. (= proposition (m))
C: I can expect you to open the window. (= proposition (k)) – You have to open the window. (= proposition (l))
A: I would like you to open the window. (= proposition (g)) – Certainly you can open the window. (= proposition (e))
E: I would prefer it if the window was open. (= proposition (a)) – There is a lack of fresh air. (= proposition (b))

The verbalizations of categories I to E display systematic differences: the request variants (from I to E) can be *misunderstood* by the partner with increasing ease. (The request (!): 'There is a lack of fresh air' is extremely indirect.) On the other hand (from I to E), it becomes increasingly more difficult for the partner to *object to* the request. The requests offer the partner increasingly greater freedom of action. An optimum for the avoidance of misunderstandings *and* strong adversive reactions on the part of the partner should be attainable by means of the verbalization of the 'half-way' condition A (cf. Herrmann & Laucht 1977). It turned out indeed that the subjects we tested most frequently produced request variants from category A.

3.2.3. Request variants R_j are the result of the verbal encoding of propositional elements of the conditions C, A or E or of the explicit obligation I. It is our opinion that people learn to select variable propositions, in which I, C, A or E are represented, when they are confronted with variable situational cues S_i, and to encode them. The *adequate* request variants resulting from S_i from the point of view of information and instrumentality (see 2.3) are the behaviour patterns R_{js}. We suggest that the competence to make requests in a way which is appropriate to the situation at hand is based upon the knowledge of the learnt relationships between S_i and R_{js}. Which situational cues S_i are connected with which adequate request variants created as verbalizations of I, C, A or E?

For a detailed theoretical description of the S_i–R_{js} connections we refer the reader once again to Herrmann & Laucht 1977, 1979; Laucht & Herrmann 1978. We claim that the following three features S_i play an important part in the selection of request variants.

(i) *The partner's understanding of the situation (SC) as assumed by the speaker*. First the speaker judges how the partner understands the situation in which the speaker and his partner find themselves. When the speaker decides that his partner does not understand the situation in the same way as he does (SC−), he justifies his request or he gives his partner specific information in some other way concerning the request conditions C, A and/or E. (Example: 'You know very well that you should offer your seat to old people' – 'You've got plenty of time now to do some shopping for me. The TV programme doesn't start till later.') In this way the speaker attempts to bring about an adequate understanding of the situation by his partner.

When the speaker decides that his partner understands the situation in the same way as he does (SC+), he checks his partner's willingness to carry out action A.

(ii) *The partner's willingness to do A as assumed by the speaker (WA)*: When the speaker decides that his partner is unwilling to do A, he does not try to reach his aim E by a simple request. (cf. proposition (f)). However, the speaker can consider the willingness of the partner to do A to be *completely unproblematic* (WA+) or he can judge it to be *doubtful or problematic* (WA?). In the case of WA+ the speaker can use many different request variants in order to get the partner to do A. However, there are important exceptions here: when the partner understands the situation in just the same way as the speaker and when he is quite prepared to do A, it would be completely inappropriate to remind him explicitly of his obligation or to ask him expressly in some other way. Probably the partner will take offence at such high-handed requests. (Under normal circumstances it would be very inappropriate to order a beer in the following way: 'You're serving here and I'm a client, so hurry up and get me a beer!') Hence, in the case of WA+, verbalizations from A and E will be preferred, not those from I and C. If the speaker is unsure of the partner's willingness (WA?) to do A, he will consider the legitimacy of his request.

(iii) *The legitimacy of the request as assumed by the speaker (LR)*. It is apparent that speakers may understand the normative legitimation of their request in different ways. If the speaker does not consider his request to be a legitimate one, he will not give his partner an order but perhaps try to establish an obligation by means of suitable strategies (see propositions (i) to (l)). On the other hand, the legitimacy for the request may be *quite unproblematic and normatively legitimate* (LR+) or there may be *problems and doubts* (LR?). The difference between LR+ and LR? can be made clear in terms of the relationship to property: if S wants P to give him back something which belongs to S, a corresponding request is highly legitimate in terms of the prevailing norms concerning property (LR+). If S wants P to give or lend him something which belongs to P, the corresponding request is no longer fully legitimate; the legitimacy is much weaker (LR?).

If the speaker decides that his partner understands the situation just as he does (SC+), considers his partner's willingness to do A as doubtful (WA?) and thinks his request to be very legitimate (LR+), he will use strong requests of the type I and C. He behaves differently when the legitimacy of his request is doubtful or normatively not very legitimate (LR?). In such a case the speaker will avoid strong requests. But he will not use weakly formulated requests because the partner might deliberately choose to misunderstand them. The speaker will use requests of average directness and verbalize propositions resulting from condition A.

3.2.4. It is hoped that these brief statements are sufficient to outline the theoretical assumptions we make with regard to the situational dependency of the choice of request variants. For the formulation of the following postulates we make use of the symbols I, C, A and E together with SC+, SC−, WA+, WA?, LR+, LR?, introduced above.

Postulate 4. When the speaker recognizes SC−, he informs the partner of conditions C, A and/or E:

S_i: SC− → R_{js}: Reason (C, A and /or E)

Postulate 5. When the speaker recognizes SC+ and WA+, his request consists of the verbalization of components of conditions A or E:

S_i: SC+ & WA+ → R_{js}: A, E

Postulate 6. When the speaker recognizes SC+, WA? and LR+, his request consists of the verbalization of I or of components of condition C:

S_i: SC+ & WA? & LR+ → R_{js}: I, C

Postulate 7. When the speaker recognizes SC+, WA? and LR?, his request consists of the verbalization of components of condition A:
S_i: SC+ & WA? & LR? → R_{js}: A

It is to be noted that we expect a dominant verbalization of condition A after postulate 5 as well as after postulate 7. Thus request variants which consist of the speaker's verbalizations of the request conditions A are over-determined in this respect. Yet postulates 5 and 7 are empirically testable, if the experimental correlates of S_i are chosen in such a way that it is obvious which of the two postulates is being tested. We have discovered specific differences in the 'surface structure' of requests, as they occur as a result of postulate 5 versus 7. There are differences in the use of modal verbs and particles and in sentence structure. Unfortunately we cannot elaborate on these phenomena here.

The empirical verification of all the postulates relating to requests obviously depends on (a) the situational features SC, WA and LR being adequately represented by the corresponding experimental conditions and (b) the presence of the preconditions for the objective and reliable matching of the observed request reactions R_j with the categories I, C, A and E.

3.3 The determination of level of speech

3.3.1. The situation-specific use of sub-languages (dialects, sociolects, idiolects), code-switching and similar phenomena have been adequately dealt with by sociolinguists and other social scientists (cf. Argyle 1969; Cazden 1972; Hymes 1972; Joos 1961; Moscovici 1967; Schlieben-Lange 1973; and the volumes edited by Fishman 1968; and Pride & Holmes 1972). We limit ourselves here to a very small part of this complex problem and discuss briefly our ideas on the situation-specific choice of words which belong to various sub-languages (cf. Herrmann 1976, 1978b; Herrmann & Deutsch 1976: 26ff., 57ff., 109ff.).

3.3.2. Children learn at an early age that there is more than one designation for objects, events and facts. Thus one and the same thing can be variously referred to as 'mother' or 'mummy', 'money' or 'dough', 'posterior' or 'arse'. Children also learn, however, that the use of such quasi-synonyms is not random. They learn that certain words which they hear from their peers in the street cannot be used at home. Soon children behave as if they were in control of two or more sub-languages to which various classes or words belong. If we simplify the matter, we can distinguish between two such word classes: *standard speech words* (W_{st}) and *non-standard speech words* (W_{non-st}). We must think of the class W_{non-st} as being divided into several sub-classes (jargon, slang, intimate speech, etc.). When children enter the phase which Piaget refers to as concrete-operational (Herrmann & Deutsch, 1976: 52ff.), they no longer use words from W_{st} and W_{non-st} arbitrarily but situation-specifically. Some years later they are able to explain W_{st} and W_{non-st} metacommunicatively (Herrmann, 1978b).

It seems likely that children learn as a result of reward and punishment that it is more risky to use W_{non-st} in the wrong situation than to use W_{st} in the wrong situation. People meet with social sanctions more often when they use 'vulgar' or 'disrespectful' words than when they use 'formal' or 'condescending' speech in situations where it is not usual. W_{st} and W_{non-st} are subject to '*asymmetric conditions of positive and negative reinforcement*'. The implicit knowledge of the following *meta-rule* seems to be an important component of communicative competence: 'If you have more than one quasi-synonym for the naming of objects, events and facts, when *in doubt* choose W_{st}.' (If we consider single languages to be divided into various strata, we can formulate this implicit meta-rule as: 'When *in doubt* choose the higher level of speech.')

3.3.3. We suggest that two specific situational cues S_i in particular are used in order to distinguish between W_{st} and W_{non-st} (cf. Argyle 1969; Creed 1972). These cues S_i are as a rule dialogue invariant, i.e. S_i have to do with the partner and the topic, which generally remain the same within the dialogue. However, there are exceptions. For example, the speaker can become increasingly more confident in the course of a dialogue and correspondingly lower his level of speech; the choice of words can suddenly become 'overbearing' for reasons of language strategy, etc. We are concerned here with the usual state of affairs, where the choice of W_{st} and W_{non-st} remains the same within the dialogue.

An initial cue S_i which governs the choice of W_{st} or W_{non-st} is the *social distance* (sD) between speaker and partner. The probability that W_{non-st} will be used increases as sD decreases. Another cue S_i is concerned with the topic. The more a conversation has to do with a subject in which the speaker feels competent and sure of himself and which is emotionally charged and relevant for the speaker (cf. Herrmann 1976), the greater the probability that the speaker will use W_{non-st}. If an adolescent is deeply interested in football and understands the game but has no emotional rapport with the disco scene, he will use standard speech when talking to his friend about the disco scene and use a specific jargon to talk about football. We suggest, therefore, that personal *topic distance* (tD) is an important situational feature, by means of which the choice between W_{st} and W_{non-st} is regulated. The probability of W_{non-st} increases as tD decreases.

Both hypothetical cues sD and tD stand in our opinion in the following relationship to one another: when the social distance between the speaker and the partner is relatively small, lack of topic distance (tD−) leads to an increase of W_{non-st}. When social distance is considerable (sD+), the use of standard speech remains constant even when there is tD−. The adolescent, who is interested in football, will use standard speech when talking to a stranger, even though he is talking about his favourite subject. If it is true that the situation-specific use of W_{st} and W_{non-st} is learnt as a result of asymmetrical positive and negative reinforcement and if the speaker chooses W_{st} in doubtful cases, he will use W_{non-st} only when he can be relatively certain that he will not evoke negative reactions from his partner by the use of these words. Such a subjective feeling of certainty should as a rule only be present when there is sD−. The use of W_{non-st} often signals confidence, emotional closeness to the partner and 'in group' behaviour, etc. When sD− exists, the speaker will choose the alternative W_{non-st} among several quasi-synonyms only when he can calculate the communicative effect of the use of such words in the given conversational context with certainty. And this is so only in the case of tD−. (There is nothing quite so embarrassing as when fathers speak to their sons in the latter's jargon.) In the case of sD−, W_{non-st} is chosen when subjects are discussed which the speaker both knows and feels an emotional rapport with.

We are considering here the case when a speaker knows several quasi-synonyms for the verbal encoding of objects, events and facts, some of which belong to the class W_{st} and others to the class W_{non-st}. Thus he has to choose between W_{st} and W_{non-st}. His language behaviour in this respect R_j, as far as instrumentality is concerned (see 2.3), can be qualified as *adequate* verbal behaviour R_{js} only when the selection of W_{st} or W_{non-st} conforms to specific cues S_i. With regard to these cues it is a matter of social distance (sD) and topic distance (tD).

3.3.4. We formulate the following theoretical postulate using the symbols sD+, sD−, tD+, tD−, W_{st} and W_{non-st} introduced above:

Postulate 8: The speaker will prefer to use words from class W_{non-st}, when he recognizes that both social distance and topic distance between himself and his partner are minimal. If there is marked social distance and/or marked topic distance he will prefer to use words from class W_{st}:

$$S_i: sD- \ \& \ tD- \ \rightarrow \ R_{js}: W_{non\text{-}st}$$
$$S_i: SD+ \ \& \ tD- \ \rightarrow \ R_{js}: W_{st}$$
$$S_i: sD- \ \& \ tD+ \ \rightarrow \ R_{js}: W_{st}$$
$$S_i: sD+ \ \& \ tD+ \ \rightarrow \ R_{js}: W_{st}$$

3.4. For the last time: 'Can you, please, give me the rubber?'

To summarize our considerations in 3.1–3.3, we return to the fictitious rubber episode described in 2.2. By means of the above postulates, we can interpret the utterance of L to H, 'Can you, please, give me the rubber?', in the following way.

(i) In the situation as we have imagined it H cannot confuse the intended rubber with other rubbers; he can, however, confuse it with other objects. The only distinguishing feature is the membership of the intended object in the class of rubbers. According to postulate 1, L chooses the word *rubber*. Multiple codability (postulates 2 and 3) is supposedly not present.

(ii) L assumes that H understands the situation just as he does (SC+) and that H is basically willing to hand over the rubber (WA+). According to postulate 5, this constellation of conditions leads to L's choosing a request from categories A or E. His utterance belongs to category A. Postulates 4, 6 and 7 are inapplicable here.

(iii) As far as L is concerned there is considerable topic distance (tD+). Furthermore, his social distance from H is fairly large. L knows two designations for the intended object; *rubber* belongs to W_{st} and *rubber-wubber* belongs to $W_{non\text{-}st}$. In accordance with postulate 8, L chooses the word *rubber*.

Admittedly this example is fictional. Also we have not sufficiently described the situational condition under which L produces his utterance. Furthermore our interpretation does not replace an empirical examination of our theoretical postulates. Many features of L's utterance can be identified which we have not taken into consideration here. Our theoretical systematization as well as our empirically obtained knowledge with regard to the situational dependency of verbal behaviour is noticeably incomplete. In what follows, we give a short review of our empirical investigations up to the present time with regard to postulates 1–8.

4. Some empirical findings

We can offer here no more than a short survey of some of our experiments to test postulates 1–8 and point out only the general tendencies indicated by the results.

4.1. Findings on the naming of objects (postulates 1–3)

A detailed account of investigations on object naming can be found in Herrmann & Deutsch (1976: 65ff.).

4.1.1. Proof that one and the same object (see postulate 1) can be referred to in different ways when it differs from alternative objects in various ways has been presented by Olson (1970). We have adopted Olson's method of investigation to a large extent and also observed a strong empirical confirmation of postulate 1.

In our *car park experiment* children play the part of car park attendants. There are varying numbers of vehicles in a car park filled with toy cars. One of these vehicles, O_i, is the object singled out by the car park attendant. The other vehicles are alternative objects O_a. The set O_i & O_a constitutes the *object constellation* C. The attendant's job is to announce over an imaginary loud speaker: 'The driver of car . . . is requested to remove his vehicle from the car park.' (The naming of the object O_i was to be inserted into the scheme.) In accordance with postulate 1 the *adequate* designation of O_i ($=R_{js}$), where O_i is invariable, is to co-vary systematically with the object constellation C (i.e. with O_a).

The vehicles used in the car park are distinguished according to the following features: object class: *bulldozer* versus *Volkswagen*; colour: *blue* versus *red*; size: *big* versus *small*. From the combination of these attributes there are eight different vehicles. In each case one of them was chosen as the object to be singled out (O_i). This object O_i can receive seven different, distinguishing designations. When O_i, for example, has the attributes *big & red & bulldozer*, O_i can be designated differently as follows: 'the big one', 'the red one', 'the bulldozer', 'the big bulldozer', 'the red bulldozer', 'the big red one' or 'the big red bulldozer'. In accordance with the object constellation C, each of these seven designation alternatives R_j can become the *adequate* designation R_{js}. We constructed seven different object constellations C in such a way that only one of the seven designations was the expected (adequate) designation in accordance with postulate 1. Since each subject named 4 objects O_i in 7 constellations C there was a total of 28 object constellations. Each subject had to display 28 naming reactions R_j.

Our subjects were 295 school children aged between 9 and 11. Other investigations have shown (cf. 4.1.2.) that children are capable of situation-specific object naming when they have reached Piaget's concrete-operational phase (Herrmann & Deutsch 1976: 133ff.). All our subjects fulfilled this condition. Since each subject had to display 28 naming reactions R_j, the total corpus of data was $n_{R_j} = 8260$. In the case of each object constellation C it could be statistically shown whether the reactions R_j of our subjects were more frequently than could be accounted for by chance *adequate* reactions in terms of postulate 1. In accordance with a statistical procedure found in Miller (1966: 215ff.) we discovered that the observed frequency of R_{js} in 27 out of 28 object constellations could not be ascribed to chance. This is a clear confirmation of postulate 1.

4.1.2. The variable designation of identical objects O_i was further investigated by us in a way which was not taken into consideration by Olson (1970). In a *relatives experiment* we assumed that a person O_i can be designated in different ways in various object constellations C, when relationship names (i.e. *father, uncle, son*) are used as naming alternatives and when the alternative objects O_a are people who are related in some way with O_i. Here the distinguishing features of O_i are realized in the form of complex predicates of the type 'X is the father of Y.' When the persons O_a are varied, a constant person O_i is to be provided with varying relationship names (R_{js}) in the correct manner.

The relatives experiment was tried out on our subjects in the form of a picture book story. In the story each subject had to display 12 naming reactions R_j: 4 objects O_i were to be named in 3 object constellations. (As in the car park experiment R_j consisted of open, verbal answers.)

According to the Montada non-verbal matrix test (1968) we classified 120 children aged from 5 to 9 years according to Piaget's criterion 'operational phase' versus 'pre-operational phase'. The relatives experiment was assessed using analysis of variance. It was shown that only children who were in the concrete-operational phase were able to give constant persons O_i variable (adequate) relationship names R_{js} with a frequency which could not be accounted for by mere chance, when O_i was placed in variable object constellations C. This also confirms postulate 1, provided that we make the reservation that postulate 1 is only valid in the case of persons who have reached the concrete-operational phase in their cognitive development.

4.1.3. We tested postulates 2 and 3 with the *candle experiment* and the *Murks experiment*. In both experiments the subjects were confronted with object constellations C, which consisted of a single intended object O_i and a *single* alternative object O_a. In the case of O_i there was multiple codability: there were always two possible adequate designations R_{js}. The *object distances* D of O_i and O_a with regard to the dimensions X and Y were varied systematically as follows: (a) $D_X > D_Y$, (b) $D_Y > D_X$, (c) $D_X \approx D_Y$. These conditions (a)–(c) were set up after prior scaling of the stimulus material (intermodal distance comparison; cf. Baird 1970; Krantz 1972).

Every experiment was preceded by a learning phase: using stimuli which were *not* used in the candle and Murks experiments and requesting *non*-verbal reactions, different groups of subjects learnt to show a preference for either the dimension X or Y (cf. postulate 3). As a result of these two conditions of learnt *preference for dimensions* (X versus Y) and the distance conditions ((a)–(c)) an experimental plan with six cells was conceived. From postulates 2 and 3 we deduce the following expectations: (i) In the case of $D_X > D_Y$ the attribute of O_i belonging to X will be verbalized. An effect of the preference for dimensions does not occur. (ii) In the case of $D_Y > D_X$ the attribute of O_i belonging to Y will be verbalized. An effect of the preference for dimensions does not occur. (iii) In the case of $D_X \approx D_Y$ the attribute of O_i belonging to the preferred dimension X versus Y will be verbalized.

In the *candle experiment* the objects O_i and O_a, which are represented by means of two dimensional drawings of candles, are distinguished according to the dimensions height (= X) and width (= Y). The *Murks experiment* was embedded in a science fiction story: There is a distant star called Murks. The people who live there have wheels instead of legs. The inhabitants of Murks are given names according to the area (= X) and the brightness (= Y) of their wheels. The wheels vary according to these dimensions. Our subjects had to name a candle or an inhabitant of Murks in changing object constellations. 59 children aged from 9 to 12 took part in the candle experiment and 51 children of the same age in the Murks experiment.

Analysis of variance of the data in the candle experiment showed that our expectations (i), (ii) and (iii) were confirmed with a high degree of statistical significance. In the Murks experiment the results of analysis of variance were not equally conclusive: the data corresponded to our expectations (i) and (iii). But expectation (ii) was not confirmed: when O_i and O_a differ more greatly with regard to brightness than to area

($D_Y > D_X$), only those children verbalize brightness who have learnt to give preference to brightness. Those children who have learnt to give preference to area verbalize – contrary to our expectations – area to a statistically significant extent. Under condition (ii) the effect of learnt preference claimed in postulate 3 prevails in the Murks experiment over the effect of object distance claimed to postulate 2.

Both experiments taken together show that postulates 2 and 3 can be experimentally confirmed. The anomaly in the results of the Murks experiment make it appear doubtful, however, whether the learnt preference for dimensions is only effective when the object difference is approximately the same ($D_X \approx D_Y$). Both postulates are largely justified from an empirical point of view. However, the predicted effects probably do not always show the relationships which we described in 3.1.2 and 3.1.3.

4.2. Findings on request variants (postulates 4–7)

In the past we have published only a small part of our continuing series of investigations on situation-specific variation of requests (Laucht 1979; Laucht & Herrmann 1978) which concern postulates 5–7. The interpretation of the results contained in these references is now in need of correction. Some publications which will contain a detailed presentation of our procedures and findings are in preparation.

4.2.1. As already pointed out (3.2.4), an important condition for the empirical testing of postulates 4–7 is that the observed verbal behaviour can be sufficiently reliably coded in terms of the thirteen propositions representing the postulated propositional structure of request. For this purpose Manfred Laucht has developed a hitherto unpublished coding manual, which is continually being checked and improved. Our findings to date on the reliability of coding are satisfactory. The reliability coefficients vary between 0.70 to 0.90 Furthermore it should be noted that inadequate coding works against the empirical confirmation of our expectations deduced from postulates 4–7.

The method used to code observed requests in terms of the thirteen structural components is based on reducing each observed utterance (request) to predicate–argument structures (cf. Engelkamp 1976; Fillmore 1968; Kintsch 1974). Since our thirteen structural components exist in the same propositional format, explicit rules for the coding of utterances (or segments of utterances) can be developed (cf. Herrmann 1978a: 19ff.).

4.2.2. Our *detective experiment* takes the form of a two-person game rather like the well-known game of Monopoly. The partners in the game – the subject and a confidant of the experimenter – were given the role of detectives who had to complete a certain task. By means of a manipulation unnoticed by the subject the latter was brought to a point at which he had to ask his partner (confidant) to relinquish an object (gun). This situation was organized in such a way that the speaker could assume that his partner understood the situation in the same way as he himself did (= SC+). Furthermore the partner needed the gun himself so that the speaker had to assume that his partner was not necessarily willing to part with the gun (= WA?). The independent variable LR was represented by variable property relationships: under the condition LR+ the gun belonged to the speaker, who then asked for it back; under the condition LR? the gun belonged to the partner, from whom the speaker wanted to borrow it. According to postulates 6 and 7, it is to be expected that in the case of LR+ utterances from categories I and C will dominate while utterances from category A will dominate in the case of LR?. Our data are derived from the free utterances of the subjects.

144 male adolescents aged between 16 and 23 took part individually in the detective game. Our expectations derived from postulates 6 and 7 were confirmed with a high degree of significance (using the χ^2 test): when the desired object belonged to the speaker, requests from categories I and C dominated; when the speaker had to borrow the object from the partner, his utterances in the majority of cases belonged to category A.

We repeated the detective experiment with the modification that the subject could assume that the partner was quite willing to hand over the gun (WA+). According to postulate 5 it was now to be expected that the subjects under both legitimation conditions (LR+ and LR?) would produce utterances from categories A and E in the majority of cases. This expectation was confirmed (Laucht 1979).

4.2.3. The *film experiment* differs from the detective experiment inasmuch as the subjects do not produce requests in order to reach some goal of their own but state which requests, in their opinion, other people should make in specific situations. In other words we tested the communicative knowledge of the subjects with regard to situation-specific request variants. The film experiment was carried out before postulates 4–7 had been formulated. Nonetheless we offer an account of this investigation – *ex post facto* – with regard to these postulates. The subjects were supposed to help in the writing of a film script. It was to be a film about a birthday party organized by a child. Specific episodes in the film were given in advance. The subjects formulated 'suitable' sections of the dialogue which contained requests. The episodes were varied in respect to the conditions WA and LR occurring in postulates 5, 6 and 7.

In one episode (a), the same conditions were created as in the detective experiment. Our expectations correspond to postulates 6 and 7. LR+ versus LR? were represented by the breaking versus the obeying of a traffic rule by the partner. Episode (b) had to do with the participation of the partner in a game which was played during the party. We assume that the participants in a birthday party are quite willing to take part in such games (= WA+). We varied the attractiveness of the games; however, according to Postulate 5 we would always expect a majority of requests from categories A and E. In episode (c), it was a matter of an offer of help which the partner was asked to give. We assumed that the partner was not completely willing to offer this help (= WA?). The legitimacy of the speaker was also somewhat problematic (= LR?). We attempted to vary the extent of the lack of legitimacy; however, according to postulate 7 we would always expect a majority of utterances from category A. In episode (d), which also had to do with an offer of help, we assumed as in episode (c) that conditions WA? and LR? were present. We attempted to vary the degree of inconvenience for the partner and thus the extent of his lack of co-operativeness (WR?); however, according to postulate 7 a majority of A-requests was always expected.

222 school children (114 boys and 108 girls) aged between 11 and 13 took part. Evaluation of the data obtained by means of the χ^2 test confirmed our expectation with regard to episodes (a), (b) and (d). In the case of episode (c) it was shown that requests from category A were, as expected, in the majority at *both* levels where there was a lack of legitimacy. However, it turned out that the frequency of A-requests varied significantly with regard to the extent of the lack of legitimacy. We also discovered considerable differences among the episodes as well as among the individual conditions, according to which the episodes were varied, with regard to the frequency of occurrence of courtesy particles. We cannot, however, go into the resulting problems of interpretation here. We gained the overall impression that the film experiment is in need of improvement with regard to the operationalization of WA and LR. Nevertheless, postulates 5–7 seem to be suitable for the explanation of the basic finding of this experiment, which – as already mentioned – was carried out before the formulation of the postulates.

4.2.4. In our *just-how-likely-would-you-be-to-say-it experiment* the subjects received written descriptions of situations, which were varied systematically in the following way: the willingness of the partner to do something (WA) varies in proportion to the partners interest (WA+) or lack of interest (WA?) in carrying out the action. The legitimacy for the request (LR) varies to the extent that the speaker can fall back on (LR+) or not fall back on (LR?) a code of rules (laws, etc.) or a previously expressed agreement between the speaker and the partner. The subjects received a list of twelve requests, which we had previously assigned to categories I, C, A or E. The subjects calculated for each of these request variants the subjective likelihood with which they would use them with regard to each individual description of a situation (= dependent variable).

The data obtained from 221 students at a vocational school aged from 15 to 21 were evaluated according to a complex analysis of variance plan. We obtained the following results: (a) The subjective likelihood for utterances of category A (versus I, C, E) is considerably higher under condition WA+ than under condition WA? (b) The subjective likelihood for utterances from category A (versus I, C, E) is considerably higher under condition LR? than under condition LR+. The analysis of our data shows that the likelihood of occurrence of requests from category A co-varies with LR even when *condition WA+* is present: even when the partner is quite willing to do something, A-requests are more likely to occur in the case of lower legitimacy than in the case of greater legitimacy. This confirms our opinion that both WA and LR are important determining factors in the choice of request variants. However, we are in some doubt as to whether the influence of WA and LR interact in quite the way we hypothesized in postulates 5, 6 and 7.

4.2.5. We repeated the investigation described in 4.2.4 with the modification that the dependent variable did not consist of statements about subjective probability but requests (utterances) produced freely by the subjects. In this case the subjects were 356 pupils aged 13 or 14 and 16 or 17. The results reported under 4.2.4 were entirely corroborated: the predominance of requests from category A varies with LR and with WA.

4.3. Findings on situation-specific choice of words (postulate 8)

More detailed presentations of the relevant studies may be found in Herrmann 1976,, 1978b and Herrmann & Deutsch 1976: 109ff. In all the experiments described in the following section three conditions were fulfilled: (a) We made certain that our subjects knew several quasi-synonyms for each object to be named, at least one of which belonged to standard speech and one to non-standard speech. (b) The tests took place in the absence of the experimenter. The utterances were recorded without the knowledge of the subjects. (c) The words used by the subjects for object naming (R_j) were classified (W_{st} or W_{non-st}) by groups of judges who were not acquainted with the purpose of our investigation. The correspondence of judgments was controlled by means of Kendall's W.

4.3.1. In our *puzzle experiment* it is not the topic distance between the partners (tD) which is varied but the social distance (sD). The subject (a child) had a puzzle in front of him in which some pieces were missing. Behind a partition there was a partner with the missing pieces. The speaker (subject) named a missing piece and was thus able to obtain it from his partner. The words used for the purposes of naming were classified as W_{st} or W_{non-st}. The independent variable consisted of the partner being either an unknown adult (sD+) or a child of the same age (sD−). The missing pieces of the puzzle showed pictures of the following objects: bank note, ball, policeman, cigarette, lavatory bowl and buttocks.

76 boys aged between 10 and 13 took part in the puzzle experiment. The expected significant difference was found: when the partner was an unknown adult, designations from category W_{st} were more frequent than when the partner was a child of the same age. Postulate 8 is thus confirmed, provided that we may assume that the topic distance in the puzzle experiment was slight. Unfortunately we did not check this explicitly.

4.3.2. In the *context experiment* children had to name objects O_i to their partner, a friend of the same age, who in turn had to match them with several other objects O_k. In each case, one object O_i and one object O_k formed a pair, e.g. lavatory bowl O_i and hardware shop O_k. We varied the experimental conditions as follows: the object O_k, which was to be matched with an object O_i, belonged either to the object class O_{kn} or O_{kd}: O_{kn} objects were illustrations of objects or scenes which are emotionally stimulating for children aged between 10 and 12. O_{kd} objects were by contrast only slightly emotionally laden. This was established by means of previous experiments. An O_{kd} object is, for example, a police car or a hardware shop. A typical O_{kn} object is the representation of a boy standing in front of a broken window being threatened by a policeman with a truncheon. Since the partner was always a friend of the same age as the subject, we assumed the constant condition sD− for the context experiment. The matching of the object O_i with the object classes O_{kn} or O_{kd} made it possible to examine topic distance: O_{kn} represents the condition tD− while O_{kd} represents the condition tD+. In accordance with postulate 8, we had the following expectation: when an object O_i is named which is to be matched with an object O_{kn}, the word used to designate the object will belong with greater probability to category $W_{non\text{-}st}$ than when we are concerned with an object from class O_{kd}, with which O_i is to be matched. An investigation involving 30 children aged between 10 and 12 yielded results which fully confirmed this expectation. One and the same object O_i is named at different levels of speech depending on the different emotional contexts.

4.3.3. In order to test postulate 8 we also conducted a number of experiments in which both variables were varied (i.e sD and tD). This was the case, for example, in our *quiz experiment*. The subject sat opposite his partner, separated by a partition. A set of photos with representations of fourteen objects (O_i) lay in front of the subject. Seven objects (O_{if}) had to do with the subject 'football', e.g. football, football shoes, referee, five objects (O_{id}) had to do with the subject 'discotheque', e.g. record, musician, public house, and there were two 'neutral' objects which were chosen to obscure the purpose of the investigation. By means of the successive naming of these objects O_i to the partner, a quiz-like game was created in which the subject had to match the object O_i with a simplified drawing. When the object was matched correctly, the subject was given the correct answer to a quiz question and received one point in the quiz game. The naming of the objects O_i was seen by the subject as an unimportant intermediate step in the acquisition of points in the quiz. All subjects named all fourteen objects O_i. (In assessing the results of the experiment, the naming of the objects was classified as W_{st} or $W_{non\text{-}st}$.)

The participants in the experiment were 50 boys aged 13 and 60 adolescents aged 17. The younger age group was told that the experiment was about a new game which they were to try out because children know best which games they like. The older subjects were given the same cover story with the modification that they were better qualified to understand children than we were.

The condition of *social distance* was varied by confronting some of our subjects with an unknown adult (sD+), while others chose a friend of the same age (sD−). After the quiz experiment the following selection of subjects took place: all the subjects (n = 110) received two questionnaires concerning 'interest in football' (Q_f) and 'interest in discotheques' (Q_d). Subjects scoring above the median in Q_f *and* below the median in Q_d were defined as being 'interested in football' (i.e. experimental group I_f). Subjects scoring below the median in Q_f *and* above the median in Q_d were defined as being 'interested in discotheques' (i.e. experimental group I_d). Two 13-year-old boys belonged to I_d and four 17-year-old adolescents belonged to I_f. After the elimination of these six subjects our experimental group I_f consisted of 23 13-year-old boys interested in football (rather than discotheques); the experimental group I_d consisted of 30 17-year-old adolescents interested in discotheques (rather than football). Twelve persons from I_f had played with an unknown partner and eleven persons with their friend. With regard to I_d the relationship was 18 to 12.

The *topic distance* (tD) from objects O_i could be defined in the following manner: with regard to subjects I_f objects O_{if} have only slight topic distance (tD−), while the objects O_{id} have marked topic distance (tD+). In the case of I_d the relationship is reversed.

The following findings resulted from our tests on I_f and I_d ($n=53$): the subjects name objects O_i to a friend (sD−) *and* with slight topic distance (tD−) significantly more often with words from the category W_{non-st} than under the three other conditions (sD− & tD+; sD+ & tD−; sD+ & tD+). Thus postulate 8 is confirmed. However, contrary to expectations, there was another finding: even when the social distance was great (sD+), W_{non-st} was used to name discotheque objects O_{id} significantly more often by those people interested in discotheques than by those interested in football. A corresponding finding was not, however, present in the case of football objects O_{if}. We have attempted to interpret this result elsewhere (Herrmann 1976: 370).

4.4. Concluding remarks

In this chapter we have not reported on two areas of research related to the topics discussed here, which we are at present working on, namely inter-individual (dispositional) differences in the flexibility of verbal encoding and threats and promises in connection with requests. In our opinion the investigations reported on here as well as the experiments which we are at present conducting in those other areas show that postulates 1–4 and 6–8 can be confirmed reasonably well. With regard to postulate 5 we have some informal confirmation, but we need further systematic investigation. Distinguishing object features, object distance and the learned preference for particular featural dimensions are essential determining factors in the naming of objects. The willingness of the partner, as recognized by the speaker, to do a particular thing and the legitimacy of the request have an influence on the choice of request variants. Social distance between speaker and partner and topic distance determine to a high degree the choice among quasi-synonyms which belong to various sub-languages. Our findings (cf. 3.2.4 and 3.3.4) also show us, however, that we do not as yet adequately understand the *interaction* between those factors in determining verbal behaviour as hypothesized in postulates 2 and 3 and 5, 6 and 7. We hope to arrive at a better understanding of these interactions through further theoretical reflection and empirical studies.

In summary, we assume that rather heterogeneous aspects of verbal behaviour, e.g. object naming and choice of request variants, can be conceptualized in terms of the *pars pro toto* principle: While participating in an episode of a dialogue the speaker retrieves mental data from memory or he produces them innovatively. These mental data can be described as structures of propositions. The speaker utilizes situational cues obtained from learning experience. These cues determine in each case which propositional *components* of the retrieved or innovatively produced mental structure are *selected – pars pro toto –* for verbalization. The guiding principles for this selection of structural components seem to be *information* for the partner and *instrumentality* for reaching the episode-specific goal intended by the speaker.

In our view utterances are conceived of as the verbalizations of selected components of propositional structures. The listener's comprehension is not only the decoding of such an utterance but also the *reconstruction* of the whole propositional structure from which the speaker has selected the verbalized component. Thus, speaking cannot be seen as a simple encoding procedure and language comprehension consists of much more than decoding language strings. The selection of the appropriate propositional input for verbal encoding remains a highly relevant topic for psychological research.

References

Anderson, J. R. & Bower, G. H. 1973. *Human associative memory*. Washington, DC: Winston.
Argyle, M. 1969. *Social interaction*. London: Methuen.
Baird, J. 1970. *Psychophysical analysis of visual space*. Oxford: Pergamon Press.
Bolles, R. C. 1972. The avoidance learning problem. In Bower, G. H. (ed.) *The psychology of learning and motivation*, vol. 6. New York: Academic Press.

Bransford, J. D., Barclay, J. R. & Franks, J. J. 1972. Sentence memory: a constructive versus interpretative approach. *Cognitive Psychology*, *3*, 193–209.

Bredenkamp, J. & Wippich, W. 1977. *Lern- und Gedächtnispsychologie*, vol. 2. Stuttgart: Kohlhammer.

Cazden, C. B. 1972. The situation: a neglected source of social class differences in language use. In Pride, J. B. & Holmes, J. (eds.) *Sociolinguistics*. Harmondsworth: Penguin Books.

Chafe, W. L. 1979. The flow of thought and the flow of language. In Givón, T. (ed.) *Discourse and syntax*. New York: Academic Press.

Clark, H. H. & Clark, E. V. 1977. *Psychology and language*. New York: Harcourt Brace Jovanovich.

Clark, H. H. & Lucy, P. 1975. Understanding what is meant from what is said: a study in conversationally conveyed requests. *Journal of Verbal Learning and Verbal Behavior*, *14*, 56–72.

Creed, C. D. 1972. Parameters of social interaction and speech variation. PhD thesis, Southampton University.

Deutsch, W. 1976. *Sprachliche Redundanz und Objektidentifikation*. Marburg: Dissertationsdruck.

Deutsch, W. & Clausing, H. 1979. Das Problem der Eindeutigkeit sprachlicher Referenz. In Ueckert, H. & Rhenius, D. (eds.) *Komplexe menschliche Informationsverarbeitung*. Bern: Huber.

Dörner, D. 1976. *Problemlösen als Informationsverarbeitung*. Stuttgart: Kohlhammer.

Engelkamp, J. 1976. *Satz und Bedeutung*. Stuttgart: Kohlhammer.

Fillmore, C. J. 1968. The case for case. In Bach, E. & Harms, R. T. (eds.) *Universals in linguistic theory*. New York: Holt, Rinehart & Winston.

Fishman, J. A. 1965. Who speaks what language to whom and when? *La linguistique*, *2*, 67–88.

(ed.) 1968. *Readings in the sociology of language*. The Hague: Mouton.

Garner, W. R. 1974. *The processing of information and structure*. New York: Erlbaum.

Gordon, D. & Lakoff, G. 1971. Conversational postulates. In *Papers from the Seventh Regional Meeting of the Chicago Linguistic Society*. Chicago: Chicago Linguistic Society.

Grice, H. P. 1975. Logic and conversation. In Cole, P. & Morgan, J. L. (eds.) *Syntax and semantics*, vol. 3: *Speech acts*. New York: Seminar Press.

Herrmann, Th. 1976. Zur situativen Determination der Sprachschichthöhe. *Zeitschrift für Sozialpsychologie*, *7*, 355–71.

1978a. *Sprechhandlungspläne als handlungstheoretische Konstrukte*. Arbeiten der Forschungsgruppe Sprache und Kognition am Lehrstuhl Psychologie III der Universität Mannheim, no. 2.

1978b. Zur Entwicklung der Sprachschichtrepräsentation in der späteren Kindheit. In Augst, G. (ed.) *Spracherwerb von 6 bis 16*. Düsseldorf: Schwann.

Herrmann, Th. & Deutsch, W. 1976. *Psychologie der Objektbenennung*. Bern: Huber.

Herrmann, Th. & Laucht, M. 1976. On multiple verbal codability of objects. *Psychological Research*, *38*, 355–68.

1977. Pars pro toto. Überlegungen zur situationsspezifischen Variation des Sprechens. *Psychologische Rundschau*, *28*, 247–65.

1979. Planung von Äußerungen als Selektion von Komponenten implikativer Propositionsstrukturen. In Ueckert, H. & Rhenius, D. (eds.) *Komplexe menschliche Informations-verarbeitung*. Bern: Huber.

Hörmann, H. 1976. *Meinen und Verstehen*. Frankfurt: Suhrkamp.

Hymes, D. H. 1972. On communicative competence. In Pride, J. B. & Holmes, J. (eds.) *Sociolinguistics*. Harmondsworth: Penguin Books.

Joos, M. 1961. *The five clocks*. New York, 1961.

Kintsch, W. 1974. *The representation of meaning in memory*. Hillsdale: Erlbaum. 1977. *Memory and cognition*. New York: Wiley.

Klix, F. 1971. *Information und Verhalten*. Bern: Huber.

Krantz, D. H. 1972. A theory of magnitude estimation and cross modality matching. *Journal of Mathematical Psychology*, 9, 168–99.

Laucht, M. 1979. Untersuchungen zur sprachlichen Form des Aufforderns. In Tack, W. (ed.) *Bericht über den 31. Kongress der Deutschen Gesellschaft für Psychologie*. Göttingen: Hogrefe.

Laucht, M. & Herrmann, Th. 1978. *Zur Direktheit von Direktiva*. Arbeiten der Forschungsgruppe Sprache und Kognition am Lehrstuhl Psychologie III der Universität Mannheim, no. 1.

Lindsay, P. H. & Norman, D. A. 1972. Human information processing. New York: Academic Press.

Metzger, W. 1954. *Psychologie*. Darmstadt: Steinkopff.

Miller, R. G. 1966. *Simultaneous statistical inference*. New York: McGraw-Hill.

Minsky, M. 1975. A framework for representing knowledge. In Winston, P. H. (ed.) *The psychology of computer vision*. New York: McGraw-Hill.

Montada, L. 1968. *Über die Funktion der Mobilität in der geistigen Entwicklung*. Stuttgart: Klett.

Moscovici, S. 1967. Communication processes and the properties of language. *Advances in Experimental and Social Psychology*, 3, 225–70.

Neisser, U. 1967. *Cognitive psychology*. New York: Appleton-Century-Crofts.

Olson, D. R. 1970. Language and thought: aspects of a cognitive theory of semantics. *Psychological Review*, 77, 257–73.

Pride, J. B. & Holmes, J. (eds.) 1972. *Sociolinguistics*. Harmondsworth: Penguin Books.

Rosch, E. 1975. Cognitive representations of semantic categories. *Journal of Experimental Psychology*, 104, 192–233.

Rosenberg, S. (ed.) 1977. Sentence production: developments in research and theory. Hillsdale, NJ: Erlbaum.

Schank, R. C. & Abelson, R. 1977. *Scripts, plans, goals, and understanding*. Hillsdale, NJ: Erlbaum.

Schlieben-Lange, B. 1973. *Soziolinguistik*. Stuttgart: Kohlhammer.

Searle, J. R. 1969. *Speech acts: an essay in the philosophy of language*. Cambridge: Cambridge University Press. 1975. Indirect speech acts. In Cole, P. & Morgan, J. L. (eds.) *Syntax and semantics*, vol. 3: *Speech acts*. New York: Seminar Press.

Treisman, A. M. 1968. *Strategies and models of selective attention*. Oxford: Oxford University Press.

Winograd, T. A. 1977. A framework for understanding discourse. In Just, M. A. & Carpenter, P. A. (eds.) *Cognitive processes in comprehension*. Hillsdale: Erlbaum.

Wunderlich, D. 1972. Sprechakte. In Maas, U. & Wunderlich, D. (eds.) *Pragmatik und sprachliches Handeln*. Frankfurt: Athenäum.

Wundt, W. 1862. *Beiträge zur Theorie der Sinneswahrnehmung*. Leipzig: Winter.

5. Conversation sequences*

DAVID D. CLARKE and MICHAEL ARGYLE

1. Introduction

Conversational patterns and sequences are interesting in their own right, and they may give a clue to more general properties of the organization of action and interaction over time. The structures of language and discourse are a part of, and may also be an analogue of, the frameworks within which social life as a whole is conducted. If characteristic patterns of talk and action can be identified and described rigorously enough, they may allow hypotheses of considerable power and generality to be tested. In the course of this chapter we shall consider various approaches to the sequential analysis of dialogue, before going on to more general considerations of the construction of socially skilled interaction over time, the structure of social episodes in different situations, and the effects of varying degrees of skill on the production of social behaviour.

What, then, are these characteristic patterns of talk and action like? If we start with a very simple notion of behavioural structure or non-randomness, it is clear that the likelihood of a given behavioural event occurring in a given interval of time varies with many things: the time of day, place, season, weather, economic climate and number of people present, together with the actors' ideas, goals, values, skills, ages, sexes, professions, states of intoxication, and so on ad infinitum. It would be hard to imagine any variable of even tenuous relevance to human affairs which could not figure in the list. However, at the heart of the matter, if there is such a thing, one seems to find the idea of *sequential* organization. Nothing gives a clearer indication of what is about to happen in most spheres of human activity than a knowledge of what has just been happening. Human activities are characteristically protracted in time,

* We are grateful to the S.S.R.C. for financial support and to Ann McKendry, Betty Hammond and Christine Smith for their help in preparing the manuscript.

and the selection of any one action fragment depends, as much as any-thing, on the architecture of the whole episode or project. This need not involve conscious planning, or even an awareness of the patterns being generated, any more than the regularity of an electrocardiogram implies that the heart sets out deliberately to reproduce a chosen trace.

The implication is that attempts to understand the regulation of action must pay special attention to its sequential construction. This should come as no surprise since the basic organizational features of the brain, which we presume to determine the basic organizational features of action, include its role as intermediary between sensory and motor nerves, or if you prefer between stimulus and response, circumstance and action. Even the crudest appraisal of the nervous system and the demands of natural selection indicates that its central function must be to organize patterns of behaviour which are contingent upon incoming information. However as the motor skill model of social behaviour (Argyle 1969) indicates, the dependency of output upon input is, in the case of social interaction, cyclical (figure 3). Output for one person is input for the other, and just as one person discharges his obligations to act he provides the very pressures and circumstances which mobilize and shape further action by the other. As this cycle of mutual contingency goes round and round it leaves a trace of its nature in the form of the sequential pattern of the interaction, rather as a revolving tyre leaves tracks in the sand. With each cycle of the process the imprint upon the world is extended, forming what appears to be a linear record, with only its regularities to betray the way it was produced (except, of course, that the pattern left by a revolving tyre consists of unvarying repetitions, whereas a conversation does not).

However, general issues concerning the nature and regulation of ac-tion have to be considered in relation to specific instances of action and specific types of action, and it is for that reason that action theory is sometimes pursued through the medium of conversational analysis, without necessarily pursuing all the facets of conversation which interest the pure conversation analyst. For those conversation analysts who are really action theorists in disguise, conversation becomes (as Homans once said of groups) not so much *what* we study, as the *place* in which we study it.

Turning to a quite different strand of argument, a sequential analysis of conversation is also suggested by the nature of language. Clearly the orderly sequential combination of units is a fundamental feature of lan-guage at all levels of structure (or 'articulation'), and yet linguistic inquiries have tended to stop short at the level of the sentence. There is just as much reason to suppose that sentences are combined systematically in discourse, as to suppose that morphemes are combined systematically in sentences. It may even turn out (as we shall see later) that the higher levels of linguistic structure, such as conversations, may be structured not only to the same degree as sentences, but to some extent *in the same way*, at least in that similar concepts and methods of analysis can be used. They may be some kind of 'syntax' of discourse at work, or even, more generally still a syntax of action (Clarke 1979a).

There is one big difficulty, however, with the idea that a characteristic sequence of events will emerge in a given set of circumstances, from which underlying processes may be inferred, and that is that for any set of circumstances, however carefully defined, there will always be a number of appropriate sequences, not just one. In practice the sequences which are observed or presumed to ensue from any given set of circumstances (including perhaps the past history of the sequence up to a certain point) are indeterminately numerous, and only in the most abstract and compli- cated sense, the members of a characterizable set. The first task then is to capture for a given set of circumstances the set of behaviour sequences that may be expected, and in this respect at least, it resembles the task of the syntactician in capturing the set of morpheme strings that are well- formed sentences in a given language.

The property of a behavioural system whereby a number of alternative courses of events may be expected under any given set of constraints is sometimes called multilinearity, and the distillation of the various possi- bilities into a single coherent formulation, with a standardized format, is called canonical description. It is important to note that canonical descrip- tions (such as that provided for the set of sentences in a language by an adequate generative grammar) are not *sufficient as*, although they may be *necessary for*, the *explanation* of the observable patterning of events. In this context a generative 'rule' or 'grammar' is likely to be a representation of an empirical law, used rather as a physicist might use an equation, rather than an alternative object of study concerning people's opinions of what *ought* to be done in given circumstances. A method for providing canoni- cal descriptions of multilinear behavioural systems would not only shed light on their nature for scientific purposes, but would also provide a powerful tool for problem solving, insofar as it would answer systemati- cally questions about the likely outcome of events, the likely effect of policies as yet untried, and so on. It is with these objectives in mind that some researchers have elected to concentrate first on the mechanics of conversational sequencing, and it is from that standpoint that we shall begin our examination of sequence-analytic research on conversations.

There is one further preliminary. The ideal of a sequence analysis of discourse can lead too easily to the assumption that the ideal *modus operandi* is to take a corpus of talk and perform some kind of pattern-identifying procedure upon it, but with linguistic precedents so much in mind we cannot overlook the idea of a generative or hypothetico-deductive approach in which speculations about organizing principles, which are not directly data or corpus based, are enshrined in some kind of generative simulation or model, charged with the task of reproducing all and only the sequences of events which are observed to be characteristic of the system in question (where system could be a person, a family, a district, culture, situation, or any number of entities with identifiable behavioural properties). We shall consider other modes of research too, since in the present state of the art it is harder and more important to answer questions about how this kind of research can best be done, than it is to identify any specific feature of our natural system of discourse.

2. Some basic parameters of conversational structure

Let us begin by considering some studies done to determine some of the basic design features of the discourse system: a sort of skeleton on which the flesh and blood of detailed analysis can later be arranged.

The most basic question must surely be whether there is a regular sequential organization at all, joining utterances of different types into a body of coherent dialogue. The difficulty here is that the regularities, if they exist at all, will be very difficult to describe, and so what is really needed is a procedure to demonstrate their existence which does not rely on a description of their form. In one attempt to provide just that, Clarke (1975a) recorded candid dialogue in a waiting room situation and then presented twenty-line extracts to new subjects in the form of a pack of twenty cards, each bearing one utterance, but out of sequence and with no clue to the speaker or its original place in the conversation. By re-shuffling these cards into what seemed a plausible order the subjects were able to reconstruct the original sequence with *far* greater than chance accuracy. (Some indices showed significance levels of 10^{-12} for parts of the task.) The same technique has been used on psychotherapy transactions with similar results. It also demonstrates very nicely the asymmetry of contingencies in non-directive forms of therapy (Shapiro 1976), with the utterances of the therapist being more predictable from those of the patient, than the patient's utterances are from a knowledge of the therapist's. It is doubtful whether the subjects could have given a general account of the sequential pattern they associate with sensible talk, but they must have had a theory of organization which was largely common to all subjects, and largely accurate, for the task to be accomplished so successfully. Accuracy implies that the regularities the subjects believed to be a feature of conversation, really are; so we may take their existence to be demonstrated even if we cannot as yet describe their form.

The experiment was run in a second version after Dr Anne Treisman (personal communication) pointed out that the cues the subjects were using may not have been the kinds of regularity the study set out to show. It could have been, for instance, that the practice of referring to new topics first by name and later with pronouns, would disambiguate the order in which two utterances had originally come. Furthermore the use of 'I' or 'you' would show for certain utterances who was speaking. The effect of context on syntax, interesting though it is in itself, was not in question. It was more the progression of semantic content through dialogue that was important, and particularly the arrangement of different speech act types (Austin 1962), such as threats, promises, invitations and insults. The second card shuffling study reduced the dialogue to a standard 'telegraphic' style with no pronouns and only present active declarative verbs. Given this (rather strange looking) dialogue, subjects were able to reconstruct the whole from the parts with *even greater* accuracy, so clearly the pattern of successive utterances does not reside in grammatical modifications alone. It may still have been that semantic or 'narrative' content was the subjects' main guideline, and it would not seem possible to test this by removing syntactic and semantic variation in a further version of the study in order to estimate the orderliness of dialogue structure as a sequence of pure speech act types alone.

Instead, the ability of subjects to reconstruct sequences of abstract utterance types was tested using Bales' (1953) matrices of reactive tendency (Clarke 1975b, forthcoming). These are data tables showing the probability of each of twelve utterance types, such as *shows solidarity*, *raises other's status*, *gives help*, *reward*, being followed immediately by each of the twelve types as the reply or continuation by another speaker.

Bales' twelve categories were to stand in for speech act types, and the reactive tendency matrix for the 'correct' sequence to be reconstructed. Subjects estimated for each of the twelve categories acting as antecedent, the likelihood, in rank order, of each of the twelve categories acting as sequitur. Rank order correlation showed that subjects had again reproduced the original data with greater than chance accuracy, but less strikingly this time ($p < 0.00025$). Even at this abstract level of description, and despite twenty years, one ocean and an unfamiliar ranking method separating the subjects who first produced Bales' discussions and those who were able to reconstruct them, it seems that the pattern comes through. The succession of utterances in casual talk, seen as categorically differing social acts *are* non-randomly arranged.

This is rather like saying that every utterance depends for its form and content on those which precede it, in which case it is now reasonable to ask how many of those which precede it have an influence on its form? In the simplest case, a kind of chain reaction called a Markov chain, each item would depend on only the one before. For instance, a type *b* item would follow a type *a* with constant probability regardless of what had preceded the *a*. This is quite different from the spelling rules of English where letter *i* is frequently followed by *e*, and *c* commonly followed by *i*, without *cie* being a permissible triplet. Here the placing of *e* depends on the use of the *two* previous letters. This is a *second order* system. Borrowing a technique from Miller & Selfridge (1950), a study was run to estimate what *order* of structure existed in dialogue (Clarke 1975b). As it turned out a very similar study was being run at the same time by Pease & Arnold (1973) with much the same result.

Unless you have elaborately compiled tables showing how common each unit is after various combinations of previous units, it is hard to ascertain what the order of a given sequence of symbols is. This approach is possible with words or letters, but difficult in principle for utterances as there is as yet no agreed typology on which to base the count. The opposite strategy, however, is straightforward. Sequences of different order may be produced and then assessed for their realism. To produce a first order 'dialogue', a number of subjects contribute one utterance each to a growing script, knowing only what the previous subject contributed. When producing second order, each subject is allowed to know the two last contributions, and so on.[1] Scripts of varying orders of structure were then rated for their plausibility as real, and ratings were found to increase up to fourth order but not beyond that. This is not to say that fourth order approximations and above were indistinguishable from real discourse, but only that higher orders produced no further improvement. On the

---

[1] Just to make life more complicated, Miller & Selfridge used *nth* order to mean that the sequence is structured over *n* item groups, or each item depends on the preceding $n-1$. In Pease & Arnold's usage and the one adopted here *nth* order means each item depends on *n* previous ones.

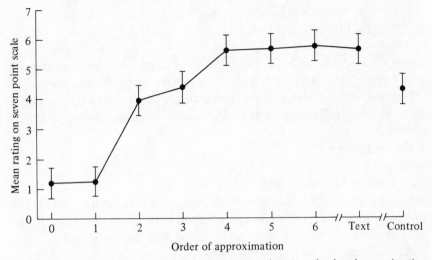

Figure 1. Mean ratings given to nine dialogue types as a function of order of approximation

contrary, the approximations of fourth order and above were rated as *more* plausible than control extracts of real dialogue. This is a common occurrence in this kind of research and probably due to the fact that the real dialogues contain disfluencies, which seem not to be recognized as a familiar aspect of real talk. It is interesting to speculate that the perception of spoken language includes a facility for editing out and forgetting false starts, errors and so on. Does all this mean then that the structure of dialogue is that of a roughly fourth order stochastic series? Regrettably not, as the next study was to show.

After the development of information theory (Shannon 1948), there was a fashion in linguistics for examining sentence construction as an instance of signal strings constrained by transitional probabilities of various orders. However as Chomsky (1957) was able to show, some perfectly regular and precisely defined patterns of sequence are not precisely expressed in transitional models of *any* order, especially those low enough to be calculable in practice. It seems that sentences, and also dialogues, are constructed so as to accommodate 'nested' or 'embedded' sequences. In the sentence

The book which X is on the table.

the X can be replaced with an infinite variety of things of indeterminate length, so *is* would have to be tabulated as a possible sequitur to all of them. This is also misleading since *is* is related to *book* anyway, rather than the tail end of the subordinate clause. It makes more sense to see

The book is on the table.

as the basic structure with

which X

somehow inserted within it. Having embarked on this reasoning, it is not long before the whole principle of sentence construction is viewed as insertions within insertions, or elaborations upon elaborations, rather than one item following another. Likewise in dialogue the implicit parentheses

Before I forget . . .

and

. . . now where were we?

can contain any amount of talk, while the subsequent items relate to the previous topic, not the most recent utterances. Pairs of question and answer often get caught up in one another like this (Jefferson 1972):

A: Who are you taking to the party?

B: Whose party?

A: Jane's of course!

B: Oh, Sue.

Here the last answer is to the first question, while the question to be asked second is answered first. The reason for this is obvious, the consequence is devastating. The commonness of such constructions in dialogue makes it unsuitable for most straightforward kinds of sequence analysis. In Clarke (1975b, forthcoming), a study is described in which three arrangements of the same pairs of question and answer were rated for their plausibility. They were called linear ($q^1,a^1,q^2,a^2,$), nested ($q^1,q^2,a^2,a^1,$) and cross-nested (q^1,q^2,a^1,a^2). Speaker order was varied as the respective questions and answers dictated. Ratings of cross-nested form were significantly lower than either linear or nested constructions, which were not significantly different from one another. It seems that nesting, and its attendant complications for analysis, *are* really part of discourse structure.

So far we have considered the relation between each utterance and the past, but it does not seem when we talk as though we only review the past course of the conversation and try to extend it. We also lead up to things, and choose utterances for their consequences, as well as their compatibility with their immediate antecedents. Is there a span of future influence to take account of in understanding utterance choice, as well as a span of past influence? How far ahead can people foresee the course of conversation? To try and answer that, a piece of apparatus was used, which subsequently acquired the nickname of the 'future machine'. The future machine itself was a simple chart recorder which drew a trace over time as the subject turned a knob. While conversing with a second subject the person operating the future machine had to lead the topic around to a point where he could insert a specific, previously chosen remark. (A third subject observed all this to ensure that the conversation was treated realistically, and all trials were aborted in which the observer was able to spot which remark had been planted.)

Throughout the conversation the knob on the future machine was used to record the intending speaker's judgment of how long it would be before the remark could be inserted. When the chosen utterance was finally used, an additional pulse on the chart recorded the time. The chart was now a graph showing on one axis the real time before the remark was made, and on the other axis the subject's expectation. Over any period when the subject could accurately foresee the time still to elapse, his trace would have formed a straight diagonal line, showing for example, that thirty seconds before the remark was made he thought there were thirty seconds to go, and so on for all time values. We expected to find that for an identifiable period before the remark was made (called the span of anticipation) the subject's trace would lie close to the ideal diagonal, whereas before that it would depart noticeably from it. The result was disappointing, and a summary curve averaged across subjects showed that the trace does finally move towards the diagonal, but only slightly and within the last ten seconds. It seems as though past information is likely to influence utterance choice more strongly than a clear and far-sighted view of where the conversation is leading.

Suppose then that the essential process of dialogue generation is a

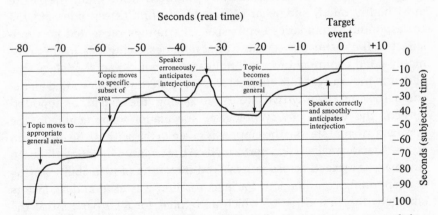

Figure 2. Example trace from condition in which speaker expectations were recorded

succession of choices as to how to follow up the immediate past. Is it possible to determine next, not *how much* of the past information, but *which aspects* of it will shape the future? In the next study that issue was raised in a slightly different form. Now we asked which selected aspects of the past course of a conversation (if any) would enable a subject to predict its immediate future development as accurately as he could if he had been given a complete transcript of the past discussion. The experiment was in four stages, and a cyclic design allowed four groups of subjects to treat four dialogues to the four stages in turn, without repeating a stage or a dialogue. The four stages will be described for one dialogue passing through the hands of the four subject groups in succession. The material was real dialogue from candid recordings, and twenty-turn extracts were used in two separate parts, consisting of the first fifteen lines and the last five. In the first stage subjects saw the first fifteen lines only, and wrote a précis which was to be as brief as possible, while being suitable for someone else to use it as a basis for predicting the last five lines. In effect subjects were asked what were, in their opinion, the most significant aspects of the first fifteen lines in shaping the likely course of the conversation.

The second group of subjects then took these summaries, but not the first fifteen lines, and made their written predictions of the last five lines. The third group of subjects predicted the last five lines from the first fifteen (but without seeing the summaries); and, finally, the fourth group rated eleven versions of the last five lines, one of which was the *real* last five lines (though not identified as such), and five versions produced from summaries and five from the first fifteen lines. The question now becomes which of the continuations produced from summaries were most highly rated, and what aspects of the first fifteen lines did the corresponding summaries emphasize. The ratings presented no problem, but the distinctive features of summaries giving rise to the most highly rated continuations were not easy to spot. So another stage was added to the study. More subjects were recruited, who now rated all the summaries on twenty-two scales, including the extent of reported speech, the extent of psychological speculation (comments on the speakers' mental states), the emphasis given to the setting, the topic, and so on. A factor analysis was performed on the twenty-two ratings for each summary (averaged across judges) and the rating of plausibility for the corresponding continuation. Varimax rotation was used and six factors emerged, the first three of which accounted for 69.0 per cent of the variance.

Factor I was 'personal versus situational' description; factor II was called 'specific-acute-foreground versus general-chronic-background', as it differentiated ratings of such things as the emphasis given by the précis writers to the motives of the speakers, and the last few lines of the transcript they were summarizing, from the emphasis they gave to the speakers' religious and political views, for example; factor III concerned 'social versus task' aspects of the dialogue, with the summary writers' emphasis on mood, personality and general psychological speculation loading on one pole, and conversational history, goals and topic on the other. Factor IV, 'role versus individual variables', had religion, year, topic and time of day loading on one pole, and age, occupation and ambitions loading on the other. Factor V was called 'content versus setting', distinguishing knowledge of the topic and emphasis given to reported speech, for instance, from time of day, place, year, speakers' occupations and political views. Factor VI was dubbed 'platonic versus carnal', since marital status, sex, time of day and speakers' ages loaded on one pole, while the other was concerned with the year, the season, previous conversations, and the speakers' long-term ambitions in life. If these six dimensions show the variety of summaries obtained, which factors were associated with the success of subsequent predictions? The ratings of continuations based on the summaries loaded most on factor IV, where role as opposed to individual description produced a loading of 0.59. On factor V there was a loading of 0.26 on content as opposed to setting, and on factor III a loading of 0.11 appeared on social as opposed to task considerations. By this time the data had passed through a long convoluted procedure, and it would be wise to reserve final judgment until there is corroboration, but they suggest that (for these dialogues at least) it is social roles and factual content which emerge from dialogue, as the best indicators of its future course.

To pursue the argument just one stage further: if dialogue is generated by a series of choices of next utterance, so as to be consistent with certain aspects of a certain number of past utterances, it seems that the speaker has two choices to make, and may well make them separately and in a definite order. On the one hand he has to choose which of the possible past remarks he will react to and, on the other, which of several appropriate reactions he will make. A study was carried out recently to test the hypothesis that speakers make those two decisions, separately and in that order. Passages of typewritten artificial dialogue with several 'loose ends' were given to subjects who produced fifteen possible continuations for each, put them in order of preference and indicated for each continuation which of the previous lines it derived from. If the hypothesis were true, we expected to find that all continuations derived from a given antecedent line would occupy a block of consecutive ranks. For this purpose the null hypothesis could be that the continuations were based on each antecedent line as often as they had been in the real data but randomly ranked, or that the ranks and antecedents were randomly assigned to continuations. The former is a stronger test of the hypothesis, while the latter has the distinct advantage of being mathematically tractable. The latter null hypothesis may be rejected in favour of the view that continuations from the same antecedent occupy consecutive ranks with $p < 0.01$.

Of course, the sequential organization of conversation does not just involve the processes whereby the next utterance at any time is fashioned so as to fit in with what has gone before, in content, style, tempo and so forth. There is also the matter of how one utterance or one speaking turn leads on to the next so smoothly, regardless of what it is to consist of, or the content it is to convey. How, for instance, is one speaker able to start talking as another stops, with so little gap or overlap? This seems unremarkable at first sight, but there does not appear to be time for the second speaker to think of something to say in the brief interval since the first speaker stopped talking. Presumably the reply was being prepared and organized beforehand, ready to go, rather like one relay runner starting off *just before* receiving the baton from his predecessor, so as to ensure a smooth changeover. Furthermore, there is not usually a chairman to allocate turns and decide how much each person shall say and at what point, and yet this seems to be a very orderly business.

Who decides and how is the decision publicized and enforced on other participants? It seems that the whole thing is managed by an intricate system of cues indicating for instance when the listener would like to become the speaker, when the present speaker wishes to continue without interruption, and when the present speaker would like one of his listeners in particular to answer his last point.

Until now we have only dealt with the sequential organization of content and illocutionary force. Now the time has come to consider the sequential organization of the turn-taking system in conversation, which has been one of the main topics of conversation-analytic research in the past.

Verbal and non-verbal factors play a part in this. Sacks, Schegloff & Jefferson (1974) found that speaker turns are constructed linguistically so that the separate 'turn constructional components' are recognizable, and, by the same token, the 'transition relevance points' between them can be identified as potential points for a change of speaker. A 'turn allocation component' may take the form either of the present speaker selecting the next (in multi-party conversation only, of course), for example by saying 'Don't you agree, John?', or of the 'self-selection' of the next speaker by his being first off the mark with a reply. Adjacency pairs such as question and answer serve, amongst other things, as devices for determining the speaker and the content of the next remark. There are additional complexities; for example, a one-word question such as 'Why?' tends to return the floor automatically to the previous speaker.

Non-verbal cues include the use of gaze to negotiate an impending speaker change (Kendon 1967). Typically during a long utterance the listener tends to look at the speaker more than the reverse. About three seconds before a speaker change, however, the pattern starts to change, with the listener looking progressively less (perhaps because of the need to prepare a reply in advance as mentioned above) and the speaker progressively more. By the changeover, the former listener is looking about a third as much as he was on average, and the former speaker about half as much again as he was. In the three seconds or so following the changeover the normal proportions are gradually restored. Duncan (1972, 1974) found a variety of gestural and paralinguistic cues variously functioning as turn-yielding signals by the speaker, attempt-suppressing signals by the speaker, 'back channel' signals by the auditor and turn-claiming signals. Beattie (1980) is critical of earlier approaches and advocates research and training in conversational skills based on the significance of higher order patterns and changes in pattern, not individual 'signals' with supposedly invariant meanings.

3. Looking for chain reactions

Now let us leave the very general structuring principles of conversation, and look in more detail at some of the structures to be found. Provided that the problem of 'nesting' is kept in mind, it will be useful to revert to some transitional probability methods to give an approximate picture of conversation structure. Transitional probabilities are tabulated between *types* of utterance, which recur, rather than between the utterances themselves which do not. The first problem, then, is to form a typology of utterances. There have been numerous attempts to do this for different purposes, one of the most interesting being the attempts of philosophers (Austin 1962; Searle 1965, 1969, 1975) to classify speech acts. If one can accept that speech act descriptions like *threat* and *promise* will be the notation in which conversational structure is to be analysed, then the only problem is with the choice and definition of labels. However it is not clear that a list of such labels, with an indication of who spoke each one, even *contains* the patterns we are after, without which it cannot be used as the basis of analysis. (For an excellent critique of conversation models using speech act labels as units see Levinson 1978.) What, to take a simple example, is the use of recording that a conversation proceeded

A: QUESTION

A: QUESTION

B: ANSWER

if we cannot tell which question was answered? On the transcript we could write ANSWER$_1$ or ANSWER$_2$ but in the context of a transitional frequency matrix that would mean nothing. Further

A: DEMAND

B: STATEMENT

leaves us wondering if B complied, while

A: DEMAND

B: COMPLY

could mean B had engaged in almost any conceivable form of speech or action but we cannot tell which. There is a lesson to learn from reported speech where the most elliptical of reports will tell us who asked whom what, or who threatened whom with what unless what (and by when). These phrases seem to suggest that a minimal coding frame for discourse will look something like:

THREAT (A, B, x, y, z)

meaning *A threatened B with x unless y by z*. This is rather like a case grammar notation (Fillmore 1968), but for recording speech act use in dialogue. Now rules of inference can be set up showing explicitly the equivalence between one type of utterance in a certain context, and another, such as:

If   COMMAND (A, B, x)

and PERFORM (B, x)

then COMPLY (B, (COMMAND (A, B, x))).

Each speech act type would thus have its own characteristic string of 'arguments' or qualifying variables. A similar notation was used in a simulation study of question–answer embedding to be reported below.

Turning back to Markov analysis, there are yet further complications. At the heart of this method lies a table of transitional probabilities showing how likely each of the n types of utterances is, after every possible *combination* of the n types, occurring in the last m events (where m is the order of analysis). That means that n^{m+1} combinations have to be tabulated, which looks fine for the simple case where there are twenty types and a first order model, giving four hundred cells. Fifty types and fifth order sequences would be more appropriate here, and by no means seem excessive, until the resulting 614 *million* data cells need to be filled. How may long chain constructions be studied without setting off this 'combinatorial explosion'? Dawkins (1976) came up with an ingenious answer, whose principle is that you only need look for long chains where you know there are shorter ones. Using a computer, the first order matrix is scanned for the commonest transition, and that pair of events is then recorded and recoded as a new single event. So far only one row and column has been added to the matrix, and already we are in a position to find a second order structure if a common transition should fall in that row or column. In this way long chains of events can be detected by adding a few rows and columns to the data table, rather than multiplying it as many fold. A word of warning is called for. This procedure may seem unnecessary as the first order table already shows which events lead immediately to which others, but in that case inferences from short chains to long ones are not valid. (Remember the case of the spelling rule in which the commonness of *e* after *i* and *i* after *c* cannot be taken to imply that *cie* is a common triad.)

Many authors have used Markovian and related analyses to uncover sequential patterns in interaction (Altman 1965; Bakeman and Dobbs 1976; Benjamin 1979; Gottman 1979; Hertel 1972; Jaffe 1964; Rausch 1965), often using some form of variable-lag analysis to overcome the shortcoming that stochastic methods would otherwise only relate contiguous elements or strings in a series.

The next empirical study (Clarke 1975b) used a transitional matrix of first order as a generative rule system rather than an analytical device. Forty-six speech act types were conjoined in pairs with 0s or 1s showing that transitions were permissible or not. Separate matrices were used for reactive and proactive transitions (i.e. with and without an intervening speaker change). The proactive matrix was dominant and could select speaker change (and the other matrix) as an optional next event after some, but not all, speech act types. So, for instance, the model would start by consulting the proactive matrix, where it would find that opening remarks after the start of a conversation could include commands, requests and questions, amongst other things, but not giving permission, promising or threatening (legal and illegal next moves being marked by 1s and 0s respectively). Choosing at random between the available options, it may select a request as the first utterance. Then, entering the matrix at the row indicating legitimate sequiturs to a request, it would find that the same speaker may go on to back it up with some justification or undertaking, but that there is also the possibility of a speaker change at this point. If that is the option selected the model then looks up in the reactive table the responses that can follow a request by the other speaker, which include a question, an offer, refusal or compliance, and so on. Having selected one of these, the model assumes the second speaker has the floor and returns to consult the proactive matrix which may or may not indicate that the next thing to happen could be another speaker change. In this way the model traces out long sentences of (reasonably) plausible dialogue, such as

A: OFFER
B: REJECT
   APOLOGIZE
A: ACCEPT
B: TERMINATE

Even this crude model of dialogue structure, which was also implemented on a computer, was able to produce reasonable facsimiles of discourse, given the limitations above on speech act labels as an output medium. Allowing for the fact that this may have obscured important differences between this simulation and real dialogue, the rule model performed well. Subjects when asked to rate its output in relation to random sequences, and 'ideal' sequences produced in the same notation by a previous group of subjects, found the ideal and model sequences to be insignificantly different, while both were significantly better than the random strings ($p < 0.05$).

When using transition probability methods as analytical tools, one of the greatest difficulties is the assignment of each utterance to the correct class. To circumvent this difficulty a study was carried out (Clarke forthcoming) in which subjects were given a repertoire of categorical speech act labels to use, and their definitions. They were also allowed to indicate topic changes, and changes from one conversation to another. Various transitional frequency and chain analysis methods were used on the resulting sequences, but as their only criterion for picking one sequence and discarding the next was frequency of occurrence, the results were mostly taken up with obvious and uninteresting connections, such as question with answer. However other analyses of the same data proved more interesting. Log survivor functions (see e.g. Clarke 1979b) were plotted for the interval between conversation beginnings and endings, and topic beginnings and endings. This procedure shows whether an event becomes more or less probable (in each unit of time) as time increases since a specified previous event. According to this, topics have a finite life, and the longer they continue the more likely they are to end, on each successive turn. With conversations, though, it is different. Their chance of finishing on any given turn remains constant, regardless of length (at least over the range of the study which was a hundred turns). The strangest result of all came from an analysis of the frequency distribution with which the available categories were used. G. K. Zipf discovered that there is a curious distribution of word frequencies in text, such that their frequency and rank frequency are inversely proportional (see e.g. Carroll 1964). That is to say that the fifth most common word, for example, is one fifth as common as the commonest word. The clearest way to show this is by plotting log frequency against log rank frequency, for a large number of words. The result is a straight line graph with a slope of -1, showing frequency varies with rank frequency to the power of -1. A similar plot with our speech act labels showed a surprisingly straight line (except for the one end which on a plot of rank frequency must contain all the least frequent, and therefore least reliable data points). The gradient, however, was -0.5, suggesting that frequency varies with rank to power of -0.5, i.e. frequency is inversely proportional to the *square root* of rank frequency. No satisfactory explanation for this observation has been forthcoming.

4. Beyond straight chains

The story so far, it seems, has run into several difficulties. The structure of conversation is not really linear, but most of the available statistical tools assume that it is. Methods of analysis which work by extracting the most commonly occurring constructions from a corpus of dialogue, tend to come up with rather obvious fragments of pattern which are by no means the whole story, nor even necessarily the most important part. Can we now start to analyse conversation in a way which incorporates its non-linear properties and some of its less obvious features? Jones & Gerard (1967) described four kinds of interaction structure which go beyond the linear assumption, in that the relevance of past utterances is not assumed to be proportional to their recency. They are described in some detail below in 7, 'Sequences in different situations'.

There are other departures from linearity too. Nesting has already been mentioned. Some interaction, such as that between teacher and pupil is cyclical (Flanders 1970), and yet other stretches of talk may have a kind of recursive structure, in which a certain pattern becomes a sub-unit of the same pattern on a larger scale. Just as in syntax there may be well-formed sentences as components of other well-formed sentences; in discourse, greetings within greetings and arguments within arguments may well show the same structure on both levels. This makes for complex descriptions, however, in that the organizing principle at work on the larger scale has somehow to be re-initiated in the generation of one of its own sub-components, and then allowed to resume from the point it had reached on the higher level. This is a common design feature of many software systems especially those like *recursive augmented transition network* programmes (Woods 1970) which have to parse natural language sentences.

It was largely to circumvent these difficulties that Chomsky (1957) proposed the particular kind of grammar he did, as a model of natural language. Of the speaker's linguistic competence he also emphatically maintained that 'Like all facts of interest and importance, this is neither presented for direct observation nor extractable from data by inductive procedures of any known sort' (Chomsky 1965: 18).

There are two lessons, then, from the field of linguistics that might be relevant for the study of conversational patterns. First, the pattern is not to be extracted from data by experimental or statistical methods, but must be thought up, precisely formulated as a generative model, and the resulting output tested for its correspondence with real data, i.e. for its adequacy. Secondly, if a model is to reproduce patterns with the kind of recursions and embeddings to be found in conversation, then it will have to incorporate special devices such as phrase structure rules, to make this possible (Clarke 1979a).

Of course the idea of generating rather than analysing discourse and interaction patterns is not new. It has long been the mainstay of artificial intelligence work on natural language production and interpretation (Boden 1977; Schank & Abelson 1977; Weizenbaum 1966, 1967). Generative grammars of discourse structure have been tried (Clarke, Ellgring & Wagner 1979; Frentz 1976), and also a number of psychological models of interaction expressed as formal mathematical models (Huesman & Levinger 1976; Simon 1952). Formal logic has also served as a basis for rule models of conversation structure (Barnett Pearce, Cronen & Johnson 1978) and the management of meaning (Cronen & Barnett Pearce 1978).

If we take seriously the idea of discourse analysis by the design and evaluation of simulations or rule models, then two questions immediately arise. The first is the problem of the interface notation, in which the model will describe the world, or its 'terminal vocabulary'. The problem is the same as the difficulty arising over the use of speech act labels. If the code is made too simple, it is unable to represent the niceties of conversation that we should like to deal with; if it is too complex, it becomes formally and computationally intractable, or at best so cumbersome that the bulk of the model is taken up with the management of its own notation. There is no equivalent problem in linguistics, since the end product of a grammar is taken to be a sequence of morphemes drawn from a finite list.

The second problem is a new one. The model, or 'grammar', of discourse must have some overall design principle. It is unhelpful, and probably impractical, to start with an inappropriate design and then add extra pieces to it, to extend its capabilities. This only results in what system designers call a 'christmas tree' – a basic object with so many extras as afterthoughts, that it loses all semblance of an integrated functioning whole. The principle design formats available for a model like this are of four main types, called finite-state, pushdown-stack, linear bounded and Turing machines in automata theory (see Minsky 1972), or finite-state, context-free, context-sensitive and transformational grammars in linguistics (Chomsky 1959). Ironically, there is a perfect correspondence within the four pairs of categories, except in the case of the finite-state models, which are the only ones to have exactly the same name and slightly *different* properties in the two schemes. Despite the fact that the four types seem to exhaust the major design categories, they are *all* inappropriate as discourse models. The finite-state varieties do not permit indefinite recursion and nesting, and the others (at least in the basic form) are deterministic and non-interactive. Behaviour grammars are being proposed most ingeniously in ethology (Westman 1978), but even here the need for probabilistic and interactive grammars, and even fuzzy-set definition of terminal and non-terminal vocabularies, as additions to the basic format, raises the spectre of the christmas tree again.

From the writing of behaviour grammars it is only a short step to artificial intelligence and computational linguistics. There has been very little work here on the structure of conversation per se, perhaps because of the difficulties mentioned above. However a central AI paradigm has used natural language interpreters and generators, in a dialogue with their operators, in the exploration of syntax and semantics, and has therefore produced some dialogue capability in its programs almost as a by-product (Winograd 1972). Winograd's program deals with the giving and carrying out of instructions on a symbolic world of stacked blocks, and the asking and answering of questions. Its dialogues are remarkable as far as they go, but as models of discourse (which admittedly they were never intended to be) they clearly lack many important capabilities such as making and keeping promises, remedial exchanges (Goffman 1971), and so on. Similarly the work by Schank & Abelson (1977) has a clear value for dialogue modellers without setting out to study dialogue in itself (see below).

A study in Oxford (Clarke forthcoming) attempted to incorporate several of the principles discussed above in a program to generate variously nested combinations of question and answer. The crux of the study was the data structure in which the present state of the conversation was stored. The presence of several unanswered questions in some circumstances suggests a tree structure with its terminal branches as conversational 'loose ends', while the priority rules determining the order of answering for embedded questions have the properties of a push-down stack. The program was finally made to behave satisfactorily by combining the two into a kind of branching stack devised by Peter Hancock, which we called a 'push-down tree'.

In its ordinary unbranching form a push-down stack is a kind of store, memory or queue with the property that the last items to be entered are the first to be retrieved, like the spring-loaded stacks of trays in a self-service cafeteria from which the name comes. A tree in its simple form is a divergent branching data structure in which each item may be linked to, or lead to the accessing of, several more, and each of those to several more still, and so on. The two are combined as a push-down tree model of question and answer queues in the following way. A question–answer sequence has to begin with one or several questions by the first speaker, and then a speaker change. This would lead to a single commitment to answer or continue being stored by the model in the former case, or in the latter case by a number of possible points of continuation of equal priority, which could be represented as the end points of a fan of lines like a hand with fingers spread apart. Each of these 'finger ends' can then give rise to direct answers, in which case it ceases to be an extant option or obligation for response and is deleted, or else some further question or questions could fan out from it, and so on. The interesting thing is that all of the complex and extensive permutations of question, counter-question and answer that make logical sense can be generated, and no ill-formed ones, if the following principles are followed:

1. The outstanding commitments are mapped as a push-down tree.

2. Items are only responded to when they form the end of a branch.

3. Terminal (branch-ending) questions may be followed in the sequence by an answer, and deleted from the tree. *Or*:

4. They may be followed by one or several counter-questions by the next speaker, in which case they become (temporarily) buried in the tree and inoperative.

This may or may not indicate something about the kind of data structure used in memory to indicate where a conversation has 'got to', but it certainly generates an array of interesting sequential combinations which are well worth trying out according to the specification given above, if only to provide (in the phraseology of board-game manufacturers), 'hours of fun and entertainment for all the family'.

5. The corpus revisited

All of this has taken us a long way from the flesh and blood of real talk, and, some would argue, into a rather sterile and overformalized view of the nature of interpersonal exchanges. How then can the richness of talk as we experience it, be reconciled with the rigour which formal approaches seem to offer? The middle ground appears to lie in an analysis of examples, not by rigidly preordained statistical methods, which we have seen to be problematic, but by using our pretheoretical everyday 'feel' for the sense and structure of talk. This may then be refined into more rigorous models, after the necessary content has been included. Ethnomethodologists and other micro-sociologists have been at the forefront of this approach (Goffman 1971; Sacks et al. 1974). The principal idea in this field is that the layman's capacity to produce and understand talk or action, which is the *topic* of our inquiry, is also the tool or *resource* by which we can tackle it. Furthermore, in the case of conversation the participants analyse it for themselves as they go along, and display the results of that analysis in what they say subsequently. So, by a kind of serial process, each utterance becomes indicative of what the speaker has made of the talk so far, and by collating similar instances it is possible to see what inferences are drawn, on the basis of what prior evidence, and possibly, although this is not as straightforward, by what process of reasoning.

Often the happiest marriage between the subtlety of our everyday understanding of discourse and the precision of explicit formal approaches has been struck by linguists, philosophers and social scientists working in the tradition of discourse analysis, or as its more specialized neighbour is called, conversation analysis. Sinclair & Coulthard (1975) and Coulthard (1977) review various aspects of discourse structure, especially the cycles of verbal interaction between pupils and teachers which typify classroom interaction, such as the sequence;

Teacher asks question.

Pupils 'bid' to answer it.

Teacher selects a pupil to answer.

Pupil answers.

Teacher evaluates answer.

Sequences of classroom behaviour are discussed in their own right in section 6.

Ethnomethodological studies have focused on particular aspects such as openings (Schegloff 1968); closings (Schegloff & Sacks 1973) and turn taking (Sacks, Schegloff & Jefferson 1974). Experiments by Rommetveit et al. (1971) and Rommetveit (1968, 1972) have pointed to the crucial role of context in the construction of real talk, and the tendency for most linguistic theories to pay far too little attention to it. Very special requirements for the formulation of utterances are produced by the attempts of speakers to be clear, relevant and brief, and the attempts of hearers to find meaning in utterances, in the form of intentions attributed to the speaker in saying them (Grice 1957, 1968).

Current work by D. D. Clarke is moving towards the incorporation of more pretheoretical information. Tape recorded conversations, arguments in particular, are being screened for their more interesting constructional features, to include in future models. The fundamental issue now seems to be multilinearity. Any single sequence can be described fairly easily. In the final analysis, it is just a question of reporting what was said and in what order, with perhaps a modicum of soul-searching over concepts and categories. The real problem comes when a single, coherent, categorical description is to be given for a variety of conversations with certain factors in common, such as the possible continuations from a given point. That seems to be the most general and fundamental question in the social psychology of conversation structure, with more to tell us than any other about basic processes and the pragmatics of managing difficult situations. As yet it has no answer.

Even if progress is slow with the discovery of over-arching principles, a lot of headway has been made with specific aspects of sequential organization, and their bearing on other psychological factors like social skill, and the influence on behaviour of social situations, and this is what we shall consider next.

One area of special concern, for example, has been the development of child language and the dialogic constructions that figure both in the process and the emerging product. Bruner (1975) has emphasized the role of speech acts and their emergence from similarly constructed acts in prelinguistic play. The use of particular speech and discourse forms in the social play of young children has also been charted by Garvey (1974, 1975a, b) and Garvey & Ben Debba (1974).

Special attention has been given to the nature of conversation in selection and survey interviews (Brenner 1980), where the normal conventions of mutual intelligibility are found to run directly counter to the philosophy of 'measurement', which claims that the same form of words should be used for all survey respondents, for instance, regardless of variations in context and the respondents' own verbal style.

Further examination of particular conversational and interactional skills has been motivated by the extensive research effort in recent years on social skills, and the social skills model of social interaction.

6. Social skills and sequences

We turn now to the performance of sequences of interaction by individuals, and to the nature of the social skills required.

(1) Adjacency pairs, two-step sequences

As we showed above, adjacency pairs play an important, though limited role in the generation of interaction sequences. It would be difficult to take part in a conversation without knowing that questions normally lead to answers. These adjacency pairs are not necessarily universal to all situations. For example, a question will only lead to a relevant answer if it is suitable in terms of the role relationship of those concerned and the situation. There is, however, a general rule that an utterance should be relevant to the one before it, and this is often taken into account in decoding utterances (Grice 1975). There is also a rule that a speaker should take for granted, i.e. not repeat, knowledge that is shared by the listener, and he should add something new to it: 'The new is nested in the old' (Rommetveit 1974). When a social psychologist looks at adjacency pairs, it is evident that several different principles are involved. (a) The speech act types are related in terms of rules of discourse, whereby a question leads to an answer rather than a question, and a joke leads to a laugh rather than an apology – though a very bad joke could perhaps lead to a farewell or sympathy. (b) The meanings of successive utterances are linked – as described by Grice's maxim of relevance. (c) Some two-step links are based on principles of social behaviour, like reinforcement, response-matching or equilibrium maintenance; these are not rules, but are more like empirical generalizations or laws. (d) Some two-step links are based on the rules of particular situations, like auction sales, card games, committee meetings, etc.

However, for the reasons given earlier, we need to go beyond two-step sequences to explore most sequences of social behaviour. One model of individual social performance which does that is the motor skill model.

(2) The motor skill model

This model draws attention to a number of analogies between social performance and the performance of motor skills like driving a car (see figure 3). In each case the performer is pursuing certain goals, makes continuous responses to feedback, and emits hierarchically organized motor responses. The model has been heuristically very useful in drawing attention to the importance of feedback, and hence to gaze; it also suggests a number of different ways in which social performances can fail, and suggests the training procedures that may be effective, through analogy with motor skills training (Argyle, 1969; Argyle & Kendon, 1967).

The model emphasizes the motivation, goals and plans of interactors. It is postulated that every interactor is trying to achieve some goal, whether he is aware of it or not. These goals may be to get another person to like him, to obtain or convey information, to modify the other's emotional state, and so on. Such goals may be linked to more basic motivational systems. Goals have sub-goals: for example a doctor must diagnose the patient before he can treat him. Patterns of response are directed towards goals and sub-goals, and have a hierarchical structure – large units of

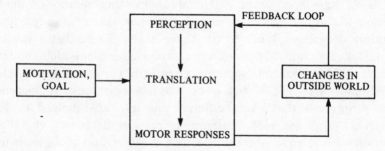

Figure 3. Motor skill model (from Argyle 1969)

behaviour are composed of smaller ones, and at the lowest levels these are habitual and automatic.

Harré & Secord (1972) have argued persuasively that much human social behaviour is the result of conscious planning, often in words, with full regard for the complex meanings of behaviour and the rules of situations. This is an important correction to earlier social psychological views, which often failed to recognize the complexity of individual planning and the different meanings which may be given to stimuli, for example, in laboratory experiments. However it must be recognized that much social behaviour is *not* planned in this way: the smaller elements of behaviour and longer automatic sequences are outside conscious awareness, though it is possible to attend for example to patterns of gaze, shifts of orientation, or the latent meanings of utterances. The social skills model, in emphasising the hierarchical structure of social performance, can incorporate both kinds of behaviour.

The social skills model also emphasizes feedback processes. A person driving a car sees at once when it is going in the wrong direction, and takes corrective action with the steering wheel. Social interactors do likewise – if another person is talking too much they interrupt, ask closed questions or no questions, and look less interested in what he has to say. Feedback requires perception, looking at and listening to the other person. It requires the ability to take the appropriate corrective action, referred to as 'translation' in the model – not everyone knows that open-ended questions make people talk more and closed questions make them talk less. And it depends on a number of two-step sequences of social behaviour whereby certain social acts have reliable effects on certain others.

The operation of this model depends on the performer's knowledge of which moves on his part will produce certain responses in the other. One of the most important of these is the effect of reinforcement. This is one of the key processes in social skill sequences. When interactor A does what B wants him to do, B is pleased and sends immediate and spontaneous reinforcements – smile, gaze, approving noises, etc., and modifies A's behaviour, probably by operant conditioning – for example, modifying the content of his utterances. At the same time A is modifying B's behaviour in exactly the same way. These effects appear to be mainly outside the focus of conscious attention, and they take place very rapidly. The result is that anyone who gives strong rewards and punishments in the course of interaction will be able to modify the behaviour of others in the desired direction.

However there are several important differences between social behaviour and motor skills.

1. *Rules*. The moves which interactors may make are governed by rules – they must respond properly to what has gone before. Similarly, rules govern the other's responses and can be used to influence his behaviour, e.g. questions lead to answers.

2. *Taking the role of the other*. It is important to perceive accurately the reactions of others. It is also necessary to perceive the perceptions of others, i.e. to take account of their point of view. This appears to be a cognitive ability which develops with age (Flavell 1968), but which may fail to develop properly. Those who are able to do this have been found to be more effective at a number of social tasks, and more altruistic. Meldman (1967) found that psychiatric patients are more egocentric, i.e. talked about themselves more, than controls, and it has been our experience that socially unskilled patients have great difficulty in taking the role of the other.

3. *The independent initiative of others*. Other interactors are pursuing *their* goals, reacting to feedback and so on as well. We shall discuss below ways of analysing the resulting sequences of interaction. The social skills model fits best in cases of 'asymmetrical contingency', i.e. interviewing, teaching, etc., where one person is effectively in charge. In such cases it is possible to compare the social skills used by effective and less effective performers.

The social skills model generates a characteristic kind of 4-step sequence.

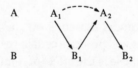

This is a case of asymmetrical contingency, with A in charge. A's first move, A_1, produces an unsatisfactory result, B_1, so he modifies his behaviour to A_2, which produces the desired B_2. Note the link A_1–A_2, representing the persistence of A's goal-directed behaviour. This can be seen in the social survey interview:

I_1: asks question.

R_1: gives inadequate answer, or does not understand question.

I_2: clarifies and repeats question.

R_2: gives adequate answer.

or:

I₁: asks question.

R₁: refuses to answer.

I₂: explains purpose and importance of survey: repeats question.

R₂: gives adequate answer.

The model can be extended to cases where both interactors are pursuing goals simultaneously, as in the following example, from a selection interview:

I₁: How well did you do at physics at school?

R₁: Not very well, I was better at chemistry.

I₂: What were your A level results?

R₂: I got a C in physics, but an A in chemistry.

I₃: That's very good.

There are two four-step sequences here: $I_1 R_1 I_2 R_2$ and $R_1 I_2 R_2 I_3$. There is persistence and continuity between R_1 and R_2, as well as I_1 and I_2. Although I has the initiative, R can also pursue his goals.

(3) Hierarchy of plans and goals

It has long been recognized that in the performance of motor skills there is a hierarchy of plans and goals, and this was embedded in the Miller, Galanter & Pribram (1960) account of behaviour. A motorist has the main goal of driving from one point to another; sub-goals involve the points in between; these in turn have several levels of subordinate goals before we reach the actual manipulation of accelerator and steering wheel. At the higher levels there are consciously chosen plans; at the lower levels automatic sequences of behaviour are run off.

Schank & Abelson (1977) show that there is often a series of sub-goals, which must be reached in a particular order; at certain points alternative routes (i.e. sub-goals) can be taken. An example is buying and selling. The customer has the following sub-goals: (a) find out what goods are available; (b) find out more about them, e.g. price, try them out; (c) agree the sale; (d) take the object away, or arrange for delivery.

We have recently studied the goals and the goal structure (i.e. the relations between goals) for a number of common situations. Samples of nurses and occupational therapists rated the relevance of a list of possible goals in each situation, and later samples rated the degree and nature of intrapersonal and interpersonal conflicts.

Figures 4 and 5 show two examples of goal structures. The figures show links between goals both within and between individuals. A high score

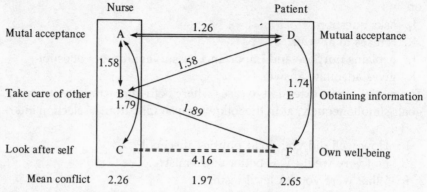

Figure 4. The goal structure of a nurse–patient encounter (from Argyle, Furnham & Graham 1981)

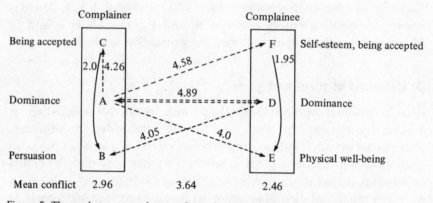

Figure 5. The goal structure of a complaint (from Graham et al. 1980)

(4–5) shows interference or two-way conflicts while a low score (1–2) shows instrumentality in one direction or both. The goal structure for a nurse–patient encounter is shown in figure 4: the only conflict is between the physical well-being of nurse and of patient. For a complaint situation (e.g. about noise at night) there is a great deal of conflict, as shown in figure 5 (Graham, Argyle & Furnham 1980). This kind of analysis can act as a map, suggesting the way to move effectively in each situation. In a complaint, the findings suggest, one should avoid trying to dominate the other, and concentrate on persuasion.

The selection interview has four main episodes: (a) greeting, informal chat; (b) interviewer asks questions; (c) candidate asks questions; (d) ending. Each of these episodes has further sub-goals, each of which in turn may have further sub-goals. Some of these units of the interview consist of repeated cycles, as will be shown below.

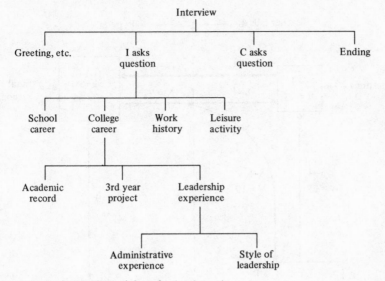

Figure 6. Episode structure of the selection interview

(4) Cycles of interaction

Some Markov chains suggest the existence of cycles of interaction, as when A usually leads to B, B to C, and C to A. Dawkins (1976) devised a way of locating such repeated cycles with his 'fly music machine', in which audible tones coded individual units of behaviour, and repeating patterns and variations emerged as recognizable 'melodies'.

The selection interview sequence shown in figure 6 contains more than one level of repeated cycle. There are repeated cycles in which the interviewer deals with a series of topics – school career, college career, etc. And there are repeated cycles within each of these topics, consisting typically of an open-ended question, and a number of follow-up questions.

Flanders (1970) found that there are repeated cycles of this kind in the school classroom, as shown in figure 7. He maintains that the skills of teaching consist partly of the ability to control these cycles, and to shift from one to another. Thus the teacher might start with a short cycle: Lecture (by teacher) – Question (by teacher) – Answer (by pupil). She could then shift to a longer cycle which included more pupil participation and initiative by stimulating and reinforcing such moves on the part of pupils. However the actual questions, answers, etc. are of course not repeated, and it is misleading to describe lessons as repeated cycles. What is happening is a progressive build-up of ideas and information as the

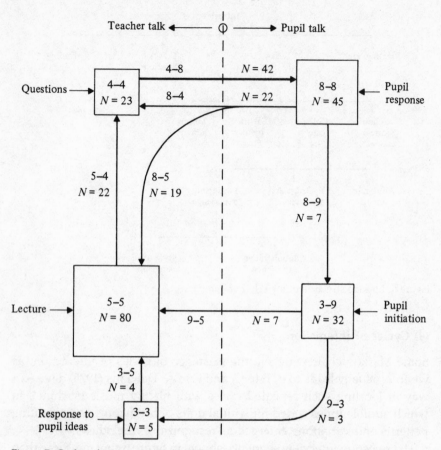

Figure 7. Cycles of interaction in the classroom (from Flanders 1970)

lesson proceeds. The cycles do not carry on indefinitely, and stop when the teacher has gone as far as she had planned with a particular topic.

There is another kind of repeated cycle in marital squabbles. Cronen (personal communication) found that many married couples had rows which took a standard form, and that this often involved a cycle of increasing antagonism or recrimination.

(5) Episodes

Several investigations of behaviour in the classroom have recognized these repeated cycles as a natural larger unit of analysis. A still larger unit of analysis is the period of cycles which ends when some pedagogical goal has been attained. Smith et al. (1967) defined a 'venture' as 'a segment of discourse consisting of a set of utterances dealing with a single topic and having a single overarching content objective'. While in a sense there are repeated cycles, there is also a continuous build-up in the complexity of the material discussed.

These two levels of larger units have been found in other social situations. We are concerned in this section with the larger units, which we shall call an 'episode'. We mentioned the episodic structure of the selection interview above. In doctor–patient encounters, for example, it has been suggested that there are six episodes, in a fixed order, though some may be omitted:

1. Relating to the patient.
2. Discussing the reason for the patient's attendance.
3. Conducting a verbal or physical examination or both.
4. Consideration of the patient's condition.
5. Detailing treatment or further investigation.
6. Terminating.

(Byrne & Long 1976)

An episode may be defined as a segment of a social encounter which is characterized by some internal homogeneity, such as pursuit of a particular goal, a particular activity, topic conversation or mood, a particular spatial location, or individuals taking particular roles. Episodes may be identified by the investigator, or a sample of judges may be used to determine the episode boundaries.

Repeated cycles and episodes are found in the play of young children. Repeated cycles are a feature of early mother–infant interaction, as in 'peek-a-boo' games (Bruner 1975). Episodes are found in the play of 3–5 year olds, whose games consist of complete episodes of 'going shopping', 'going to the doctor', etc. (Garvey 1977).

We are conducting studies of episode structure. The beginnings of a number of situations were briefly introduced, and subjects asked to write a sketch of how the situation might develop. They were then asked to parse their scripts into the main episodes, and then to parse the episodes into sub-episodes. There was considerable agreement on the main episodes, and these were described in fewer words than the sub-episodes. There was considerable agreement on the phase sequence for each situation. For example when a wife calls on a new neighbour, it was agreed that the following episodes would occur: (a) greeting; (b) visitor admires house; (c) other provides coffee, etc.; (d) exchange of information about jobs, husbands, interests, etc.; (e) arrange to meet again, introduce husbands; (f) parting.

We suggest that social encounters usually have a five-episode structure.
1. Greeting.
2. Establishing the relationship, clarifying roles.
3. The task.
4. Re-establishing the relationship.
5. Parting.
The task, episode 3, in turn often has several episodes, which come in a fixed order, as in the doctor–patient case described above. What is the 'task' in encounters which are primarily social occasions? It appears to be a combination of eating and drinking combined with exchange of information, though there may also be pseudo-tasks like dancing and playing games.

7. Sequences in different situations

We have seen that the sequence of events in the classroom, the doctor's, a selection interview, and when shopping are quite different. And all of these are different from an informal chat between friends, or other primarily social occasions. However some features of these sequences may be universal, for example people take turns to speak. In this section we shall explore the extent to which the differences can be explained in terms of the goals or other features of situations.

(1) Reacting and initiating

Jones & Gerard (1967) suggested that there are four different kinds of dyadic encounter, in terms of who is reacting to whom.

Pseudo-contingency. Here neither interactor is reacting to the other, except as regards timing. Examples are people acting in a play, or enacting a ritual, like greeting and saying farewell. Greetings and farewells are a little different, in that there is some variation and interaction. Such formal sequences are taken by Harré & Secord (1972) and Goffman (1971) as a model for other situations; our view is that they lack some of the key properties of other kinds of sequence. In pseudo-contingencies, the sequence is totally predictable from the rules; there is no variation within the rules, except in style.

Reactive contingency. Here each person reacts to the last move by the other. Examples are rambling conversations. The sequence is limited by the universal rules of all social behaviour, and the particular rules of the

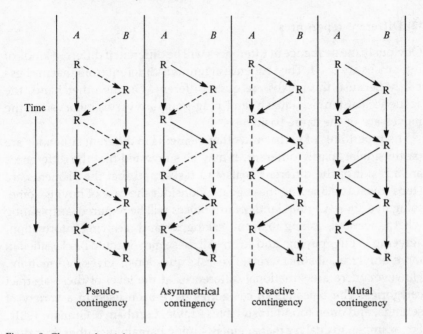

Figure 8. Classes of social interaction in terms of contingency (from Jones & Gerard 1967)

situation, which will allow only certain kinds of utterances, for example, and certain sequences. Thus a conversation in a pub is somewhat different from a conversation at a polite dinner party. In either case the sequence could be described, and to a limited extent predicted by the rules governing which sequences are allowable, as sensible sequences of social behaviour, and the probabilities (in each situation) that the allowable moves will be made.

Asymmetrical contingency. Here only one person has a plan, while the others are mainly reacting to what he does. Examples are teaching and interviewing. However the person being interviewed does have some initiative; he gives longer or shorter replies, he may pursue his own plan, e.g. to impress the interviewer (figure 6), and he may ask questions.

Mutual contingency. Here each interactor is pursuing his own goals, is reacting to the moves made by the other, and neither is in charge of the situation. Examples are negotiation and serious discussion. There are no sharp dividing lines between this kind of encounter and asymmetrical (where the subordinate person has *some* initiative) and reactive contingency (where neither person is pursuing a particular goal) (see Argyle 1979).

(2) Different repertoires

Obviously the sequence of utterances will be different if different kinds of utterances are used. The sequence at tennis is different from that in chess partly because the moves are quite different. On the other hand, the sequences at tennis, squash, and ping-pong are very similar, since the moves are of the same basic type.

The repertoires of verbal and other elements in different situations are partly similar, partly different. It may be suggested that the differences are a result of the different goals and tasks, and that the elements are steps towards achieving these goals. Consider the case of buying something in a shop. Certain kinds of utterances will be required – explaining what is wanted, asking to see it, asking for and receiving information, agreeing to buy, paying, and so on. All these moves could be classified in more universal, abstract terms, like 'asks questions', 'gives information'. However there are situational differences at the level of these abstract categories. The Bales (1950) categories have been used in a variety of settings, and often found unsuitable (Argyle, Furnham & Graham 1981). For example, to analyse management–union bargaining rather finer divisions are needed, and other sets of categories have been devised for this situation (Morley & Stephenson 1977; Rackham, Honey & Colbert 1971). Similar considerations apply to psychotherapy interviews (cf. Mann, Gibbard & Hartman 1967), and other situations.

Repertoires of utterances also differ in content; there is no general way of classifying contents though the General Inquirer program has been used for this purpose in psychotherapy interviews (Stone et al. 1966). On the other hand, the categories of non-verbal communication do not appear to vary much between situations, perhaps because interpersonal tasks are similar in all situations.

We can see how the use of a different repertoire will affect the sequence, by looking at negotiation. Morley & Stephenson's scheme has nine main categories – procedure, settlement point, limits, positive consequences of proposed outcome, rejection consequences of proposed outcome, other statements about outcomes, acknowledgment (praise, etc.), acknowledgment (blame, etc.), information (other statements of fact or opinion). There are also eight 'referents', i.e. of persons whose activities or behaviour are being described – self, opponent, own side, etc. This repertoire makes for a much more intricate sequence than that in another kind of negotiation, the auction sale, where only one move is possible.

Speech styles vary between situations in a number of ways: (a) different language may be used as in multilingualism; (b) high and low forms of the language may be used, as in diglossia – the Bernstein elaborated and restricted codes are an example; (c) vocabulary may be larger or smaller, or specialized, as for cooking, surgery, etc.; (d) grammar and sentence construction may be simple or complex; (e) accent, volume and speed vary between situations (Argyle et al. 1981).

It may be suggested that just as the elements of the repertoire used in a situation are functional in relation to situational goals, the same is true of the structure of the elements, i.e. the way in which they are grouped and contrasted. We studied this by asking subjects to rate the elements of a work and a social situation along a number of scales, and carried out hierarchical cluster analyses of the ratings. There were a number of interesting differences, as expected. For example discussion of work and personal matters was sharply contrasted in the work situation, but not in the social situation (Argyle, Graham & Kreckel 1981).

(3) Different rules

Situations also differ in their rules, including rules about the order of events. This is most obviously true of games, and of formal situations like rituals and ceremonies, but it is also true of less formal situations. Schank & Abelson (1977) have given an account of this in terms of the knowledge a person would need to have, or how a computer would need to be programmed to cope with common social situations, like going to a restaurant. It needs a certain body of knowledge to understand stories like the following.

(1) John went to a restaurant. He ordered a hamburger. It was cold when the waitress brought it. He left her a very small tip.

(2) Willa was hungry. She took out the Michelin guide.

Schank & Abelson say that we know the 'scripts' for these situations, i.e. have organized knowledge about the situation.

Their central concept is the *script*: the restaurant script for example describes the sequence of events at a restaurant for the four main episodes – enter, order, eat and exit. Scripts incorporate the kind of features we have been considering: *goals* and the relations between them; *plans* – knowledge of the sequence of elements which will realize the goals; *elements* of behaviour, e.g. order, eat, pay, leave, tip; *roles*, e.g. of waiter and diner, and *physical equipment* – menu, food. The *rules* are implicit in the scripts, especially role scripts. And there are 'interpersonal themes' which are scripts for love, father–son interaction; etc. This scheme does not include the skills or difficulties of situations, but it does formalize much of the conceptual knowledge needed in a situation.

The way in which one utterance or other element would follow another depends on the properties of the situation. Thus the significance of 'Can I pay the bill?' would be quite different and lead to different answers if addressed to (a) a waiter, (b) another diner, (c) a bank manager. The same applies to the sequence of events in a game of cricket; it is necessary to understand the game to know what will happen next after (a) six balls have been bowled, (b) ten men are out, (c) the ball reaches the boundary, etc.

Sequences also depend on the role-relations between people, as the paying the bill example showed. Victorian parents liked their children to be 'seen and not heard', which is one kind of discourse (Fishman 1972). Wittgenstein (1953) thought that the conversation between a builder and his assistant would consist solely of directions from the builder. With more enlightened skills of supervision, the builder would ask the assistant for his suggestions, listen to his ideas, and ask him how he was getting on. The motives of the builder here are more complex – he wants to tell the assistant what to do, but he also wants to motivate him, make use of his skills and knowledge, and keep him happy (Argyle 1972).

We carried out a study of the rules of twenty-five situations, in terms of agreed beliefs about what should and should not be done. There were clear rules for informal situations as well as formal situations, though some situations were much more rule-bound than others. Some rules were thought to apply to all situations ('be polite', 'don't embarrass other people', etc.). Other rules applied only to one or two situations, and could be interpreted as functional for those situations. For example 'don't pretend you've understood when you haven't' (tutorial), and 'make sure your body is clean' (at the doctor's). The method used to elicit rules however did not produce any information about rules of sequence (Argyle et al. 1979).

(4) Cultural differences

Interaction sequences which appear to be universal in our own culture may take somewhat different forms in other cultures. Here are some examples:

Question–answer. In the Gonja, and elsewhere, people do not ask questions unless they have the power to extract an answer (Goody 1978). School children do not ask questions in class. Information is regarded as a form of property in some cultures, not to be given away for the asking. In Japan, questions are not asked where the answer might be 'no', since the second speaker would lose face. In fact similar rules to these operate in our own culture, in that only certain kinds of questions may be asked, or will be answered, in any given setting.

Disagreement and polite usage. In some cultures great emphasis is placed on politeness. To disagree is to insult the other person. To give him information that he doesn't like is avoided, and inaccurate information given instead. In South American countries subordinates in business organizations do not speak their minds when more senior officials are present, so less use is made of group meetings.

Episode structure. This takes much the same form everywhere, but the second episode, of chatting and establishing relationships, is much longer in some cultures. In Arab countries this is rarely less than twenty minutes.

Rules. Particular situations have different rules in different cultures. Buying and selling may be done by a long drawn-out process of bargaining; business may not proceed at all unless the usual 'dash' or bribe is paid, and this must be negotiated too. Requests for others to go away, to cease their sexual advances, or to decline food, may not be believed unless these are made three times, or very vehemently.

The use of non-verbal signals. In some cultures a lot of use is made of non-verbal signals, either replacing verbal utterances, or commenting on them. In Botswana there is no word for 'thank-you'; instead the cupped hands are held out. In Southern Italy there is an extensive gesture language, over 200 hand-signals having familiar meanings; these are often used to replace verbal utterances, or make sotto voce comments, e.g. about the honesty or sexual desirability of others present (Morris et al. 1979).

8. Sequences and social competence

Social competence requires not only the skilled use of certain utterances, but also the ability to produce them at the right point in the sequence, and to produce a number of related utterances in sequence.

(a) The analysis of skilled performance. The usual method of discovering the most effective social skills is to compare the performance of samples of effective and ineffective practitioners – defined in terms of some objective

index of success. The difference may lie in the use of particular kinds of utterance; successful teachers make more use of praise, illustrative examples, developing pupils' ideas, and structuring, and they are warm and enthusiastic (Rosenshine 1971).

A socially skilled person is someone who is able to realize his goals in social situations. A skilled teacher teaches his pupils more, a skilled therapist's patients recover, and so on. For such professional social skills the goals are fairly obvious, though there may be more than one goal present. In everyday situations it is less clear what the goals are. Graham, Argyle & Furnham (1980) asked samples of people to rate lists of goals for their relevance in different situations, and extracted factors of highest relevance. There were usually three such factors: (a) social acceptance, making friends, etc.; (b) eating, drinking and other bodily needs; (c) task goals specific to the situation.

There is considerable skill in the construction of single utterances. Bates (1976) found that Italian children aged 2 would say the equivalent of 'I want a sweet', but by 6 years could add 'please', rephrase it as a request, without question intonation, as a conditional ('I would like'), and use formal pronouns in addressing the other. Adult polite speech goes a long way beyond this, as in 'If you're passing the letter box could you post this letter for me', for which it might be hard to provide grammatical rules. Being polite cannot entirely be reduced to the grammar of the sentences however; how polite is 'Please could you tell me why you gave us such a terrible lecture this evening?' Giving orders or instructions needs skill: 'Do X' does not get things done, in most settings, even when the speaker has the power to command. Orders are usually disguised as suggestions, or even questions.

There is an important non-verbal component in skilled utterances. The amount of warmth, directiveness, or questioning is shown by the tone of voice and pitch pattern. Elaboration and comments on the utterance are provided by special ways of delivering words or phrases – in special accents, volume, pitch, etc., which Fonagy (1971) has called 'double-coding'.

What is usually regarded as 'tact' requires more social skill. Tact could be defined as the production of socially effective utterances in difficult situations; these are usually utterances which influence others in a desired way, without upsetting them or others present. How do you congratulate the winner without upsetting the loser? What do you say to a child who has just been expelled from school? This is clearly an area of social skills where the skill consists in finding the right verbal message;

again it seems to have little to do with grammar. McPhail (1967) presented teenagers with written descriptions of a variety of difficult social situations and asked them what they would say. The younger ones opted for boldly direct, often aggressive, utterances, but the older ones preferred more skilled, indeed 'tactful' remarks (figure 9).

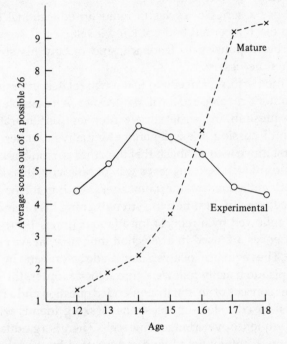

Figure 9. Experimental and mature solutions to social problems (from McPhail 1967)

Similar considerations apply to professional social skills. A selection interviewer may want to assess candidates in terms of adjustment, authoritarianism, judgment, motivation, social competence, etc. He needs to ask the best questions to produce useful information in these areas. Asking 'Are you neurotic?', for example, wouldn't be very useful. The usual approach is to explore the candidate's performance in past situations which called for judgment, hard work, stability, etc. Tactful skills are required to explore areas of failure, or to find out the truth where a candidate is concealing it. A skilled interviewer can control the length of the other's replies by using open-ended or closed questions, by the amount of head-nodding and other reinforcement given while the other answers, and by the use of interruptions.

(b) Skilled sequences. Complex professional skills require the construction of quite elaborate·sequences. Here are some of the points we have made about teaching:

1. A teacher should follow the statement of a principle by an example.
2. He should be able to establish certain cycles of interaction, such as lecture–question–answer–comment.
3. He should use a series of cycles to build up educational episodes, intended to teach a certain body of knowledge.
4. He should be responsive to feedback, and modify his style of behaviour when necessary.

Sometimes the performer needs to make two related utterances, separated by the other's response to the first utterance. An example is the use of a follow-up question, in a social survey interview, as illustrated above in section 6, in discussing 'the independent initiative of others'. In persuasion the first move is to establish that the other person has some goal or need; the second step is to suggest a way of satisfying this need – in a way that is advantageous to the persuader. An ingratiator starts by flattering, agreeing with, or otherwise strengthening his rewards for the others; this is followed by a request for a favour (Jones 1964).

Longer sequences are used in a selection interview, as was shown in figure 6 above. The sequence follows a plan made beforehand by the interviewer. The episode usually follows a chronological order; the sequence within episodes consists of an initial open-ended question and a number of more sharply focused follow-up questions. Making friends with someone involves a sequence over a longer time scale. There is a gradual increase in self-disclosure, carefully timed, and reciprocated by the other.

(c) Failures of social competence; social skills trainings. Many people are lacking in social skills – they can't make friends, they suffer acute social anxiety, they can't cope with certain social situations. They are lacking in assertiveness, they can't establish relationships with the opposite sex, and so on. About 7–10 per cent of the normal population are quite seriously handicapped in this way, 25–30 per cent of neurotics and virtually all psychotics are socially inadequate (Argyle 1980).

This may be due to failure of several kinds. Socially inadequate neurotic patients are usually very poor conversationalists, and we have observed a number of characteristic types of failure:

1. Failure to make non-verbal responses and feedback (head-nods, smiles, 'uh-huh' noises) as a listener.
2. Failure to pursue any persistent plan, producing only passive responses.

3. Attempts to make conversation by producing unwanted information ('I went to Weston-Super-Mare last year').
4. Failure to make a proactive move after replying to a question ('Where do you come from?', 'Swansea . . .' – end of conversation).

In order to identify these forms of failure, it is necessary to understand the structure of normal conversation. It is then possible to train people in how to do it. The general procedure is instruction and demonstration followed by role-playing and play back of tape or video-tape recordings. Sometimes special exercises are used. For example, lack of persistent planning can be tackled by practice at a simple skill, like interviewing, where the performer is in charge. He is asked to make notes beforehand, and plan the whole session. Failure to make non-verbal responses can be dealt with by playing back a video-recording (Trower, Bryant & Argyle 1978).

People with social skills problems often have difficulty with particular social situations – parties, dates, interviews, etc. This is often because they have failed to understand the situation, for example thinking that an interview is an occasion for vocational guidance, that a date is a kind of philosophy tutorial, or bidding less than the last person at an auction sale. In some cases they lack the special skills needed for the situation. The training consists partly of working through the main features of the situation with the trainee – the goals, conflicts between them, the main rules, the roles, the repertoire of verbal and non-verbal elements, the special difficulties, and the skills needed. This is followed by training in the skills needed in the situation (Argyle et al. 1981). Situations which have been the object of workshop training include parties, dating, assertiveness situations, and making friends.

A great deal of detailed information has now accumulated about people's habits and practices in the organization of interpersonal encounters. How far are these principles of sequence universal to all situations, or to all cultures? Some two-step links are very common, though not universal, like question–answer, request–comply or refuse, joke–laugh, etc. The four-step goal-directed sequence is probably universal, though the actual goals and sequences vary. Similarly the details of repeated cycles vary between situations. We suggested earlier that encounters have a basic five-episode structure, though episode 3, the task, divides up into a series of sub-episodes specific to each task.

Some of these principles of sequence are clearly functional in relation to situational goals. In our study of doctor–patient interaction we found that one of the main goals of patients is 'seek help, advice, reassurance', and that a common two-step sequence is 'ask if disease is serious – reassure that illness/disease is not serious'. Four-step goal-directed sequences are clearly functional. Cycles of the type 'lecture–asks question–answer–comment' (in the classroom) are processes of social interaction which have been found to be successful, in this case in attaining the goal of teaching. Rules governing the order of events have presumably emerged, like other rules, because they help in goal attainment. Episodes are often ordered – e.g. the six doctor–patient episodes – because tasks have to be done in a particular order.

All in all the state of the art seems to be that interest in conversation structure is growing, and a number of recurring constructions have been found and described already, so that many conversation types can be viewed in terms of their middle-sized building blocks. What remains is to find the overall structuring principles that govern the global levels of conversation structure, if indeed such principles and such patterns exist.

References

Altman, S. A. 1965. Sociobiology of rhesus monkeys, ii: stochastics of social communication. *Journal of Theoretical Biology, 8,* 490–522.

Argyle, M. 1969. *Social interaction.* London: Methuen.

1972. *The social psychology of work.* London: Allen Lane.

1979. Sequences of social behaviour as a function of the situation. In G. P. Ginsburg (ed.) *Emerging strategies in social psychology.* London: Wiley.

1980. Interaction skills and social competence. In M. P. Feldman & J. Orford (eds.) *The social psychology of psychological problems.* New York and London: Wiley.

Argyle, M. & Kendon, A. 1967. The experimental analysis of social performance. *Advances in Experimental Social Psychology, 3,* 55–98.

Argyle, M., Furnham, A. & Graham, J. A. 1981. *Social situations.* Cambridge: Cambridge University Press.

Argyle, M., Graham, J. A., Campbell, A. & White, P. 1979. The rules of different situations. *New Zealand Psychologist, 8,* 13–22.

Argyle, M., Graham, J. A. & Kreckel, M. 1981. The structure of behavioural elements in social and work situations. In Argyle et al. *Social situations.* Cambridge: Cambridge University Press.

Austin, J. L. 1962. *How to do things with words.* Oxford: Clarendon Press.

Bakeman, R. & Dobbs, J. M. Jr. 1976. Social interaction observed: some approaches to the analysis of behaviour streams. *Personality and Social Psychology Bulletin, 2,* 335–45.

Bales, R. F. 1950. *Interaction process analysis.* Cambridge, Mass.: Addison-Wesley.

1953. The equilibrium problem in small groups. In T. Parsons, R. F. Bales & E. A. Shils (eds.) *Working papers in the Theory of Action.* Glencoe, Ill.: Free Press.

Barnett Pearce, W., Cronen, V. E. & Johnson, K. 1978. The structure of communication rules and the form of conversation: an experimental simulation. Paper to Speech Communication Association, Minneapolis.

Bates, E. 1976. *Language and context: the acquisition of pragmatics.* New York: Academic Press.

Beattie, G. W. 1980. The skilled art of conversational interaction. In W. T. Singleton, P. Spurgeon & R. B. Stammers (eds.) *The analysis of social skills.* New York: Plenum.

Benjamin, L. S. 1979. Use of structural analysis to study social behaviour (SASB), and Markov chains to study dyadic interaction. *Journal of Abnormal Psychology, 88,* 303–19.

Boden, M. 1977. *Artificial intelligence and natural man.* Hassocks: Harvester.

Brenner, M. 1980. Patterns of social behaviour in the research interview. In M. Brenner (ed.) *Social method and social life.* London: Academic Press.

Bruner, J. S. 1975. The ontogenesis of speech acts. *Journal of Child Language, 2,* 1–19.

Byrne, P. S. & Long, B. E. L. 1976. *Doctors talking to patients.* London: HMSO.

Carroll, J. B. 1964. *Language and thought.* London: Prentice Hall.

Chomsky, N. 1957. *Syntactic structures.* The Hague: Mouton.

   1959. On certain formal properties of grammar. *Information and Control, 1,* 91–112.

   1965. *Aspects of the theory of syntax.* The Hague: Mouton.

Clarke, A. H., Ellgring, H. & Wagner, H. 1979. Situational effects on the syntax of speech and gaze behaviour in dyads. Paper for symposium on 'Temporal aspects of speech', Social Psychology and Language Conference, Bristol, July 1979.

Clarke, D. D. 1975a. The use and recognition of sequential structure in dialogue. *British Journal of Social and Clinical Psychology, 14,* 333–9.

   1975b. *The structural analysis of verbal interaction.* DPhil thesis. Bodleian Library Oxford.

   1979a. The syntax of action. *Oxford Review of Education, 4.3,* 239–55.

   1979b. The linguistic analogy: when is a speech act like a morpheme? In G. Ginsburg (ed.) *Emerging strategies in social psychology.* London: Wiley.

   forthcoming. *Future-grammar: a generative account of interaction sequences.* Oxford: Pergamon Press.

Coulthard, M. 1977. *Introduction to discourse analysis.* London: Longman.

Cronen, V. E. & Barnett Pearce, W. 1978. The logic of the coordinated management of meaning: an open systems model of interpersonal communication. Paper to International Communication Association Convention, Chicago.

Dawkins, R. 1976. Hierarchical organisation: a candidate principle for ethology. In P. P. G. Bateson & R. A. Hinde (eds.) *Growing points in ethology.* Cambridge: Cambridge University Press.

Duncan, S. Jr. 1972. Some signals and rules for taking speaking turns in conversation. *Journal of Personality and Social Psychology, 23,* 283–92.

   1974. On signalling that it's your turn to speak. *Journal of Experimental Social Psychology, 10,* 234–47.

Fillmore, C. J. 1968. The case for case. In E. Bach & R. T. Harms (eds.) *Universals in language.* New York: Holt, Rinehart and Winston.

Fishman, J. A. 1972. *The sociology of language.* Rowley, Mass.: Newbury House.

Flanders, N. A. 1970. *Analyzing Teaching Behavior*. Reading, Mass.: Addison-Wesley.

Flavell, J. H. 1968. *The development of role-taking and communication skills in children*. New York: Wiley.

Fonagy, I. 1971. Double coding in speech. *Semiotica*, 3, 189–222.

Frentz, T. S. 1976. A generative approach to episodic structure. Paper presented to the University of Southern California Western Speech Communication Convention, San Francisco, November.

Garvey, C. 1974. Some properties of social play. *Merrill-Palmer Quarterly of Behavior and Development*, 20, 163–80.

    1975a. Requests and responses in children's speech. *Journal of Child Language*, 2, 41–63.

    1975b. Contingent queries. Draft MS.

    1977. *Play*. London: Fontana and Open Books.

Garvey, C. & Ben Debba, M. 1974. Effects of age, sex and partner on children's dyadic speech. *Child Development*, 45, 1159–61.

Goffman, E. 1971. *Relations in public*. London: Allen Lane the Penguin Press.

Goody, E. N. 1978. Towards a theory of questions. In E. N. Goody (ed.) *Questions and politeness*. Cambridge: Cambridge University Press.

Gottman, J. M. 1979. *Marital interaction*. New York: Academic Press.

Graham, J. A., Argyle, M. & Furnham, A. 1980. The goal structure of situations. *European Journal of Social Psychology*, 10, 345–66.

Grice, H. P. 1957. Meaning. *Philosophical Review*, 66, 377–88.

    1968. Utterer's meaning, sentence meaning and word meaning. *Foundations of Language*, 4, 225–42.

    1975. Logic and conversation. In P. Cole & J. L. Morgan (eds.) *Syntax and semantics. III Speech acts*. New York: Academic Press.

Harré, R. & Secord, P. 1972. *The explanation of social behaviour*. Oxford: Pergamon.

Hertel, R. K. 1972. Application of stochastic process analysis to the study of psychotherapeutic processes. *Psychological Bulletin*, 77, 421–30.

Huesman, L. R. & Levinger, G. 1976. Incremental exchange theory: a formal model for progression in dyadic social interaction. In L. Berkowitz (ed.) *Advances in experimental social psychology 9*. New York: Academic Press.

Jaffe, J. 1964. Verbal behavioural analysis in psychiatric interviews with the aid of digital computers. In D. Mck. Rioch & E. A. Weinstein (eds.) *Disorders of communication*. Research Publication of the Association for Research in Nervous and Mental Disorders, 42. Baltimore: Williams and Wilkins.

Jefferson, G. 1972. Side sequences. In D. Sudnov (ed.) *Studies in social interaction*. New York: Free Press.

Jones, E. E. 1964. *Ingratiation: a social psychological analysis*. New York: Appleton-Century-Crofts.

Jones, E. E. & Gerard, H. B. 1967. *Foundations of Social Psychology*. New York: Wiley.

Kendon, A. 1967. Some functions of gaze direction in social interaction. *Acta Psychologica*, 26.1, 1–47.

Levinson. S. 1978. Some pre-observations on the modelling of dialogue. MS. Department of Linguistics, University of Cambridge.

Mann, R. D., Gibbard, G. S. & Hartman, J. J. 1967. *Interpersonal styles and group development*. New York: Wiley.

McPhail, P. 1967. The development of social skill in adolescents. Unpublished MS. Cited in M. Argyle. *Social interaction*. London: Methuen, 1969.

Meldman, M. J. 1967. Verbal behaviour analysis of self-hyperattentionism. *Diseases of the Nervous System*, 28, 469–73.

Miller, G. A. & Selfridge, J. A. 1950. Verbal content and the recall of meaningful material. *American Journal of Psychology*, 63, 176–85.

Miller, G. A., Galanter, E. & Pribram, K. H. 1960. *Plans and the structure of behavior*. New York: Holt.

Minsky, M. 1972. *Computation: finite and infinite machines*. London: Prentice-Hall.

Morley, I. E. & Stephenson, G. M. 1977. *The social psychology of bargaining*. London: Allen and Unwin.

Morris, D., Collett, P., Marsh, P. & O'Shaughnessy, M. 1979. *Gestures: their origins and distribution*. London: Cape.

Pease, K. & Arnold, P. 1973. Approximations to dialogue. *American Journal of Psychology*, 86, 769–76.

Rackham, N., Honey, P. & Colbert, M. J. 1971. *Developing interaction skills*. Northampton: Wellers.

Rausch, H. L. 1965. Interaction sequences. *Journal of Personality and Social Psychology*, 2, 487–99.

Rommetveit, R. 1968. *Words, meanings and messages*. London: Academic Press.

1972. Language games, syntactic structures and hermeneutics. In J. Israel & H. Tajfel (eds.) *The context of social psychology*. London: Academic Press.

1974. *On message structure: a conceptual framework for the study of language and communication*. London: Wiley.

Rommetveit, R., Cook, M., Havelka, N., Henry, P., Herkner, W., Pecheux, M. & Peeters, G. 1971. Processing utterances in context. In E. A. Carswell & R. Rommetveit (eds.) *Social contexts of messages*. London: Academic Press.

Rosenshine, B. 1971. *Teaching Behaviours and Student Achievement*. Slough: NFER.

Sacks, H., Schegloff, E. A. & Jefferson, G. 1974. A simplest systematics for the organisation of turn-taking for conversation. *Language 50.4*, 696–735.

Schank, R. C. & Abelson, R. P. 1977. *Scripts, plans, goals and understanding*. Hillsdale, NJ: Erlbaum.

Schegloff, E. A. 1968. Sequencing in conversational openings. *American Anthropologist*, 70, 1075–95.

Schegloff, E. A. & Sacks, H. 1973. Opening up closings. *Semiotica*, 8, 289–327.

Searle, J. 1965. What is a speech act? In M. Black (ed.) *Philosophy in America*. London: Allen and Unwin & Cornell University Press.

1969. *Speech acts*. Cambridge: Cambridge University Press.

1975. A taxonomy of illocutionary acts. In K. Gunderson (ed.) *Language, mind and knowledge*. Minnesota Studies in the Philosophy of Science, 7. Minneapolis: University of Minnesota Press.

Shannon, C. E. 1948. A mathematical theory of communication. *Bell System Technical Journal*, 27, 379–423.

Shapiro, D. A. 1976. Conversational structure and accurate empathy: an exploratory study. *British Journal of Social and Clinical Psychology*, 15, 213–15.

Simon, H. A. 1952. A formal theory of interaction in social psychology. *American Sociological Review*, 17, 202–11.

Sinclair, J. & Coulthard, R. M. 1975. *Towards an analysis of discourse: the English used by teachers and pupils*. London: Oxford University Press.

Smith, B. O., Meux, M. O., Coombs, J., Nuthall, G. A. & Precians, R. 1967. *Studies of the strategies of teaching*. Urbana, Ill.: Bureau of Educational Research, University of Illinois.

Stone, P. J., Dunphy, D. C., Smith, M. S. & Ogilvie, D. M. 1966. *The general inquirer: a computer approach to content analysis*. Cambridge, Mass.: MIT Press.

Trower, P., Bryant, B. & Argyle, M. 1978. *Social skills and mental health*. London: Methuen.

Weizenbaum, J. 1966. ELIZA – A computer program for the study of natural language communication between man and machine. *Communications of the ACM, 9*, 36–45.

 1967. Contextual understanding by computer. *Communications of the ACM, 10*, 474–80.

Westman, R. S. 1978. Environmental languages and the functional bases of animal behaviour. In B. Hazlett (ed.) *Quantitative methods in animal behaviour*. London: Academic Press.

Winograd, T. 1972. Understanding natural language. *Cognitive Psychology, 3*, 1–191.

Wittgenstein, L. 1953. *Philosophical investigations*. Oxford: Blackwell.

Woods, W. A. 1970. Transition network grammars for natural language analysis. *Communications of the ACM, 13*, 591–606.

6. Psychological and linguistic parameters of speech accommodation theory*

JITENDRA N. THAKERAR, HOWARD GILES
and JENNY CHESHIRE

In this chapter, we begin by reviewing some limitations of traditional sociolinguistics, arguing that it could benefit from theoretical innovations derived from social psychology. A social psychological theory of language usage is then discussed, whose basic tenets are that when interlocutors desire each other's approval they will converge their speech patterns, whereas when they wish to differentiate from each other socially, they will diverge them. A series of empirical studies are reported which suggest that under certain conditions interlocutors' shifts of speech, objectively measured as divergence, more accurately reflect their subjective attempts to integrate linguistically and psychologically with their partners than to dissociate from them. The interpretation of these data led to the elaboration of speech accommodation theory and to the formulation of a systematic distinction between the linguistic and the psychological processes, and the objective and the subjective processes that operate in interpersonal communication. This in turn led to a reformulation of the theory in propositional terms.

1. From sociolinguistics to speech accommodation theory

The study of linguistic variation in social contexts has captured the imaginations of scholars in various social and language-related sciences. The desire to understand the relationship between linguistic and social variables gave rise to the multidisciplinary field of sociolinguistics,

* Data reported in this chapter are more fully described in the first author's doctoral dissertation. We acknowledge with great appreciation the statistical advice afforded us by David Green, the computational assistance by Sue Evans as well as valuable discussions about the data herein with Richard Bourhis, W. P. Robinson, Philip Smith and John Turner. We are also indebted to Donald Taylor for drawing our attention to the crucial roles of speech functions in accommodation and to Colin Fraser and Klaus Scherer for their insightful comments on an earlier draft of this chapter.

which, according to Hymes (1972), has at its heart the study of speech diversity in different social settings. While acknowledging the fact that this field has in the last decade made great strides forward by informing us how, when and where we modulate our speech, some writers have nevertheless voiced dissatisfactions with the current state-of-the-art. Expressed reservations have in the main been primarily on theoretical grounds, and they include the following. First, traditional sociolinguistics has been more descriptive than explanatory, thus lacking power of prediction (Giles, 1977a; Scotton & Ury 1977). Secondly, sociolinguistics have mainly highlighted correlations between linguistic and large-scale, objectively defined social variables (e.g. socio-economic classes, age and sex groups), thereby neglecting the idea that speakers' own subjective attitudes, perceptions of situations, cognitive and affective dispositions and the like may interact to determine their speech outputs (Giles, Smith & Robinson 1980; Smith, Giles & Hewstone 1980). Thirdly, sociolinguists, in line with their tendency to exclude language from definitions of social and structural variables, cannot entertain fully the idea that language can often assume the role of an independent variable by creating, defining and negotiating social settings (Giles, Hewstone & St Clair in press). Finally, traditional sociolinguists have been unable to specify adequately the conditions under which, and the reasons why, speech can be more salient than other non-linguistic variables in influencing social relations, situations and structures (Giles, Smith, Ford, Condor and Thakerar 1980; Smith 1980). Admittedly, certain sociolinguists (e.g. Labov 1970; Scotton 1980; Sankoff 1972) have attempted to address some of these issues by employing social psychological phenomena such as attitudes, intentions and motivations as determinants of verbal behaviour and by considering some of the creative and negotiative functions of speech.

Of late, and in some ways due to a desire to take into account the above omissions, social psychologists have established a new paradigm in sociolinguistics, which, it can be argued, has focused essentially upon the cognitive processes mediating between individuals' social perceptions of the environment and their communicative behaviours (Giles 1977b; Giles & Powesland 1975; Giles & St Clair, 1979, in press; Giles, Robinson & Smith 1980; Marková 1978; Robinson 1972; Rommetveit & Blakar 1979; St Clair & Giles 1980; Scherer & Giles 1979). In order to elucidate the nature of cognitive organization, researchers have relied upon a number of social psychological processes underlying both the encoding and decoding of language behaviour. This interest in exploring the mediating cognitive processes has been the central concern of one of the few theories which have evolved out of the socio-psycholinguistic paradigm, namely speech accommodation theory (Bourhis 1979; Giles 1977a; Giles & Powesland 1975). This theoretical framework developed out of a desire to demonstrate explicitly the value and potential of social psychological concepts and processes for increasing our understanding of the dynamics of speech diversity in social settings – an area of inquiry which has previously relied upon basically static norms and rules for its explanatory potential (Bourhis & Genesee 1980; Giles 1977a).

Speech accommodation theory was devised to explain some of the motivations underlying certain shifts in people's speech styles during social encounters, and some of the social consequences arising from them. More specifically, it originated in order to elucidate the cognitive and affective processes underlying speech convergence and divergence. Convergence has been defined as a linguistic strategy whereby individuals adapt to each other's speech by means of a wide range of linguistic features, including speech rates, pause and utterance lengths, pronunciations, etc. (for a review, see Giles & Powesland 1975),[1] whereas divergence refers to the manner by which speakers accentuate vocal differences between themselves and others (Giles 1973). Central to this framework is the notion that during social interaction, participants are motivated to adjust (or to accommodate) their speech styles as a means of gaining one or more of the following goals: evoking listeners' social approval, attaining communicational efficiency between interactants and maintaining speakers' positive social identities. The theory has been elaborated by recourse to a number of social psychological principles, speech convergence being handled primarily in terms of similarity–attraction (Byrne 1969) and causal attribution (Heider 1958), and speech divergence by means of intergroup processes (Tajfel 1974). A brief overview of the two speech strategies will be presented next; a more elaborate discussion appears elsewhere (Giles 1980).

1.1. Speech convergence[2]

Accommodation theory proposes that this phenomenon may profitably be considered a reflection (often non-conscious) of a speaker's or a

[1] For a discussion of the value of speech accommodation theory for understanding the dynamics of non-vocal, non-verbal behaviours, see von Raffler Engel 1980.

[2] It should be noted that other models have been adopted to account for convergent behaviours (e.g. Jaffe & Feldstein 1970; Matarazzo et al. 1968; Natalé 1975). A comparative study of some of these has recently been presented by Street & Giles (in press) in favour of the speech accommodation framework.

group's desire for social integration or identification with another. The theory has its basis in research on similarity–attraction which, in its simplest form, suggests that as person A becomes more similar to person B, this increases the likelihood that B will like A. Interpersonal convergence through speech, then, is but one of the many devices a person may adopt in order to become more similar to another person. Specifically, it involves the reduction of linguistic dissimilarities between two people in terms of their dialects, pause lengths, etc. Since increasing similarity between people along such an important dimension as communication is likely to increase a speaker's attractiveness (Bishop 1979) as well as his or her predictability (Berger 1979) and intelligibility (Triandis 1960) in the eyes of the recipient, convergence may be best considered as a reflection of an individual's desire for social approval.

A study by Giles & Smith (1979) supports the notion that speech convergence evokes positive reactions in its recipients (see also Bourhis, Giles & Lambert 1975). A Canadian male tape recorded eight versions of the same short message on North American education for an English audience in Britain. One of these, a non-converging version, was a message where the speaker did not converge towards the audience from a standard version supposedly spoken to Canadians back home on any of three linguistic dimensions, namely pronunciation, speech rate and message content. The other seven versions represented the remaining combinations of convergence and non-convergence with regard to these three speech features. Although listeners appreciated accommodation on each of the linguistic levels, the English listeners upgraded the speaker more highly in attractiveness when he converged in speech rate than when he converged in either pronunciation or content (cf. Street under review). In addition, it was found that there was a non-linear relationship between convergence and attraction. The most positively evaluated convergent strategy of the eight was the combination of content plus speech rate convergences; the effect of adding pronunciation to this optimum was to reduce the favourableness of listeners' perceptions of the speaker. According to listeners' ratings, they thought that the speaker had an uncomplimentary view of them when he converged on all three linguistic features. The addition of pronunciation shifts (in *this* instance) could have been seen as patronizing, ingratiating or (despite the authenticity of the accent) as a caricature.

Therefore, if one accepts the notion that people find approval from others satisfying, and that speech convergence goes some way towards achieving this end, it would not seem unreasonable to suppose that there may be a general tendency for people to converge towards others in many social situations. It follows, then, that the greater the speaker's need to gain another's approval or attraction, the greater the magnitude of convergence there will be, up to a certain optimal level (at even perhaps an optimal rate). Many factors could affect the intensity of such a need, including the probability of future interactions with the other, the extent of their social power over the interlocutor, recollections of previous convergences from that person, etc. Hence, Natalé (1975) found that speakers who gained a high score on a social desirability scale, indicating a strong trans-situational need for social approval, converged more to their partner's vocal intensity and pause length than speakers who gained a low score on this personality measure. Probably among the most crucial determinants of the amounts of speech convergence encoded is the power dimension. This can be illustrated, for example, by the linguistic relationship between Puerto Ricans and Blacks in New York City. By common consent, the latter hold more power and prestige than the Puerto Ricans, and therefore it would not be surprising to learn from an accommodation perspective that Puerto Ricans assimilate the dialect of Blacks far more than vice versa (Wolfram 1973). Moreover, the vast literature on language and dialect assimilation of immigrant groups in alien dominant cultures (e.g. Fishman 1966) can also be viewed from this perspective. Typically, language shifts are unilateral, with the subordinate group converging to the powerful dominant group in their use of language to a far greater extent than vice versa (Giles & Bourhis 1976; Taylor, Simard & Papineau 1978).

Research reported by Aboud (1976) suggests that even six year olds are aware of power and status differences in language usage which mediate their accommodative strategies. She and her associates studied the communication patterns of Chicano and Anglo-American children, who, of course, represent respectively low and high power groups. These children were asked to explain how to play a game which they had just learned to two listeners of their own age. The listeners themselves solicited the explanations by saying 'Tell me how to play the game'; one inquired in English and the other in Spanish. The authors found that 71 per cent of the Spanish-dominant Chicanos converged by adopting the language of their English listener. Only 17 per cent of the English-dominant Anglos accommodated to the Spanish listener, despite the fact that half of them were in a bilingual programme. None of the non-convergers used any alternative forms of accommodation (see Giles, Taylor & Bourhis 1973), such as saying a few key words in Spanish, or apologizing for their supposed lack of Spanish fluency. In a similar study involving the investigation of Spanish–English code-switching from an accommodation perspective, Valdés-Fallis (1977) found that bilingual Mexican American women tended to follow a language-switch initiated by a male, and also tended to imitate the relative frequency of language-switching, as well as the kinds of switching patterns selected by a 'male' speaker throughout a conversation. Bilingual accommodation was notably more limited or non-existent in speech exchanges between two females. Such a finding again confirms an accommodation theory prediction based on the higher values and social power that are traditionally associated with male roles rather than with female roles in society. Similarly, it has been shown that the more an individual desires another's approval, the more the latter's speech will sound similar to that of the former's. Larsen, Martin & Giles (1977) found that speakers who anticipated interaction with a prestigious, authoritative figure perceived his speech as sounding more similar to their own than did subjects who were told little about him and who did not expect to meet him. This *perception* of a reduced language barrier between oneself and another no doubt facilitates the convergence process, since the recipient will appear to be a more attainable target to shift towards.

It should also be mentioned that speech accommodation theory also relies upon notions of social exchange (Homans 1961), in that in order for convergence to come about, it should incur more potential rewards for the speaker than costs. Such rewards could include a gain in the listener's approval, as already indicated, whilst the potential costs could include expended effort or a loss of personal (and sometimes, as we shall see in the next section, social) identity. However, the specific social rewards that accrue may depend on the particular linguistic features by means of which convergence takes place (see Giles 1977a, 1980, for further discussion).

Much of the work testing the above assumptions about convergence has been conducted in the bilingual setting of Québec, since this speech shift can easily be measured in terms of the use of one language or the other (i.e. French or English). However, as we shall see, even bilingual convergence is not such a simple all-or-nothing process, but can take a number of different forms. Giles et al. (1973) derived two predictions from the theory: the greater the effort in convergence perceived from a speaker, the more favourably he will be evaluated by the listener and the more the listener in turn will converge back.

A request was made at McGill University for bilingual English Canadian (EC) students to participate in an experiment. They were randomly assigned to one of four stimulus conditions but in such a manner that their self-reported French-speaking skills were matched across the groups. The students were told that it had been hoped that a face-to-face situation could have been created for them to speak with French Canadians (FCs). However, due to the enormous difficulties involved in transporting FCs to McGill University and ECs to l'Université de Montréal at convenient times for all, taped messages were being used. They were told that bilingual FC students had been recorded in their own university, describing a picture for bilingual EC students. They were then informed that they would each hear one of these FC bilinguals, and from his taped description were expected to draw the picture he was talking about. The informants were assured that the quality of their drawing was completely unimportant as the experimenters just wanted to see if the message had been effectively communicated. They were then provided with paper and pencil and told to draw the picture as the speaker was describing it. The experimenter turned on the tape recorder when the subjects were ready, but *apparently* did so a little too far back on the tape (and apologized) as the FC speaker was heard receiving his instructions in French. He could be heard being told that his recipient would be an EC bilingual, and was then heard to inquire of the experimenter which language he should use for his audience. The experimenter asked (in English) whether he could speak English – the reply was affirmative (also in English) – and told him he could speak in the language of his choice. The purpose of this procedure was to ensure that the EC listeners were made fully aware that the speaker was known to be a FC bilingual, that they were aware of the fact that their speaker knew that they themselves were bilingual, and that they knew their speaker's language form was the result of a conscious choice on his part.

Members of all groups heard the same description of a very simple harbour scene composed in such a manner that another person could draw it while listening to the description. Each group heard the same male FC bilingual student read a different version of this passage: (a) totally in French; (b) in mixed French and English; (c) in fluent English but with a distinct FC accent; and (d) in non-fluent but comprehensible English that contained many pauses, speech disturbances and a few grammatical errors. It was thought that descriptions (a)–(d) would be considered by EC bilinguals as reflecting a series of messages increasing with regard to their perceived effort in convergence. After drawing the picture from one of these descriptions, students were presented with a questionnaire on which they were required to rate their reactions to their speaker and his performance. They were then presented with a similar picture to the one they had just drawn, and asked to describe this for the same FC bilingual whom they were told would draw it the following week. The informants were handed a microphone and were tape recorded giving their description. They were then asked to fill in another short questionnaire about their performance.

The results supported the predictions in that the greater the amount of effort in convergence a speaker was perceived to have put into his message, the more favourably he was perceived. More specifically, the non-fluent English speaker was viewed as the most considerate and concerned about bridging the cultural gap between English and French Canadians, and more people converged back to him by use of French in their descriptions than any of the other speakers. In all, though, we identified fourteen types of convergence, some of which included no French at all. These convergent messages included: returning the description totally in French; returning it in 50 per cent French; providing just the salutation and valediction in French; expressing an intention in English on the tape of slowing down the speech rate so that the FC could understand the speaker better. Most of the messages to the non-converging FC were presented back to him simply in English without any verbally expressed regrets for doing so.

Cross-cultural interaction in a *realistic* context, however, suggests the need for an elaboration of accommodation theory. In the above experiment, the EC listeners were fully aware of the speaker's bilingual skills, and of the fact that he had voluntarily chosen to speak the language he adopted on the tape. In everyday life, however, we are often unaware of the background to a convergent or non-convergent act. For instance, when a person has shifted his speech towards us, we cannot always be sure whether he wanted to make the effort to reduce the dissimilarities himself or whether he was under pressure from elsewhere to do so. Hitherto, such attributed motives had not been taken into account, and this could be where causal attribution principles come into the picture.

Recent developments in causal attribution provide useful guidelines for an extension of accommodation theory. It has been suggested that we understand a person's behaviour and hence evaluate the person himself in terms of the motives and intentions that we attribute as the cause of his actions (Jones & Davis 1965; Kelly 1973). It has been proposed that a perceiver considers three factors when attributing motives to an act – the other's ability, his effort and the external pressure impelling him to perform in the manner in which he did. Heider (1958) has given the example of someone rowing a boat across the stream where the perceiver's evaluation of the actor will depend on the perception of the actor's ability to row, the amount of effort exerted and the external factors such as the wind and the current prevailing at the time. The implication of this for the present context is that a listener can attribute both convergence and non-convergence in a variety of ways. In a follow-up study, Simard, Taylor & Giles (1976) found that the mere perception of convergence was not in itself sufficient to engender positive feelings in the recipients. Listeners who attributed the motives behind another's convergence to them as a desire to break down cultural barriers (so-called internal attribution) perceived this act very favourably. However, when this same shift towards them (actually the use of French by an EC to an FC audience) was attributed externally to some pressures in the situation forcing the speaking to converge, such positive feelings were not so readily evoked. Similarly, when non-convergence (i.e. the maintenance of English by the EC) was externally attributed to situational pressures which demanded own-group language, negative attitudes were not as pronounced as when the behaviour was internally attributed to a lack of effort on the part of the speaker.

1.2. Speech divergence

Thus far, we have considered convergence as an active process while non-convergence has assumed a more passive, subordinate role considered only from the perspective of the decoder. This orientation is unfounded, particularly given that non-convergence (or speech maintenance, see Bourhis 1979) can be used by ethnic groups as a symbolic tactic for maintaining their identity and cultural distinctiveness (Giles 1977b; Giles & Saint-Jacques, 1979; Lambert 1979). This was exemplified recently when for the first time the Arab nations issued their oil communiqué to the world not in English, but in Arabic. Likewise, one witnesses the attempts of many ethnic minorities throughout the world to maintain their own language varieties as an expression of cultural pride, e.g. Québecois, Basques, Catalans, Welsh (Ryan 1979). Moreover, it may well be that under certain conditions people not only want to maintain their own speech styles, but wish to emphasize them in interaction with others. In such cases, speakers may wish to accentuate the linguistic and social differences between themselves and others, perhaps because of the others' outgroup membership, undesirable attitudes, habits or appearance. This process of dissociation, termed divergence (Giles 1973) is, of course, the opposite of convergence in that it involves speakers modifying their speech away from their interlocutors and increasing the communicative distance between them. If both participants in a dyad are similarly dissociatively motivated, then they may be symmetrical in their efforts towards progressive divergence.

To the extent that divergent strategies are probably adopted most often in dyads (or in larger group contexts, see Ros & Giles 1979) where the participants derive from different social or ethnic backgrounds, the incorporation of ideas from Tajfel's (1974, 1978) theory of intergroup relations and social change provides an appropriate framework within which to consider divergence more generally. People do not always react to each other as individuals qua individuals; there are occasions when they react (and are seen to react) to each other as representative members of different social groups. In this vein, Tajfel & Turner (1979) conceived of an interindividual–intergroup continuum, where at one extreme (the interindividual pole) would be found encounters between two or more people which were fully determined by their interpersonal relationships and individual characteristics, and at the other extreme (the intergroup pole) would be encounters which were fully determined by the participants' knowledge of their memberships in contrastive social categories. The more participants in an encounter view the situation as being towards the intergroup end of the continuum 'the more they tend to treat members of the outgroup as undifferentiated items in a unified social category rather than in terms of their individual characteristics' (p. 36). Tajfel's theory, which is concerned with understanding behaviour found at this latter extreme, enables us to predict that the more individuals define situations in intergroup terms and desire to maintain or to achieve a positive social identity, the more likely speech divergence is to occur.[3]

Tajfel describes a sequence of processes simply defined as follows. Social categorization of the world involves knowledge of our membership in certain groups: the values associated with these group memberships (defined as our social identity) have meaning only through social comparison with other groups and form part of the self-concept. Since we seem to derive great satisfaction from possessing a positive social identity, we perceive and act in such a way as to make (or keep) our own social

---

[3] This is not to suggest that definitions of encounters in intergroup terms, particularly amongst speakers possessing inadequate social identities, will not give rise to *convergence* (for a discussion of this issue in terms of 'passing' and 'group assimilation' strategies, see Giles 1978).

group favourably distinct from other groups: a process termed 'psychological distinctiveness'. This means that when a particular group affiliation is important to individuals, and interaction with a member (or members) of a relevant outgroup occurs, the former will attempt to differentiate themselves from the latter on dimensions that they value. Given the importance of language to group identity (see in the ethnic context, Giles, Llado, McKirnan & Taylor 1979; Giles et al. 1976; Taylor 1976), we have argued that language in its broadest sense would be an extremely important dimension along which speakers may wish to differentiate from each other in an intergroup context. By diverging and emphasizing their own language, dialect, slang (Drake 1980), discourse structures or even phrases or isolated words, members of an ingroup can accentuate differences between themselves and the outgroup on a salient and valued dimension of their group identity in order to achieve a positive 'psycholinguistic distinctiveness' (Giles, Bourhis & Taylor 1977).

Bourhis & Giles (1977) designed an experiment to demonstrate the use of *accent* divergence amongst Welsh people in an interethnic context, and to investigate the conditions which would facilitate its occurrence. The study was conducted in a language laboratory where people who placed a strong value on their national group membership and its language were learning the Welsh language (only 26 per cent of Welshmen can speak their national tongue). During one of their weekly sessions, Welshmen were asked to help in a survey concerned with second language learning techniques. The questions in the survey were verbally presented to them in English in their individual booths by a very English-sounding speaker, who at one point arrogantly challenged their reasons for learning what he called 'a dying language with a dismal future'. Such a question was assumed to threaten their feelings of ethnic identity, and the informants broadened their Welsh accents in their replies, compared with their answers to a previously asked, emotionally neutral question. In addition, some informants introduced Welsh words and phrases into their answers while one Welshman did not reply for a while and then was heard to conjugate Welsh verbs very gently into the microphone. Interestingly, even when asked a neutral question beforehand, the informants emphasized their Welsh group membership to the English speaker, in terms of the content of their replies (or 'content differentiation'), demonstrating that psycholinguistic distinctiveness can occur in many different forms. Moreover, it has been shown that certain social groups positively evaluate members of their ingroup who diverge in accent when conversing with speakers from relevant outgroups (Bourhis 1977; Bourhis et al. 1975;

Doise, Sinclair & Bourhis 1976). At the same time, speech divergence from an outgroup member is often, perhaps not surprisingly, viewed negatively as insulting, impolite or hostile (Sandilands & Fleury 1979).

It may well be that there is a hierarchy of strategies of psycholinguistic distinctiveness, some being more symbolic of social dissociation than others. Perhaps from the perspectives of both ingroup speaker and outgroup listener a few pronunciation and content differentiations may be considered as of low level psycholinguistic distinctiveness, whereas various forms of accent and dialect divergences may be considered instances of stronger social dissociations. Verbal abuse and abrasive humour and the maintenance of or switch to another language in the face of an outgroup speaker may be among the most potent forms of psycholinguistic distinctiveness, given their extremely overt, dissociative character.

The notion of *language* divergence was investigated by Bourhis et al. (1979). The study involved different groups of trilingual Flemish students (Flemish–English–French) being recorded in 'neutral' and 'ethnically threatening' encounters with a Francophone (Walloon) outgroup speaker. As in the previous study, the context of the interaction was a language laboratory, where participants were attending classes to improve their English skills. Many Flemish and Francophone students converse together in English, it being an emotionally neutral compromise (cf. Scotton 1979) between maintaining rigid linguistic distinctiveness and acquiescing to pressures to converse by using the other's language. In this experiment, the speaker spoke to students in English, although revealing himself as a Walloon by means of distinctive Francophone pronunciations in that language. It was found that when the speaker demeaned the Flemish in his ethnically threatening question, listeners rated him as sounding more Francophone (a process termed 'perceptual divergence'), and themselves as feeling more Flemish, than when a neutral question was asked. This cognitive dissociation was manifested behaviourally at a covert level by means of muttered or whispered disapproval whilst the Walloon was speaking which was tape recorded, unknown to the informants, and at an overt level through divergent shifts to own-group language (Flemish). However, this divergence only occurred under certain specific, experimental conditions and then for only 50 per cent of the sample. It was found that only when their own group membership and that of the speaker was emphasized by the investigator, and when the speaker had been known from the outset to be hostile to Flemish ethnolinguistic goals did these listeners diverge in language when they spoke. In a follow-up study, however, language divergence into Flemish did occur for nearly 100 per cent of the informants under these same conditions, but only when the Walloon speaker himself diverged into French in his threatening question. Interestingly, the form of the language divergence in the first of these Belgian studies differed from that in the second. It was found that in the former, the ingroup first replied to the outgroup threat in English; and then switched into Flemish. In the latter (more threatening situation), listeners replied in a directly divergent manner by a complete shift into Flemish. A study by Taylor & Royer (1980) has also examined language divergence, this time in the context of Québec. They found that FC subjects who were led to believe that they would meet an Anglophone who was in total disagreement with their ethnolinguistic values anticipated speaking more French than did a matched group of FCs who expected to be conversing with an EC who completely agreed with their language views. Interestingly, individual's anticipated divergence was accentuated for the former group of subjects after they had discussed their probable language behaviours towards the EC in the context of a *group* discussion. Post-experimentally, Taylor & Royer also investigated, by means of a questionnaire, the FCs' own rationales for anticipating their language strategies, which confirmed the notion that speech divergence is strongly related to manifestations of positive ethnic identity. Language divergence, then, like convergence, can take on many forms and may, of course, be influenced by a number of factors that we have discussed elsewhere, including the perceived legitimacy–illegitimacy of the intergroup status positions for ingroup members, the perceived strength of ingroup and outgroup boundaries, as well as the perceived socio-structural factors operating on both groups, and the speakers' intragroup status and identification with other meaningful social categories (see Giles 1978, 1979; Giles & Johnson 1981).

In a number of situations a speaker might, with a mind to being intentionally ambiguous, attempt to converge with regard to one linguistic feature (e.g. speech rate), while not converging, or even diverging, on another (e.g. pronunciation). An example of this can be found in Montréal, where, on occasions, FC shoppers have been known to address Anglophone store assistants in fluent English while requesting the services of a Francophone assistant instead. This is an instance of convergence in terms of linguistic form, but psychologically the message content is, of course, one of social dissociation. Holt (1973) describes a similar phenomenon (which she calls 'linguistic inversion') by reference to certain terms used by black slaves in the United States in the last century. The meaning of many phrases and words (e.g. *nigger*) when said to a White was quite different (and even positive among the ingroup) from anything the outgroup would ever have imagined. In fact, Blacks often used phrases that would have seemed to Whites to be overtly convergent, but that for other Blacks in the situation would indicate covert divergence.

Finally, and in complete contrast, simultaneous shifts away from and towards the other in a dyad can occur in ways that can be regarded as totally integrative for both participants. This occurs in many role-defined situations where a status or power discrepancy exists in a dyad, such as between doctor and patient, and employer and employee. The acceptance of the role differentiation by the participants will, of course, be manifested behaviourally. Someone entering an interaction where they accept a subordinate role will signal this by modifying his or her speech patterns in a complementary way to that of the other. Such speech shifts have been termed instances of 'speech complementarity' and can be regarded as divergence in a simple descriptive linguistic sense, yet psychologically may involve acceptance of the situation rather than dissociation (Giles 1980). Classic examples of speech complementarity might be when two young people are out on a date. Each accentuates their respective masculine and feminine qualities by means of linguistic as well as non-linguistic strategies. This does not, however, preclude the possibility of convergence simultaneously occurring on other linguistic dimensions. For instance, a woman may adopt a soft voice and certain paralinguistic and intonational features with an eligible bachelor lawyer, yet wish to gain his attraction, approval and respect by not only fulfilling her feminine role requirements but also by converging to his higher prestige dialect.

1.3. Speech accommodation theory: propositions, status considerations and pilot data

In summary, speech accommodation theory proposes that:

1. People are more likely to converge towards the speech patterns of their recipients when they desire their approval and when the perceived costs for doing so are proportionally lower than the anticipated rewards.
2. The magnitude of speech convergence will be a function of the extent of the speakers' repertoires and of the factors (personality and environmental) increasing the need for approval.

3. Speech convergence will be positively evaluated by recipients when the resultant behaviour is perceived to be at an optimal sociolinguistic distance from them and is attributed positive intent.
4. People will be more likely to maintain their speech patterns or even diverge them away from those of their interlocutors either when they define the encounter in intergroup terms and desire a positive ingroup identity, or when they wish to dissociate personally from another in an interindividual encounter.
5. The magnitude of speech divergence will be a function of the extent of the speakers' repertoires as well as of contextual factors increasing the salience of group identification and the desire for a positive ingroup identity, or undesirable characteristics of another in an interindividual encounter.
6. Speech maintenance and divergence will be unfavourably evaluated by recipients when they attribute them with negative intent, but favourably evaluated by observers of the encounter who define the interaction in intergroup terms and who share a common, positively valued group membership with the speaker.

Most of the *empirical* work relating to speech accommodation theory has centred around interactions with people of equal status, leaving encounters involving participants of unequal status unexamined. This seems an important oversight since many everyday interactions involve people of differential status, and this dimension was accorded important theoretical influence in the theory itself (see above p. 209). The remainder of this chapter reports on studies which were designed to rectify the situation and whose findings, as we will see, have significant implications for the further development of speech accommodation theory.

A review of the literature reveals that the effects of status differences between dyadic partners on speech measures have attracted rather little research attention (see Jablin 1979). Studies have shown that high and low status speakers adopt different address forms (Brown & Gilman 1960; Brown & Levinson 1979; Lambert & Tucker 1976), communicative styles (Alkire et al. 1968) and amounts of verbal productivity (Siegman, Pope & Blass 1969). Interestingly, Good (1979) has suggested that in some situations, particularly casual contexts, an equal distibution of power and status is essential for effective communication to occur. Good discusses the way in which interlocutors attempt to maintain equal status (to achieve what he terms the 'parity principle') by recourse to various linguistic and discourse strategies. Of course, the reasons why interactants may wish to maintain differential status can be manifold. One reason of interest to us has been the attainment of a common goal or solution. Encounters involving such an orientation (hitherto termed 'co-operative') between people of differential status, and in the following cases different roles, would be professor–lecturer, lecturer–student, ward sister–student nurse, doctor–patient, etc. (cf. Brown & Fraser 1979; Giles 1980; Miller & Steinberg 1975; Watzlawick, Beavin & Jackson 1967). In co-operative relationships, both interlocutors make genuine attempts to contribute to the attainment of the common goal. What A does fits in with what B does, but is essentially different from it. This pattern of behaviour is based on the acceptance and enjoyment of difference (Grush, Clore & Costin 1975) and does not function without the consensus of the participants involved. Given the interlocking nature of the co-operative relationship, one partner does not impose his demands on the other, but rather each behaves in a manner which presupposes their common definition of the situation (cf. Blakar in press) whilst at the same time providing a reason for the behaviour of the other. How can such interactions be analysed in psychological and linguistic terms? Some insight into the possible speech modifications of interlocutors can be derived from speech accommodation theory. This would predict that if high and low status individuals wish to co-operate, gain each other's social approval and attain a high level of communicational efficiency, mutual convergence would occur. However, it would be predicted that the lower status speaker would converge more in the direction of the higher status speaker, rather than vice versa, given their supposed differential desires for each other's approval.

These predictions were put to the empirical test in two pilot studies which had, in addition, two further aims. First, to observe in global terms the effects of differential status upon speech dimensions. As there is little published work in this domain, it seemed worthwhile to get the 'feel' of what may be happening psychologically and linguistically in such dyads. Secondly, to determine which speech dimensions are most influenced by status manipulations and thereby select the appropriate dependent measures for the investigation proper. In the first pilot study, 4-minute recordings were made of two female students in equal status and unequal status conditions (ES and US respectively).[4] In the ES condition, the speakers discussed topics for which they had previously been given

---

[4] A number of different dyads were in fact recorded under these conditions. The one ultimately chosen seemed to us to be typical of the others, clearest in acoustic quality as well as 'natural' in conversational structure.

similar ratings of knowledge and competency (e.g. films and music), whilst in the US condition the same speakers discussed topics on which one of them had been given superior ratings (e.g. biological issues). Twenty-six listeners rated these two taped conversations in terms of the speakers' behaviours on a number of linguistic dimensions (pitch, speech rate, pronunciation, enunciation) and psychological dimensions (e.g. competence, knowledge, anxiety). The results showed that relative to their performance in ES, speakers in the US condition were judged to differ in their speech rates and pronunciations as well as in their levels of knowledge and perceived status ($p < 0.01$).

The second pilot study involved 3-minute recordings of twenty dental students representing two levels of experience in the subject. Two conditions were used. In one of them, the baseline monologue condition, each subject was recorded individually talking into the microphone about biological issues. In the second condition, subjects were paired together on the basis of their clinical experience to discuss and reach some agreement about certain orthodontic and prosthetic issues: each pair had a high and low status participant. Two linguistically naïve raters evaluated edited 30-second samples of each individual's speech in the baseline and the dialogue conditions on the same scales that were used in the first pilot study. The results showed a similar pattern as before, but this time they demonstrated more clearly that when two people of differential status interact to achieve a mutual goal, they diverge in their speech rates, as judged by the independent judges. More specifically, it was found that the high status speakers decreased their speech rates, whilst the low status speakers increased them, compared to their performances in the baseline condition ($p < 0.01$). In addition, there was a strong though non-significant tendency for the high status speakers to be judged to have become less standard in their accents, whilst the low status persons were judged to have standardized them. For the speech rate and pronunciation dimensions, the interrater reliabilities were 0.53 and 0.93 ($p < 0.01$) (for further discussion see Thakerar, 1981).

These pilot studies tested predictions from speech accommodation theory which suggest that mutual convergence would occur in dyads where interlocutors of different status are interacting to attain a mutual goal. However, the results have not confirmed the hypotheses. Participants appeared to linguistically *diverge* in speech rates and possibly in pronunciation also. In the light of these findings, it appears necessary to distinguish, as in table 1, the psychological from the linguistic processes. Such a distinction has always been implicit in discussions of speech

Table 1. *Linguistic and psychological dichotomies of speech accommodation*

| | | Linguistic | |
		Convergence	Divergence
Psychological	Convergence	A	B
	Divergence	C	D

accommodation theory (e.g. Giles 1980), but it has never been system-atized formally before. The psychological dimension refers to speakers' social motivations with respect to their interlocutors, whereas the linguistic dimension refers to the former's speech behaviour in relation to the latter. More specifically, psychological convergence and divergence can be defined as individuals' *beliefs* that they are integrating with and dif-ferentiating from others respectively, while linguistic convergence and divergence can be defined as individuals' speech shifts towards and away from others respectively. Indeed, previous work has mostly been con-cerned with the assumption that linguistic convergence equals psycho-logical integration, and linguistic divergence equals psychological dif-ferentiation (i.e. cells A and D in table 1). However, our pilot data suggest that linguistic divergence can occur in the context of psychological con-vergence under certain conditions (cell B), and it is also plausible, as mentioned previously, that linguistic convergence can under certain conditions be a manifestation of psychological divergence (cell C). In the remainder of the chapter, we shall maintain our focus on the effects of differential status on accommodative behaviour whilst attempting to provide stronger evidence for the existence of cell B phenomena. The hy-potheses for the studies which follow were formulated on the strength of the pilot findings, as was our decision to study further the speech rate and pronunciation dimensions (Giles & Smith 1979; Siegman & Feldstein 1978).

2. Status effects on speech rate and pronunciation: two studies

2.1. A first study of status effects

This study was concerned primarily with testing the following new hypothesis: compared to the ES condition, interlocutors in US would diverge from each other in terms of speech rate and pronunciation; high status speakers would decrease their speech rate and non-standardize their accents, whilst lower status speakers would increase their rates of speech and standardize their accents.

Secondary aims of the study were to investigate: (a) the extent to which speakers were aware of their own linguistic adjustments; (b) listeners' perceptions and evaluations of linguistic shifts in co-operative interaction; and (c) some objective linguistic correlates of divergent behaviour.

Method. The study was divided into three phases. In the first phase, 5-minute tape recordings were made of subjects talking in both ES and US conditions. The main focus of attention was on a group of State Enrolled Nurses (SENs) who were chosen from the population studied (see below). Subsequently, these same subjects rated their own performances. In the second phase, a panel of linguistically naïve subjects (henceforth termed 'listeners') evaluated edited samples of the speeches. The last phase attempted to provide a less subjective analysis of the edited taped performances using an objective speech rate measure and a phonological analysis of a socially significant consonant variable (namely glottal stop in place of final /t/). The procedures for Phases 1 and 2 will be described before introducing an overview of the findings emerging from Phases 2 and 3.

Phase 1. The speakers were 56 female nurses between the ages of 18 and 29 years, chosen randomly from the population of nurses at a local city hospital. Of these, 14 were student learner nurses (SLNs), constituting a low status group, 28 were State Enrolled Nurses (SENs), comprising a medium status group and 14 were State Registered Nurses (SRNs), the highest status group. Previous work had indicated a clear perception of status differences as described above within the nursing profession (Skevington 1980). SRNs are accorded higher status than SENs not only because of their higher entrance requirements, but also because they can ultimately reach more prestigious positions, e.g. sister-in-charge.

Prior to the experiment, contact between any of the individual nurses had been minimal. Materials consisted of discussion topics which were chosen with the help of the Assistant Nursing Director and which made the status differences between the nurses more explicit. Their speech was recorded on a stereophonic reel-to-reel recorder. The experimental design is presented in table 2.

Phase 1 was divided into two conditions: first, 28 SENs were tape recorded in pairs discussing a given topic (should unconscious patients over the age of 60 be resuscitated?), where all concerned were similarly competent (baseline, ES condition); secondly, they were recorded in a US condition, which was another unstructured dialogue requiring two speakers to discuss the topic together. In the second condition, half of the

Table 2. *Experimental design: first study*

Status	NURSES			
	SRN (N = 14)	SEN (N = 14)	SEN (N = 14)	SLN (N = 14)
Phase 1 Equal		ES ←————————→	ES	
Phase 2 Unequal	HS ←————————→	LS	HS ←————————→	LS

ES = equal status; HS = high status;
LS = low status, ←————————→ = interaction

SENs each took part in a discussion with a different SLN on a topic favouring the greater competence of SENs (how best to prepare a patient for a major operation). This was the HS condition. The remaining 14 SENs were each assigned a different SRN as an interlocutor on a topic favouring the supervisory status of SRNs (how best to organize a day-ward). This was the LS condition. Subsequently, all SENs filled in a response questionnaire which required them to rate on 7cm continuous lines their performances in each dyadic situation on seven psychological dimensions, namely, competitiveness (high–low), acceptance of situation as fair and just (readily–reluctantly), confidence (high–low), overall feeling (at ease–tense), competent and knowledgeable (high–low), sympathetic–unsympathetic, and status (high–low), plus two linguistic dimensions, speech rate (fast–slow) and pronunciation (standard–non-standard). Speakers had not been informed of the fact that they were to be required to fill out a set of questionnaires concerning their performances, so as to avoid a determined effort on their part to monitor or to memorize their verbal and non-verbal responses.

Phase 2. The listeners were 15 first year female nursing students, aged between 18 and 22 years, chosen randomly from the same population as the speakers. A stimulus tape was prepared by editing approximately 30 seconds of each SEN's speech in the ES and US conditions, and 30 seconds of each SLN's and SRN's speech in the second of these conditions. This provided a total of 56 sets of stimulus voices randomized across speakers which were rated individually by the listeners on the same 9 scales used by the speakers. The listeners were not informed of the existence of different categories of nurses on tape nor of the fact that each speaker supposedly held a different status on two occasions. Moreover, these voice samples were edited so that inferences regarding speaker status could not be made from speech *content* cues. In other words, if any rating differences did emerge, they would be the result of various para-linguistic, prosodic and phonological features. The stimulus tape was presented to listeners through stereo headphones, and the total rating time, including a post-judgment discussion, was one and a half hours. Although this was a very lengthy procedure, the listeners did not claim to be too bored or fatigued.

Results and discussion. The SEN speakers' ratings of their own perform-ance and the listeners' judgments of the SENs' speech were analysed separately. For both sets of data, separate 2 × 2 (status: HS–LS vs. con-dition: ES–US) split-plot analyses of variances were conducted on each of the nine dependent measures. However, in the listeners' case, both speakers and listeners were treated as random effects which necessitated the computation of estimation of F ratio (quasi F (F′)) from the expected values of the mean squares and its degrees of freedom, approximated to the nearest integral value (Winer 1971: 375–8). Quasi Fs were computed in order to ensure that the results could be generalized to populations of both speakers and listeners. Separate one-way ANOVAs on all depen-dent measures were also performed with the appropriate F′ procedure to determine differences between high status SENs' and SLNs' perform-ances and between low status SENs' and SRNs' performances. To attain a more conservative measure, Scheffé's procedure was followed where appropriate (Snedecor & Cochran 1967: 271) to guard against compar-isons appearing significant by reason of their size.

Let us deal first with the SENs' self-ratings. An interaction effect between status and condition ($F = 32.15$, df $= 1,28$, p. < 0.01) confirmed that the experimental manipulation of ES and US conditions was success-ful in terms of the speakers' own definitions of the situations. In the ES condition, as might be expected, no differences were reported in per-ceived status, whereas in the US condition, HS speakers rated themselves as higher in status than LS speakers. In addition, main effects for con-dition emerged for the acceptance of situation ($F = 23.98$, df $= 1,28$, p < 0.01) and competitiveness ($F = 24.36$, df $= 1,28$, p < 0.01) scales indicating that both groups of SENs, irrespective of their statuses, considered the US condition to be more acceptable and legitimate but less competitive than the ES condition. No significant effects in the case of speakers' ratings of their own linguistic performances on the two specified scales emerged, suggesting that, in retrospect, the SENs were unaware of any changes in their speech rates or pronunciations.

Several significant differences emerged in the listeners' ratings of the

SENs' speech on both the psychological and the linguistic measures.[5] An interaction effect ($F' = 81.23$, df = 1,30, $p < 0.01$) between status and condition on the perceived status of speakers measure indicated that in the ES condition no differences emerged, as again might be expected, whereas in the US condition, the HS speaker was perceived higher in status than the LS speaker. Main effects for condition were obtained for the measures of competitiveness ($F' = 93.33$, df = 1,28, $p < 0.01$) and acceptance of situation ($F' = 129.13$, df = 1,35, $p < 0.01$), showing that interlocutors were judged to be less competitive and to have more readily accepted the situation as legitimate in the US than in the ES condition. These findings of course mirror the SENs' own self-perceptions as reported above. In addition, however, interaction effects ($p < 0.01$) between status of SEN and condition were found for the dimensions of confidence ($F' = 124.64$, df = 1,31), overall feeling ($F' = 192.52$, df = 1,40), competence and knowledgeability ($F' = 121.05$, df = 1,40) and sympathy ($F' = 57.06$, df = 1,20), indicating that differences were not perceived between the HS and LS speakers in the ES but that they were in the US condition. More specifically, HS speakers were judged to have been more confident, relaxed, competent and more sympathetic towards their partners in the US than in the ES condition, whilst in contrast the LS SENs were viewed as being more tense, less confident and were judged as less sympathetic towards their partners in the US than the ES conditions.

Interaction effects between status and condition also emerged for the speech rate ($F' = 338.75$, df = 1,40) and pronunciation ($F' = 212.98$, df = 1,34) measures. These interactions are schematically presented in figure 1 and indicate that no differences were perceived between the HS and LS SENs' speech in the ES condition, but that they were in the US condition. The HS speakers were perceived to have significantly slowed down their speech rates and to have non-standardized their accent in the US condition, whereas the LS nurses increased their speech rates and standardized their accents. As we shall see later, these perceived shifts were validated and in some ways specified more distinctly by more objective analyses conducted on the SENs' speech in Phase 3.

Similar patterns of perceptions and evaluations appear when the SLNs' and SRNs' data are brought into focus. Significant differences appeared in the ratings of LS SENs' and their SRN partners' speech in the US

---

[5] From the analyses, it is evident that the interaction effects between the variables are consistently greater than their separate main effects. The observed large F' ratios for these interactions suggest that linear effects relative to interactions account for substantially *less* of the variance in the data.

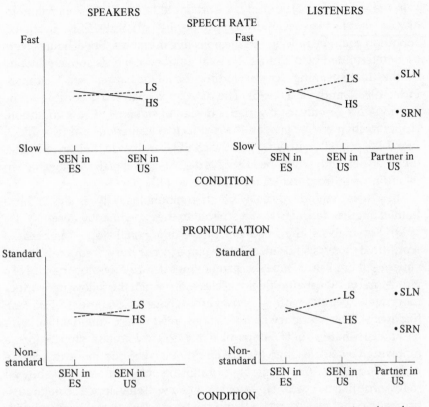

Figure 1. Schematic representation of perceived speech rate and pronunciation of speakers across equal status (ES) and unequal status (US) phases (LS = low status; HS = high status; SEN = State Enrolled Nurse; SLN = Student Learner Nurse; SRN =State Registered Nurse)

condition (p < 0.01). SRNs were perceived to be more confident (F′ = 69.01, df = 1,34), relaxed (F′ = 46.02, df = 1,38), competent (F′ = 95.8, df = 1,39) and were viewed as more sympathetic towards their partners (F′ = 93.51, df = 1,26). As will be appreciated from figure 1, SRNs were perceived to be speaking more slowly (F′ = 175.32, df = 1,26) and with a more non-standard accent (F′ = 60.68, df = 1,27) than the LS SENs. Differences also emerged between the ratings of HS SENs' and their SLN partners' speech in the US condition (p < 0.01); SLNs were perceived to be more tense (F′ = 64.33, df = 1,38), less confident (F′ = 22.49, df = 1,42), less competent (F′ = 86.78, df = 1,35) and were viewed as being less sympathetic towards their partner (F′ = 55.59, df = 1,36). On the linguistic measures, the SLNs were judged to be speaking faster (F′ = 126.91, df = 1,38) and with a more standard accent (F′ = 47.18, df = 1,38).

In the last phase of the study, we attempted to see if these perceptions of what in effect is speech divergence on the part of the SENs in the US condition could be reflected in the objective measures. Speech rates were then determined by counting the total number of words spoken divided by the total speaking time excluding the silent pauses (see Goldman-Eisler 1968; Smith et al. 1975). The data were analysed according to the previous 2 × 2 analysis of variance design of status of SEN × condition. An interaction effect between the two factors again emerged (F = 77.73, df = 1,26, p < 0.01) showing that the LS SENs increased their speech rates (by 47.20 per cent) while the HS SENs decreased theirs (by 46.46 per cent) when moving from the ES into the US condition.

The SENs' edited voices were then phonologically analysed by a trained linguist, Jenny Cheshire, 'blind' to the experimental design (Giles 1973). For analysis, the frequency of use of a glottal stop [ʔ] in place of word-final /t/ was chosen. Glottal stops occur very frequently in all varieties of English. RP speakers sometimes use a glottal stop in place of a word-final or morpheme-final voiceless stop when the following word or morpheme begins with a consonant (Gimson 1962), e.g. *that man* [ðæʔmæn]. This tendency is more widespread in most regional varieties of English; here, glottal stops also replace a voiceless stop before a following vowel, although less frequently than before a following consonant. Trudgill's (1974) study of the English spoken in Norwich showed that word-final or morpheme-final /t/ was a well-developed sociolinguistic variable that was correlated with the social class of speakers and with their speech style. Middle-class speakers used fewer glottal stops than working-class speakers, and speakers of all social classes used more glottal stops when they were speaking in a relaxed and informal situation than when they were speaking in more formal contexts. Other surveys carried out in other parts of Britain confirm that the use of glottal stops in word-final and morpheme-final positions is correlated with the social class of the speaker and with speech style (see e.g. Macaulay 1977; Petyt 1977). The linguistic analysis of the present data showed (see table 3) that compared to the ES condition, HS SENs used more glottal stops than LS SENs in the US condition, both before a vowel (χ^2 = 9.96, df = 2, p < 0.01) and before a consonant (χ^2 = 12.16, df = 2, p. < 0.01). This can be seen as confirming the subjective reactions of the listeners. The fact that more HS nurses used an increased number of word-final glottal stops in the US situation (relative to the ES situation) than their LS counterparts suggests that they were more relaxed in that situation, and that the LS nurses were less relaxed.

Table 3. *Number of high status (HS) and low status (LS) State Enrolled Nurses (SENs) using different frequencies of glottal stops(2) before a vowel (—V) and a consonant (—C) in equal status (ES) and unequal status (US) phases*

	Before vowels			Before consonants		
	2 same in ES & US	2 increase in US	2 decrease in US	2 same in ES & US	2 increase in US	2 decrease in US
HS SEN	2	9	3	–	13	1
LS SEN	5	1	8	1	4	9

Thus, the hypotheses predicting that mutual divergence in terms of speech rate and pronunciation would occur in dyads where participants of different statuses interact to achieve a mutual goal were fully supported both by listeners' reactions to the speakers as well as by more objective analyses of the data. It was found that relative to ES, HS speakers in US diverged away from their interlocutors (SLNs in this case) by slowing down their speech rates and by non-standardizing their accents, whereas LS speakers under the same conditions increased their rates of speech and standardized their accents, thereby diverging from their interlocutors (SRNs). With respect to the perceived psychological dimensions, HS speakers in the US condition were judged to have become more confident, relaxed, competent and sympathetic towards their partners than in the ES condition, whereas the LS speakers were judged to have done the opposite. Moreover, speakers were perceived to have judged the US situation as more acceptable psychologically and as more legitimate than the ES encounter.[6] In terms of the secondary aims of the investigation, we have afforded speech accommodation theory some linguistic precision for the first time and produced evidence that often speakers themselves are completely unaware of shifts in their speech styles across two conditions (cf. Berger 1980; Nisbett & Wilson 1977). The fact that speakers themselves failed to report changes in their own speech, but listeners detected changes which were also objectively demonstrated, is a salutary warning against blind optimism that

[6] Although it could be claimed that an order effect could be responsible, at least in part, for these findings, we cannot afford any credence to the view that discussing a second topic per se can account for the emergence of mutual divergence in the US condition. Indeed, the results of the second study lend strong support to this contention. At the same time, it is reasonable to assume that particular experiences of the LS and HS participants occurring immediately prior to their interaction are likely to affect the magnitude, and perhaps even the nature, of the speech strategies they adopt.

speakers' accounts are the best guide to understanding their speech behaviour.

2.2. A replication with extensions

Thus, we have further and more concrete data demonstrating the existence of cell B, table 1. However, before attempting to explain this phenomenon by elaborating the boundaries of speech accommodation theory, it seemed wise to collect more concrete data under different circumstances, not only in order to justify a theoretical reformulation but also to make it ultimately more viable. The study reported above, Investigation 1, had provided data about mutual speech divergences under the following three constraints. First, divergence had been measured in terms of the speakers' speech in the ES condition compared to their speech in the US condition but with *different* individuals. Secondly, given that each of the 30-second speech samples in the US condition (and in the ES condition) had been edited out of different sections of the entire 5-minute conversation, it was not possible to locate precisely when the divergence occurred. In other words, we do not know whether speakers diverged immediately upon confronting the US condition, or whether they did so later on when the interaction got more underway. Thirdly, the status manipulation, while admittedly being perceived as acceptable and legitimate by the subjects, was nevertheless imposed upon them by the investigators. In many situations of course, status relations between two people have to be negotiated by them, and in any case are in some instances being constantly modified (Blakar in press; Good 1979; Scotton 1980). This second investigation, therefore, was concerned with developmental issues, both by measuring potential divergences at more than one point in time after status differences had been established between the interactants, and also by studying the linguistic manifestations of the prior status negotiation process which led up to the mutual acceptance of status differences by the speakers. More particularly, the study was designed to explore the following issues: would divergence as previously obtained in Investigation 1 still emerge when the same interactants who had been in an ES condition were confronted with a co-operative situation where they held differential status? Is divergence more or less likely to emerge at the beginning or at the end of such encounters? What are some of the speech correlates of a conversation where the speakers are attempting to negotiate their relative statuses?

Method. This study was divided into two phases. In the first phase, recordings were made of dyads in three different 6-minute discussion sessions, where speakers were encouraged to provide solutions to problems related to tasks they had undertaken. In Session 1 they held ES, in Session 2 they had to negotiate their relative statuses, and in Session 3 they then held US on the basis of this negotiation. In the second phase of the investigation, a group of linguistically naïve listeners evaluated edited samples of each discussant's voice from the different sessions in which they had been engaged.

Phase 1. Speakers were thirty first year female undergraduate students, aged between 18 and 20 years. Materials consisted of a block-design task which required subjects to make designs from patterns increasing in difficulty, with four, nine and sixteen wooden blocks. Speakers interacted in pairs in three different sessions. In each, they first had to perform a block-design task and then discuss it for 6 minutes, during which their speeches were recorded, and at the end of which participants rated their own and their partner's status on a continuum, high to low. In *Session 1*, participants independently solved a simple, four block-design task and subsequently discussed with another subject who had completed the task 'the various strategies of solving the task'. Since both members of the dyad had had the same amount of practice and had successfully completed the task, an ES condition was assumed (and later confirmed by means of their self-ratings). In *Session 2*, each member of the dyad was tested separately, and her performance timed on a nine block-design task. On completion they were informed that although both had successfully completed the task, only one of them had in fact done so in the standard time set and was therefore far superior at co-ordination tasks (and, implicitly, intelligence-related tasks) than the other. This was a manipulation induced to create perceived differences in their status relevant skills. They then discussed the question 'which of you is better at co-ordination tasks and what strategy was used to complete the task quickly?' In this session, then, they had to negotiate their relative competences at co-ordination tasks and to reach agreement about their relative abilities (and statuses). Each dyad did in fact reach agreement about the superior performance of one of the members, which, interestingly enough, did not necessarily bear any relationship to their actual relative performances. Nevertheless, this agreement about relative competency was reflected in their ratings of their own and the other's status ($t = 2.37$, $df = 28$, $p < 0.01$), and on this basis, subjects were accorded either high or low status within the dyad. In *Session 3*, they had to solve a sixteen block-design task together, after which they discussed the 'advantages and disadvantages of various strategies in solving such a task' with a view to agreeing upon the best strategy to adopt.

Phase 2. Listeners were ten female undergraduates from the same population as the speakers. A stimulus tape, which was played to the listeners over stereo headphones, was prepared as follows. Each discussion session was sub-divided into initial (first 3 minutes) and final (last 3 minutes) sections, from each of which speech extracts of approximately 20 seconds were edited out for each speaker. As in Investigation 1, listeners were not informed about the nature of the experimental design, and in this instance were told simply that they would hear six samples of speech from each of thirty different speakers. Once again, an attempt was made to control for content cues of speaker status. The listeners heard the six voice samples of any one speaker in succession before moving on to the next speaker and were required to rate each sample separately. The voice samples were presented in random order for each speaker and the speakers themselves were randomized across the stimulus tape. This provided a total of 180 voice samples to be rated separately on eight of the dimensions used in Investigation 1. The total experimental time for Phase 2 listeners including debriefing was two and a half hours.

Results and discussion. Listeners' ratings for each of the eight dependent measures were analysed separately in a $2 \times 3 \times 2$ (status: high–low $\times$ session: ES–negotiation–US $\times$ section: initial–final) analysis of variance with repeated measures on the last two factors. Main effects for status, session and section were qualified by interaction effects between them (for details, see Thakerar 1981). Results indicated that except for the dimension of acceptance of situation, where a session $\times$ section interaction effect emerged ($F = 254.16$, df $= 2,18$, $p < 0.01$), three-way interactions ($p < 0.01$)[7] were obtained: speech rate ($F = 270.26$, df $= 2,18$), pronunciation ($F = 338.54$), overall feeling ($F = 255.99$), sympathy ($F = 115.1$), relative status ($F = 247.5$), confidence ($F = 163.11$) and acceptance of situation ($F = 5.22$, df $= 2,18$, $p < 0.05$). In order to determine more fully these foregoing effects of status on listeners' judgments in different sessions and between sections, further comparisons between cell means were carried out and will be considered session by session below; all t values reported are $p < 0.01$. Figure 2 graphically represents listeners' ratings of the speakers' perceived speech rates and pronunciations and may aid assimilation of the findings to be outlined.

[7] The reader is referred to note 5 above, the content of which also applies in these cases.

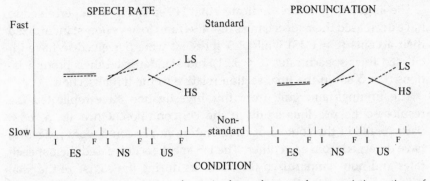

Figure 2. Schematic representation of perceived speech rate and pronunciation ratings of speakers across initial (I) and final (F) sections of each of the three sessions (LS = low status; HS = high status; ES = equal status; NS = negotiating status; US = unequal status)

Session 1: ES condition. No significant differences between pairs of means across any of the sections emerged, suggesting that speakers were not perceived to have changed their patterns of speech nor impressions during the interaction.

Session 2: negotiation condition. Significant shifts from section 1 to 2 emerged for both participants on the dimensions of competitiveness (HS t = 6.26, LS t = 6.39, df = 18) and acceptance of situation (HS t = 4.88, LS t = 5.47), indicating that compared to the initial section speakers were perceived to have been more competitive and to have less readily accepted the situation as legitimate in the final section. LS speakers were perceived as less sympathetic (t = 3.37), whereas HS were perceived as being more confident (t = 4.60) and as having higher status than LS speakers (t = 11.32) in the final rather than the initial sections. On the linguistic dimensions, HS speakers (but not LS speakers) were judged to have become more standard accented (t = 5.83) and faster in speech rate (t = 5.56) from initial to final section.

Session 3: US condition. Significant shifts from section 1 to 2 emerged for both participants on the dimensions of competitiveness (HS t = 11.42, LS t = 9.64) and acceptance of situation (HS t 6.98, LS t = 5.94), indicating that speakers were perceived to have been less competitive and as having more readily accepted the situation as legitimate in the final section rather than in the initial section. Significant differences emerged for the dimensions of confidence (t = 10.19), overall feeling (t = 10.27), status (t = 11.12) and sympathy (t = 6.86) showing that HS persons in the final section were judged to have been more confident, relaxed and sympathetic towards their partners, and as having a higher status than LS persons.

The linguistic measures indicated that HS speakers were perceived to have decreased their speech rates ($t = 4.94$) and to have non-standardized their accents ($t = 6.13$) whilst LS speakers were perceived to have increased their speech rates ($t = 5.21$) and standardized their pronunciations ($t = 5.03$) in the final section relative to the initial section.

The findings emerging from this investigation have replicated the results of the previous study in the US condition. Once again, both participants in the context of co-operation in Session 3 were judged to have diverged from each other. The HS speakers decreased their speech rates and non-standardized their accents during the course of the final session, whilst the LS speakers increased their rates of speaking and standardized their accents. Moreover, this mutual divergence was complemented by the interactants being judged as less competitive and to have more readily accepted the situation as legitimate in the final section than in the initial section of the US condition, with the HS speakers being perceived as correspondingly more confident and relaxed, and as more sympathetic towards their partners than LS speakers.

The results of the status negotiation session (i.e. Session 2) underlined the fact that the same speech features function in different ways, depending on the purpose of the interaction (Argyle 1980; Brown & Fraser 1979). In this session (see figure 2), both participants increased their speech rates and standardized their pronunciations, yet only in the case of the speakers who ultimately assumed the higher status positions were those trends significant. In this more competitive session, where participants were vying for relative superiority or status over each other, it can be seen that both participants were adopting speech styles that would enhance their perceived competences by increasing their speech rates (Brown 1980; Brown, Strong & Rencher 1975) and by standardizing their accents (Giles & Powesland 1975; Ryan 1979; Ryan & Giles 1982). In future research it would be interesting to determine whether this linguistic phenomenon that we term 'speech competitiveness' is a dependent variable of the negotiation process or whether it is itself an independent variable influencing the negotiation process; obviously, it is possible that both were happening (cf. Giles, Hewstone and St Clair in press).

It is interesting to note that in Sessions 2 and 3 (and of course in the initial section as well) no significant differences emerged between the judged performances of either speaker in the initial sections of the session. Although previous studies which have investigated language behaviours over a series of interactive sessions between the same speakers have found differences between the initial sections of the encounters, the situational definitions of each of them were likely to have been viewed as very similar by the participants (Lennard & Bernstein 1960; Welkowitz & Feldstein 1970). Not so in our present investigation where the perceived relationship and function of the dialogue was changing from session to session. Under such conditions of potential uncertainty about how best to negotiate each encounter, both speakers appear to have opted 'for the security' of a standard, baseline speech style (at least in terms of speech rate and pronunciation) for the commencement of each session. The data indicated that differences accrued *during* the session, and more specifically after the first three minutes of the conversation, in this particular context. Thus, Investigation 2 within the terms of its own situational constraints has suggested that divergence takes place in the latter half of a short dialogue. This finding then affords more credence to the view espoused earlier that there may be optimal *rates* of speech accommodation.

3. Towards an understanding of linguistic divergence and psychological convergence

Having now established the phenomenon of apparent linguistic divergence coupled with psychological convergence, how can we explain it? In an attempt to do just this, we wish to re-introduce notions of similarity–attraction and ally them with a more functional approach to speech shifts. Grush et al. (1975) found that similarity along certain behavioural dimensions does not always lead to attraction as proposed by the earlier versions of similarity–attraction research. Indeed, positive *dis*similarities, i.e. differences on task-relevant traits in complementary role situations, seemed to mediate attraction. Analogous processes may be operative in the US conditions of our two investigations as well. Since both interlocutors differed in status, they may both have expected each other to have different speech patterns reflecting this disparity. Thus, on the basis of research mentioned earlier linking perceived status and competence with accent (Giles & Powesland 1975; Ryan 1979) and speech rate (Brown 1980), it may well be that speech stereotypes exist such that high status speakers are expected to talk with a standard accent and at a fast rate whilst low status speakers are expected to talk with a more non-standard accent and slower. Hence, the speakers in our investigations may not only have been converging psychologically towards their partners but may also have been attempting to converge linguistically to what they *believed* the speech of the other to be. That is, the lower status speaker increased her speech rate and standardized her accent to comply with the speech stereotype associated with a higher status speaker, whereas the higher status speaker decreased her speech rate and became less standard accented so as to comply with the speech stereotype associated with her lower status partner. We would suggest that such vocal stereotypes are so strong that they would operate to bias (obviously within limits that require empirical exploration) perceptions of speech already heard. Indeed, many middle-class individuals have reported anecdotes to us of their having been aware on encountering a manual worker of converging their speech 'downwards' (cf. Giles & Powesland 1975) towards that which they expected of him. Moreover, they reported the tendency to continue adopting this strategy tenaciously throughout the duration of the conversation despite the worker having sounded quite contrary to their expectations!

Findings of a study by Thakerar & Giles (1981) are consistent with these speculations. In this study, independent groups of listeners in three conditions listened to a stimulus 'neutral' speaker. The stimulus material for the experiment was a 1-minute monologue recorded by a male speaker, the content of which had been transcribed from one of the speakers in the ES condition of the previous investigation. All groups were told before listening to him that the speaker was describing a block-design task that he had just completed. After listening to him, subjects in the control condition were told nothing further about him and were required to evaluate him on traits of competence and benevolence (Brown et al. 1975) and also to rate his speech rate and accent. In the remaining two experimental conditions, subjects were provided with more information about the speaker between listening to his taped voice and rating him on the same scales as the control group. One of these groups (the HS condition) was told that the speaker had in actual fact completed the task he was describing in less time than the average time taken by students, and that he was doing very well in his university examinations. The other experimental group (the LS condition) was told that he had completed the task much more slowly than the average student, and that he was doing poorly in his examinations. Results showed that compared to the control group, subjects in the HS condition rated the same stimulus speaker as sounding significantly more standard accented, and as talking more quickly, and that he also was perceived as more competent. The subjects in the LS condition, in contrast, rated this same stimulus speaker as sounding significantly more non-standard, talking more slowly, and as being less competent than the speaker in the control condition (see figure 3). The experiment actually had another section to it where listeners were afforded a second opportunity of hearing the speaker and were asked to rate him yet again. In other words, they had the chance of modifying their previous ratings. Nevertheless, the same findings emerged after the second set of ratings, with judgments of speech rate being polarized by the two experimental groups in their respective directions on this occasion. These data, then, clearly suggest that listeners have non-content speech stereotypes associated with speakers of different statuses, and that these expectations greatly bias their impressions of people even after they have heard them, and that they are, in addition, extremely resistant to subsequent reversals.

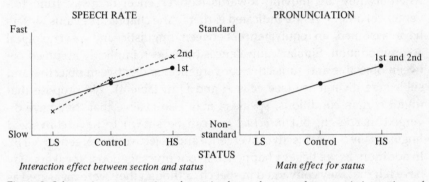

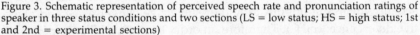

Figure 3. Schematic representation of perceived speech rate and pronunciation ratings of speaker in three status conditions and two sections (LS = low status; HS = high status; 1st and 2nd = experimental sections)

Hence, on the basis of the Thakerar & Giles findings, it can be argued that people expect HS speakers to speak at a faster rate and with a more standard accent than LS persons. It will be recalled that the results of the foregoing studies reported in this chapter show that HS speakers in co-operative contexts adopted slower rates of speech and non-standardized their accents, while LS speakers became faster in speaking rate and standardized their accents. In an attempt to explain this intriguing divergence, we would argue that in co-operative situations, HS persons may *subjectively* be attempting to shift their speech patterns in the direction *expected* of their LS counterparts, and that LS persons are also attempting to shift their speech towards where they *believe* their HS partners are linguistically. In other words, we are suggesting that HS speakers adopt slower rates of speech with more non-standard accents because, at least in part, they expect LS persons to possess these speech styles, and that LS speakers become faster and more standard accented because they expect, at least in part, HS persons to speak in this way. The reasons why the speakers may attempt to become more similar to each other will be discussed shortly.

In table 1 we distinguished conceptually between psychological and linguistic processes of speech accommodation. Our present data on what we believe to be psychological convergence reflected by linguistic divergence therefore now need to be further elaborated. This can be achieved by means of a dichotomy of the linguistic process into an *objective* dimension, defined as speakers' shifts in speech independently measured as moving towards (convergence) or away (divergence) from others, and a *subjective* dimension, defined as speakers' *beliefs* regarding whether they are moving towards (convergence) or away from (divergence) others. As we indicated earlier in the chapter, previous writers have assumed an equivalence between linguistic and psychological accommodation. Similar equivalences have been implicitly assumed between objective and subjective convergence, and between objective and subjective divergence (see cells A and D in table 4). We propose that under certain conditions, speakers may also believe that they have diverged in speech, but *in actual fact* can be shown to have converged linguistically (i.e. subjective divergence and objective convergence: cell B). In addition, as we believe happened in our investigations, speakers may have felt that they converged in speech, although they were measured as actually diverging linguistically (i.e. subjective convergence and objective divergence: cell C). Therefore, in order to attain a fuller understanding of speech accommodation, we need to subject people's speech shifts to *subjective* analyses as well as to objective analyses. Research along these lines would attempt a reply to the question: what do speakers think they are converging or diverging to in interpersonal encounters?

Our argument thus far can be summarized as follows. Although the

Table 4. *Subjective and objective linguistic dimensions of speech accommodation*

	SUBJECTIVE LINGUISTIC	
	Convergence	Divergence
OBJECTIVE LINGUISTIC Convergence	A	B
Divergence	C	D

shifts appearing in figures 1 and 2 can objectively be represented as divergence, we believe the speakers themselves in the spirit of psychological integration and co-operation thought they were converging to where they believed their partners to be. However, we need to extend the argument somewhat further. Another assumption in speech accommodation theory has been the notion that the functions underlying speech accommodation do not differ for mutually converging (or even diverging) speakers. More specifically, if a speaker converges 'downwards' to his or her partner, and the latter converges 'upwards' (Giles 1973; Giles & Powesland 1975) then such mutual accommodation simply reflects a reciprocal desire for each other's approval. Data emerging from the present experiments suggest that such a view is untenable, and that subjective linguistic convergence on the part of the HS speakers may have occurred for quite different functional reasons than the subjective linguistic convergence produced by the LS speakers. It is interesting to recall that the HS speakers were consistently judged by our listening samples as becoming sympathetic to their partners, whereas the LS speakers were not. It is quite possible then that the two speakers are shifting with separate aims in mind.

What psychological functions may such shifts fulfil? Many writers have discussed the complex functional components of speech (e.g. Dabbs 1980; Halliday 1970; Robinson 1972). However, for our present purposes we prefer the more simplistic distinction between the social psychological functions served by speech styles introduced by Giles, Scherer & Taylor (1979): those of cognitive organization and identity maintenance. Indeed, these functions bear a close resemblance to the cognitive and affective functions of mothers' talk to babies, as suggested by Brown (1977). The cognitive organization function involves speech markers being used by interlocutors to organize events into meaningful social categories, thereby allowing the complex social situation to be reduced to manageable proportions. In this way, the speaker may organize his or her output to take account of the requirements of the listener (Applegate & Delia 1980; Blakar in press; Higgins 1980), and the latter may select from this and organize it according to the cognitive structures most easily available for comprehension. At the same time, interlocutors may wish to speak in the way that will allow them to present themselves most favourably (Scherer 1979), and in turn listeners may wish to select from the linguistic input in a manner that maintains or even enhances their self or social esteem. In this way, the identity maintenance function of speech serves to fulfil the emotional needs of participants by their seeking to attend to speech markers that positively reinforce their egos and by failing to process any information that may have a negative effect on their images. Although Taylor & Giles (1979) suggested that in uncertain conditions, these two functions may operate simultaneously, it would seem beneficial to consider them as occupying a two-dimensional space, where speakers and listeners can be considered as functioning simultaneously as either high, medium or low in both these respects.

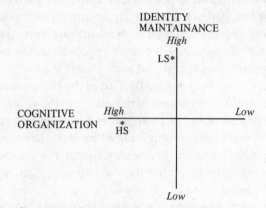

Figure 4. Proposed cognitive organization and identity maintenance perspectives of high status (HS) and low status (LS) interacting speakers

In a co-operative encounter between participants of differential status, it may well be that they place different emphases on the cognitive organization and identity maintenance functions. We in fact propose that HS speakers in our studies may have been more concerned with the former, whilst LS speakers may be relatively more concerned with the latter (see figure 4), given their respective social statuses for the tasks at hand. Therefore, LS speakers were found to increase their speech rates and standardize their accents. On the basis of findings reviewed earlier, it is argued that such speakers adopt this speech style in order to become linguistically more similar to the expected speech characteristics of their HS interlocutor and that they are subsequently evaluated more favourably on competence dimensions. This shift, then, would be motivated by the need to attain a higher self-esteem in the task-related situation, and also perhaps to show respect to the HS partner. In any case, the speech shift here can be seen more as an expression of identity maintenance than as cognitive organization. HS speakers were found to decrease their speech rates and to non-standardize their accents in US conditions. Again on the basis of findings reported earlier, it is argued that HS speakers adopt this kind of speech style in order to become subjectively more similar to what they imagine the linguistic behaviour of their partners to be, and in order to be perceived as sympathetic, by helping them out. Given their positive self-esteem in the situation, this linguistic shift is likely to be motivated by their desire to relax their partners and to make their messages more easily comprehensible. Hence, the shift here can be seen more as an expression of cognitive organization than as identity maintenance. Moreover, in co-operative encounters between participants of differential status where no status alternatives exist (cf. Tajfel 1974; Turner & Brown 1978), competition between the interlocutors to 'out-do each other' is greatly reduced, and they are more likely therefore to accept the situation as legitimate.

4. An interpersonal simulation of speech accommodation

On the basis of the previous discussion, a third investigation was designed, the main purposes of which were as follows. First, to demonstrate that the objective shifts of divergence observed in the previous two investigations reflect speakers' subjective attempts to converge linguistically towards the way that they thought their partners spoke and secondly, to determine the cognitive and affective functions of these speech shifts. However, it is obviously extremely difficult, if not impossible, to discover, whilst they are actually conversing, what speakers think they are doing linguistically, and why they believe they are doing them psychologically without disturbing the natural flow of interaction. In order to obtain some insight into these processes, therefore, we adopted the 'interpersonal simulation' technique (Bem 1965, 1972). The subjects in this experiment were asked to listen to a tape recording of a typical co-operative interaction between two people of different statuses. In the control conditions, subjects were not in fact informed of the speakers' relative status, whilst in the experimental conditions they were. Half of the subjects were asked to imagine being one of the speakers, and the remainder were asked to imagine being the other. They were subsequently required to fill in questions regarding 'their own' and the other speakers' performances: see table 5 for an outline of the experimental data. The following hypotheses were tested:

1. Under the control conditions where no information regarding the speakers' relative statuses was provided, listeners would assess the former's speech patterns in the divergent manners indicated in the previous investigations.

Table 5. *Experimental design of interpersonal simulation*

GROUPS	MANIPULATION
Control 1 (N = 10)	Information A → Imagine 'X' → Listen → Rate
Control 2 (N = 10)	Information A → Imagine 'Y' → Listen → Rate
Experimental 1 (N = 10)	Information A → Imagine → 'X' → HS → Listen → Rate
Experimental 2 (N = 10)	Information A → Imagine → 'Y' → LS → Listen → Rate

X = high status (HS) speaker, Y = low status (LS) speaker

2. In the experimental conditions where information regarding the relative statuses of the speakers was provided, listeners taking the role of the HS person on the tape would perceive the LS person to be speaking at a slow rate and with a non-standard accent, and would perceive 'themselves' to be converging to these speech patterns, whilst listeners taking the role of the LS person on the tape would perceive the HS person to be speaking at a fast speech rate and with a standard accent, and would perceive 'themselves' to be converging to these speech patterns.
3. HS speakers on tape would be perceived to be shifting their speech patterns more for reasons of cognitive organization than the LS speakers, who in turn would be perceived as shifting more than the former, for identity maintenance reasons.

Method. Subjects were forty female undergraduates, twenty of whom participated in two groups of subjects for the control conditions (C1 and C2) whilst the remaining two groups of ten subjects each participated in the experimental conditions (E1 and E2). The subjects in each group were presented with a stimulus tape, which was a conversation between two women, of 6 minutes in length, divided into two sections of 3 minutes each by means of a long pause. The stimulus conversation was one of the taped dialogues from the third session, the US condition, of Investigation 2. This particular discussion had been selected as it reflected one of the most extreme mutual divergences as judged by the listeners in that investigation; it seemed to us an exaggerated version of the norm for US interactions. In C1 condition, the group of subjects was asked to imagine that they were one of the persons on the tape (in fact, unknown to them, the HS speaker) and to listen to the conversation as though they were this person. The C2 group of subjects was asked to take on the role of the other person (unknown to them, the LS speaker) while they were listening to the conversation. In E1 a similar procedure to C1 was followed, but in addition the subjects were told that the person they were to imagine was the higher status person, who had done much better than the other person on the tape in a previous co-ordination task – a task that incidentally was related to standard intelligence tests. Subjects were further told that the content of the dialogue was a discussion of the best strategy to adopt to complete a co-ordination task on which they had co-operated. E2 was afforded a similar set of instructions to C2 except that in addition the subjects in this condition were told that the speaker they had to imagine was the lower status person, who had done much worse than the other person on the tape in a previous co-ordination task. The subjects were told, as were E1 subjects, about the implications of scoring well on this task for intelligence and also about the background to the conversation they were about to hear. Listeners heard both initial and final sections of the conversation consecutively, and were then required to rate their 'own' as well as the 'other' speaker on two continuous rating scales, namely speech rate (fast–slow) and pronunciation (standard–nonstandard), separately, in retrospect for each section of the conversation. Subjects were then required to rate their 'own' speaker's reasons for acting the way she had. More specifically, there were four continuous 7 cm lines tapping speech functions: the extent (high–low) to which the role-takers' own speakers had attempted to attain communicational efficiency and comfort their interlocutor (cognitive organization) and the extent to which they had attempted to show respect and attain higher self-esteem (identity maintenance). Finally, subjects were asked whether they believed their speaker had (a) attempted to reduce, maintain or emphasize *linguistic* differences with her partner, and (b) attempted to reduce, maintain or emphasize the *psychological* distance between herself and her interlocutor.

Results and discussion. Listeners' two linguistic ratings were submitted to separate $2 \times 4 \times 2$ analyses of variance (section: initial/final × condition: control 1/2/ experimental 1/2 × status: high/low) with repeated measures on the first factor. The four speech function scales were submitted to separate 2×4 analyses of variance (status: high/low × condition: control 1/2/ experimental 1/2). Data for the two remaining multiple choice items were subjected to χ^2 tests.

The findings regarding the two linguistic measures are graphically represented in figure 5. For both dimensions, significant three-way interactions emerged (F = 18.35, df = 3,36, p < 0.01; F = 16.95, p < 0.01) for speech rate and pronunciation respectively. Comparisons between the means showed that while no differences in speech rate and pronunciation between the HS and LS speakers were perceived in the initial section of the conversation by either C1 or C2 subjects, subjects assuming the role of the HS speaker in C1 did perceive their LS partner as having a faster speech rate (t = 10.0, df = 36, p < 0.01) and a more standard accent (t = 11.93, p < 0.01), while subjects in C2 assuming the role of the LS speaker did perceive their HS partner as having a slower speech rate (t = 7.48, p < 0.01), and more of a non-standard accent (t = 10.64, p < 0.01) than they themselves had in the final section of the conversation. Therefore, when listeners had no information about the relative statuses of the speakers (C1 and C2 in figure 5), they perceived the divergence in speech rate and pronunciation as did listeners in Investigation 2, thereby confirming the first hypothesis. In the experimental condition, subjects in E1, assuming the role of the HS speaker, perceived both the HS speaker and the LS speaker as becoming slower in speech rate (HS t = 6.19, LS t = 7.33, p < 0.01) and more non-standardly accented (HS t = 8.17, LS t = 8.19, p < 0.01) from the initial to the final section of the conversation. Subjects in the E2 condition, who had assumed the role of the LS speaker, perceived both the LS speaker and the HS speaker as becoming faster in speech rate (HS t = 3.70, LS t = 4.40, p < 0.01) and more standard accented (HS t = 2.97, LS t = 3.03, p < 0.01) from the initial to the final section of the conversation. As can be seen from figure 5, no differences emerged between the ratings of the HS and LS speakers when judged in the experimental conditions.

Main effects emerged on all four of the function scales (p < 0.01)

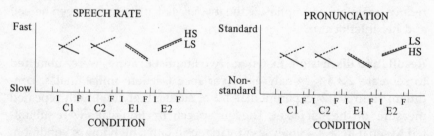

Figure 5. Schematic representation of perceived speech rate and pronunciation ratings for high status (HS) and low status (LS) speaker across initial (I) and final (F) sections for both control (C1 and C2) and experimental (E1 and E2) groups

indicating that, compared to LS speakers, HS speakers were thought to have modified their speech styles to make their speech more easily comprehensible ($F = 6.7$, df $= 3,36$) and to make their partners more comfortable ($F = 13.44$). On the other hand, LS speakers were thought to have modified their speech styles relative to HS to show respect for their partners ($F = 11.14$) and to attain a higher self-esteem ($F = 6.95$). With regard to the two remaining multiple choice items, it was found that all listeners felt their speakers were attempting to reduce linguistic differences between themselves and their partners as opposed to any other tactic ($\chi^2 = 65.4$, df $= 3$, $p < 0.01$), and also that they felt their speakers were attempting to converge psychologically towards their interlocutors ($\chi^2 = 46.11$, $p < 0.01$) rather than trying to do anything else.

These data, then, confirm the experimental hypotheses of Investigation 3. When listeners were provided with no information about the status of a speaker whose role they were to imagine, no status-related speech stereotypes could have been readily evoked which could have affected their perceptions of either person's speech patterns on tape. Hence, when speakers shifted away from each other linguistically in the control conditions, they were also heard as mutually diverging by listeners, thereby confirming hypothesis 1. This was not the case, however, when status-relevant information regarding speakers was provided for listeners in the experimental conditions. Under these circumstances, subjects perceived the speaker whose role they were asked to see themselves in whilst listening to her, as moving towards a speech style characteristic of her partner's status-related speech stereotype. In other words, HS speakers (in E1) are heard to become, in the final section of the conversation, as slow and as non-standard as their LS partners are supposed to sound, whilst LS speakers (in E2) are heard to sound as fast and as standard as their HS partners are supposed to sound in the final section, thereby confirming hypothesis 2. Moreover, data were elicited from the role-taking listeners that suggested that they thought the speakers on tape would be converging towards each other psychologically as well as linguistically *despite the fact* that in objective terms each partner was actually moving away from the other; such is the power and influence of speech stereotypes once evoked under these conditions. Finally, hypothesis 3 was confirmed, in that subjects considered that the HS speaker was shifting more for cognitive organizational reasons, whereas the LS speaker was believed to have shifted more for identity maintenance objectives. Thus, not only do speech stereotypes affect listeners' perceptions and evaluations of speakers, but they also have a profound effect on how and why the former actually talk to the latter. In future research, attention ought to be directed towards elucidating, with greater precision than has been attempted here, the component dimensions of the cognitive organization and identity maintenance functions.

It should be acknowledged openly that there need not be a one-to-one correspondence between the role-taking data elicited in Investigation 3 and the cognitive activity of speakers in the first two investigations; there are obvious problems in generalizing from a simulation procedure to actual speakers' intentions. Indeed, while these suggestive data are strongly supportive of our theoretical stance, we do admit to the need for further empirical data derived from other methodologies on these issues. In addition, we do not consider that there are any fundamental contradictions between the role-takers in this last investigation being able to report speakers' linguistic intentions and behaviour whilst the Investigation 1 speakers did not report retrospectively any changes in their speech behaviour on two *specific* dimensions, namely speech rate and pronunciation. Obviously, the sets to provided subjects in the simulation procedure as well as the questions asked of them and the task itself were vastly different from the procedure undertaken by the interacting nurses. Furthermore, it could have been that had the nurses been asked at the time whether they had attempted to become more similar to the *speech style* of their partners in the US condition, they would have replied in the affirmative.

5. Concluding remarks: a new model and reformulated propositions

The empirical research reported in this chapter developed out of a desire to determine whether predictions from speech accommodation theory suggesting mutual convergence would occur when interlocutors of different statuses interact to achieve a mutual and co-operative goal. However, data from the first two investigations did not confirm the original hypothesis, in that the speakers actually diverged from each other: the HS speakers slowed down their speech rates and became more nonstandard in their accents, whilst the LS speakers increased their speech rates and became more standard in their accents. The apparent conflict between the predictions of speech accommodation theory and the nature of the data emerging from these investigations was resolved by means of the *exploratory* findings of the third investigation. It appeared that the interactants had subjectively converged to their partners in the direction of the way that they expected them to speak. Furthermore, it was shown that the participants were psychologically converging to fulfil different cognitive and affective functions.

Three main conclusions emerge from these investigations which we have no reason to believe should not be pertinent for male speakers. First, the view that speech convergence always implies social integration and that speech divergence always implies social differentiation is rather naïve. In accordance with table 1, we believe *linguistic* convergence and divergence to be orthogonal from *psychological* convergence and divergence. Secondly, measured linguistic shifts of convergence and divergence need not necessarily reflect the direction in which speakers themselves believe they are moving. In accordance with table 4, we believe *objective* linguistic convergence and divergence to be orthogonal from *subjective* convergence and divergence. Thirdly, subjective linguistic convergence implying psychological convergence has also been shown to be more complex, in that it can fulfil different functions for different interlocutors, e.g. cognitive organization for HS and identity maintenance for LS speakers.

Nevertheless, there is not necessarily a contradiction between the original predictions of speech accommodation theory and the empirical findings reported here. From the outset, we predicted that convergence would occur in mixed status dyads where there was a spirit of cooperation. Convergence did in fact occur, but not at the objectively measurable level that was initially anticipated. Instead, it emerged at the psychological and subjective linguistic levels. Indeed, the fact that speech accommodation theory is robust enough to entertain these subtle distinctions within its theoretical boundaries may help explain why Cappella (1980) found that some dyads he tested converged towards each other on temporal indices of speech whilst others *diverged* under the same cooperative conditions. Unless we take into account the notion of speech stereotyping and consider the process whereby speakers themselves think they are shifting too, then researchers will be unable to take account of such variations and of superficially 'erroneous' results. Moreover, the potential misattribution of objectively diverging speech shifts to interpersonal differentiation from another speaker who in actual fact considers himself or herself to be converging *subjectively* could result in a breakdown of communication as well as an unfolding of mutually negative attitudes.

Let us now clarify and elaborate upon our current version of speech accommodation theory by recourse to table 6, which is a conceptual amalgam of the distinctions already made. Logically, eight possible com-

Table 6. *Some linguistic and psychological parameters of speech accommodation*

| | LINGUISTIC | | | |
| | Convergence | | Divergence | |
	Objective	Subjective	Objective	Subjective
PSYCHOLOGICAL Convergence	A	B	C	D
Divergence	E	F	G	H

binations of linguistic and psychological accommodations emerge from table 6 (namely A + B: C + B: A + D: C + D: G + H: E + H: G + F: E + F), each of which could possibly be labelled with neologisms. Note that A + B was our original, 'pure' convergence, G + H our original, 'pure' divergence, and C + D encapsulates our notion of 'speech complementarity' (see 1.1 and 1.2 above). However, as we pointed out, B + C has strong converging properties at two levels while E + H has strong diverging ones as well. We will now also reformulate the basic propositions associated with speech accommodation presented earlier. Our position is now:

1. People will attempt to converge linguistically towards the speech patterns *believed* to be characteristic of their recipients when they (a) desire their social approval and the perceived costs of so acting are proportionally lower (identity maintenance function) than the rewards anticipated; and/or (b) desire a high level of communicational efficiency (cognitive organization function).

2. The magnitude of such (subjective) linguistic convergence will be a function of (a) the extent of the speakers' repertoires, and (b) factors (personality and environmental) that may increase the need for social approval and/or high communicational efficiency.

3. Objective speech convergence will be positively evaluated by recipients when the resultant behaviour is (a) perceived as such, psychologically; (b) perceived to be at an optimal sociolinguistic distance from them; and (c) attributed with positive intent.

4. People will attempt to maintain their speech patterns or even diverge linguistically away from those *believed* characteristic of their recipients when they either (a) define the encounter in intergroup terms and desire a positive ingroup identity, or (b) wish to dissociate personally from another in an interindividual encounter (both identity maintenance functions).

5. The magnitude of such (subjective) linguistic divergence will be a function of (a) the extent of speakers' repertoires, and (b) either contex-

tual factors increasing the salience of group identification and the desire for a positive ingroup identity, or undesirable characteristics of another in an interindividual encounter.

6. Objective speech maintenance and divergence will be negatively evaluated by recipients when the acts are perceived as psychologically diverging, but favourably reacted to by observers of the encounter who define the interaction in intergroup terms and who share a common, positively valued group membership with the speaker.

This reformulation makes speech accommodation theory an even more *social psychological* perspective on language behaviour than ever before. Moreover, the present chapter has not only elucidated some of the important linguistic and psychological parameters involved in speech accommodation, but it has also pointed to the crucial cognitive role of speech *stereotypes* (cf. Giles, Scherer & Taylor 1979; Kramer 1977; Smith 1979; Snyder in press) in mediating between subjective and objective linguistic convergence. In this vein, and given that speech stereotypes are probably formed from social learning of the prevailing sociolinguistic folklore, the 'individual-speaker' character of speech accommodation theory is beginning to attend to larger scale, societal processes.

References

Aboud, F. E. 1976. Social development aspects of language. *Papers in Linguistics, 9*, 15–37.

Alkire, A. A., Collum, M. E., Kaswan, J. & Love, L. R. 1968. Information exchange and accuracy of verbal communication under social power conditions. *Journal of Personality and Social Psychology, 9*, 301–8.

Applegate, J. L. & Delia, J. G. 1980. Person centered speech, psychological development and the context of language usage. In R. St Clair & H. Giles (eds.) *The social and psychological contexts of language.* New Jersey: Erlbaum.

Argyle, M. 1980. Language and social interaction. In H. Giles, P. W. Robinson & P. M. Smith (eds.) *Language: social psychological perspectives.* Oxford: Pergamon Press.

Bem, D. J. 1965. An experimental analysis of self-persuasion. *Journal of Experimental Social Psychology, 1*, 199–218.

    1972. Self-perception theory. In L. Berkowitz (ed.) *Advances in experimental social psychology.* New York: Academic Press.

Berger, C. R. 1979. Beyond initial interaction: uncertainty, understanding and development of interpersonal relations. In H. Giles & R. St Clair (eds.) *Language and social psychology.* Oxford: Blackwell.

    1980. Self-consciousness and the study of interpersonal interaction: approaches and issues. In H. Giles, P. W. Robinson & P. M. Smith (eds.) *Language: social psychological perspectives.* Oxford: Pergamon Press.

Bishop, J. 1979. Perceived similarity in interpersonal attitudes and behaviours: the effects of belief and dialect style. *Journal of Applied Social Psychology*, 9, 446–65.

Blakar, R. in press. Towards a theory of communication in terms of preconditions. In H. Giles & R. St Clair (eds.) *Recent advances in language, communication and social psychology*. New Jersey: Erlbaum.

Bourhis, R. Y. 1977. Language and social evaluation in Wales. Unpublished Doctoral dissertation, University of Bristol.

    1979. Language in ethnic interaction: a social psychological approach. In H. Giles & B. Saint-Jacques (eds.): *Language and ethnic relations*. Oxford: Pergamon Press.

Bourhis, R. Y. & Genesee, F. 1980. Evaluative reactions to code switching strategies in Montreal. In H. Giles, P. W. Robinson & P. M. Smith (eds.) *Language: social psychological perspectives*. Oxford: Pergamon Press.

Bourhis, R. Y. & Giles, H. 1977. The language of intergroup distinctiveness. In H. Giles (ed.) *Language, ethnicity and intergroup relations*. European Monographs in Social Psychology, 13. London: Academic Press.

Bourhis, R. Y., Giles, H. & Lambert, W. E. 1975. Social consequences of accommodating one's style of speech: a cross-national investigation. *International Journal of the Sociology of Language*, 6, 53–71.

Bourhis, R. Y., Giles, H., Leyens, J.-P. & Tajfel, H. 1979. Psycholinguistic distinctiveness: language divergence in Belgium. In H. Giles & R. St Clair (eds.) *Language and social psychology*. Oxford: Blackwell.

Brown, B. L. 1980. Effects of speech rate on personality attributions and competency ratings. In H. Giles, W. P. Robinson & P. M. Smith (eds.) *Language: social psychological perspectives*. Oxford: Pergamon Press.

Brown, B. L., Strong, W. J. & Rencher, A. C. 1975. Acoustic determinants of personality from speech. *International Journal of the Sociology of Language*, 6, 11–32.

Brown, P. & Fraser, C. 1979. Speech markers of situation. In K. R. Scherer & H. Giles (eds.) *Social markers in speech*. Cambridge: Cambridge University Press.

Brown, P. & Levinson, S. 1979. Social structure, groups and interactions. In K. R. Scherer & H. Giles (eds.) *Social markers in speech*. Cambridge: Cambridge University Press.

Brown, R. 1977. Introduction. In C. E. Snow & C. A. Ferguson (eds.) *Talking to children: language input and acquisition*. Cambridge: Cambridge University Press.

Brown, R. & Gilman, A. 1960. The pronouns of power and solidarity. In T. A. Sebeok (ed.) *Style in language*. Cambridge, Mass: MIT Press.

Byrne, D. 1969. Attitudes and attraction. *Advances in experimental social psychology*, 4, 35–89.

Cappella, J. M. 1980. Turn by turn matching and compensation in talk and silence: new methods and new explanations. In H. Giles, W. P. Robinson & P. M. Smith (eds.) *Language: social psychological perspectives*. Oxford: Pergamon Press.

Dabbs, J. M. 1980. Temporal patterning of speech with gaze in social conversation. In H. Giles, P. W. Robinson & P. M. Smith (eds.) *Language: social psychological perspectives*. Oxford: Pergamon Press.

Doise, W., Sinclair, A. & Bourhis, R. Y. 1976. Evaluation of accent convergence and divergence in cooperative and competitive intergroup situations. *British Journal of Social and Clinical Psychology*, 15, 247–52.

Drake, G. F. 1980. The social function of slang. In H. Giles, P. W. Robinson & P. M. Smith (eds.) *Language: social psychological perspectives*. Oxford: Pergamon Press.

Fishman, J. A. 1966. *Language loyalty in the United States*. The Hague: Mouton.

Giles, H. 1973. Accent mobility: a model and some data. *Anthropological Linguistics*, 15, 87–105.

1977a. Social psychology and applied linguistics: towards an integrative approach. *ITL: Review of Applied Linguistics*, 35, 27–42.

(ed.) 1977b. *Language, ethnicity and intergroup relations*. European Monographs in Social Psychology, 13. London: Academic Press.

1978. Linguistic differentiation between ethnic groups. In H. Tajfel (ed.) *Differentiation between social groups: studies in the social psychology of intergroup relations*. European Monographs in Social Psychology, 14. London: Academic Press.

1979. Sociolinguistics and social psychology: an introductory essay. In H. Giles & R. St Clair (eds.) *Language and social psychology*. Oxford: Blackwell.

1980. Accommodation theory: some new directions. In S. de Silva (ed.) *Aspects of linguistic behaviour*. York: University of York.

Giles, H. & Bourhis, R. Y. 1976. Methodological issues in dialect perception: a social psychological perspective. *Anthropological Linguistics*, 19, 294–304.

Giles, H. & Johnson, P. 1981. Intergroup behaviour, ethnicity and language. In J. C. Turner & H. Giles (eds.) *Intergroup behaviour*. Oxford: Blackwell.

Giles, H. & Powesland, P. F. 1975. *Speech style and social evaluation*. European Monographs in Social Psychology, 7. London: Academic Press.

Giles, H. & St Clair, R. (eds.) 1979. *Language and social psychology*. Oxford: Blackwell.

(eds.) in press. *Recent advances in language, communication and social psychology*. New Jersey: Erlbaum.

Giles, H. & Saint-Jacques, B. (eds.) 1979. *Language and ethnic relations*. Oxford: Pergamon Press.

Giles, H. & Smith, P. M. 1979. Accommodation theory: optimal levels of convergence. In H. Giles & R. St Clair (eds.) *Language and social psychology*. Oxford: Blackwell.

Giles, H., Bourhis, R. Y. & Taylor, D. M. 1977. Towards a theory of language in ethnic group relations. In H. Giles (ed.) *Language, ethnicity and intergroup relations*. European Monographs in Social Psychology, 13. London: Academic Press.

Giles, H., Hewstone, M. & St Clair, R. in press. Cognitive structures and a social psychology of language: new integrative models and an introductory overview. In H. Giles & R. St Clair (eds.) *Recent advances in language, communication and social psychology*. New Jersey: Erlbaum.

Giles, H., Llado, N., McKirnan, D. J. & Taylor, D. M. 1979. Social identity in Puerto Rico. *International Journal of Psychology*, 14, 185–201.

Giles, H., Robinson, P. W. & Smith, P. M. (eds.) 1980. *Language: social psychological perspectives*. Oxford: Pergamon Press.

Giles, H., Scherer, K. R. & Taylor, D. M. 1979. Speech markers in social interaction. In K. R. Scherer & H. Giles (eds.) *Social markers in speech*. Cambridge: Cambridge University Press.

Giles, H., Smith, P. M., Ford, B., Condor, S. & Thakerar, J. N. 1980. Speech style and the fluctuating salience of sex. *Language Sciences, 2,* 260–82.

Giles, H., Smith, P. M. & Robinson, W. P. 1980. Social psychological perspectives on language: prologue. In H. Giles, W. P. Robinson & P. M. Smith (eds.) *Language: social psychological perspectives*. Oxford: Pergamon Press.

Giles, H., Taylor, D. M. & Bourhis, R. Y. 1973. Towards a theory of interpersonal accommodation through language: some Canadian data. *Language in Society, 2,* 177–92.

Giles, H., Taylor, D. M., Lambert, W. E. & Albert, G. 1976. Dimensions of ethnic identity: an example from Northern Maine. *Journal of Social Psychology, 100,* 11–19.

Gimson, A. C. 1962. *An introduction to the pronunciation of English*. London: Edward Arnold.

Goldman-Eisler, F. 1968. *Psycholinguistics: experiments in spontaneous speech*. London: Academic Press.

Good, C. 1979. Language as social activity: negotiating conversation. *Journal of Pragmatics, 3,* 151–67.

Grush, J. E., Clore, G. L., & Costin, F. 1975. Dissimilarity and attraction: when differences makes a difference. *Journal of Personality and Social Psychology, 32,* 783–9.

Halliday, M. A. K. 1970. Language structure and language function. In J. Lyons (ed.) *New Horizons in linguistics*. Harmondsworth: Penguin Books.

Heider, F. 1958. *The psychology of interpersonal relations*. New York: Wiley.

Higgins, E. T. 1980. The 'communication game': implications for social cognition and persuasion. In E. T. Higgins, C. P. Herman & M. P. Zanna (eds.) *Social cognition: the Ontario symposium*. New Jersey: Erlbaum.

Holt, G. S. 1973. Inversion in Black communication. In T. Kochman (ed.): *Rappin' and stylin' out: communication in urban black America*. Illinois: University of Illinois Press.

Homans, G. C. 1961. *Social behaviour*. New York: Harcourt, Brace and World.

Hymes, D. 1972. Models of the interaction of language and social life. In J. Gumperz & D. Hymes (eds.) *Directions of sociolinguistics*. New York: Holt, Rinehart and Winston.

Jablin, F. M. 1979. Superior–subordinate communication: the state of the art. *Psychological Bulletin, 86,* 1201–22.

Jaffe, J. & Feldstein, S. 1970. *Rhythms of dialogue*. London: Academic Press.

Jones, E. E. & Davis, K. E. 1965. From acts to dispositions: the attribution process in perception. In L. Berkowitz (ed.) *Advances in experimental social psychology*. New York: Academic Press.

Kelly, H. H. 1973. The process of causal attribution. *American Psychologist, 28,* 107–28.

Kramer, C. 1977. Female and male perceptions of female and male speech. *Language and Speech, 20,* 151–61.

Labov, W. 1970. Language in social context. *Studium Generale, 23,* 30–87.

Lambert, W. E. 1979. Language as a factor in intergroup relations. In H. Giles & R. St Clair (eds.) *Language and social psychology*. Oxford: Blackwell.

Lambert, W. E. & Tucker, G. R. 1976. *Tu, vous, usted: a social psychological study of address patterns*. Rowley, Mass.: Newbury House.

Larsen, K., Martin, H. & Giles, H. 1977. Aniticipated social cost and interpersonal communication. *Human Communication Research, 3*, 303–8.

Lennard, H. L. & Bernstein, A. 1960. Interdependence of therapist and patient verbal behaviour. In J. A. Fishman (ed.) *Readings in the sociology of language*. The Hague: Mouton.

Macaulay, R. K. S. 1977. *Language, social class and education*. Edinburgh: Edinburgh University Press.

Marková, I. (ed.) 1978. *The social context of language*. London: Wiley.

Matarazzo, J. D., Weins, A. N., Matarazzo, R. G. & Saslo, W. G. 1968. Speech and silence behaviour in clinical psychotherapy and its laboratory correlates. In J. Schlier, H. Hunt, J. D. Matarazzo & C. Savage (eds.) *Research in psychotherapy*, vol. III. Washington, DC: American Psychological Association.

Miller, G. & Steinberg, M. 1975. *Between people: a new analysis of interpersonal communication*. USA: Science Research Association Inc.

Natalé, M. 1975. Convergence of mean vocal intensity in dyadic communication as a function of social desirability. *Journal of Personality and Social Psychology, 32*, 790–804.

Nisbett, R. E. & Wilson, T. D. 1977. Telling more than we know: verbal reports on mental process. *Psychological Review, 84*, 231–59.

Petyt, K. M. 1977. 'Dialect' and 'Accent' in the industrial West Riding: a study of the changing speech of an urban area. Unpublished PhD thesis, University of Reading.

Raffler Engel, W. von. 1980. The unconscious element in inter-cultural communication. In R. St Clair & H. Giles (eds.) *Recent advances in language, communication and social psychology*. New Jersey: Erlbaum.

Robinson, P. W. 1972. *Language and social behaviour*. Harmondsworth: Penguin Books.

Rommetveit, R. & Blakar, R. (eds.) 1979. *Studies of language, thought and verbal communication*. London: Academic Press.

Ros, M. & Giles, H. 1979. The language situation in Valencia: an accommodation theory perspective. *ITL: Review of Applied Linguistics, 49*, 1–24.

Ryan, E. B. 1979. Why do low prestige language varieties persist? In H. Giles & R. St Clair (eds.) *Language and social psychology*. Oxford: Blackwell.

Ryan, E. B. & Giles, H. (eds.) 1982. *Attitudes towards language variation: Social and applied contexts*. London: Edward Arnold.

St Clair, R. & Giles, H. (eds.) 1980. *The social and psychological contexts of language*. New Jersey: Erlbaum.

Sandilands, M. L. & Fleury, N. C. 1979. Unilinguals in des milieux bilingues: une analyse of attributions. *Canadian Journal of Behavioural Science, 11*, 164–8.

Sankoff, G. 1972. Language use in multilingual societies: some alternative approaches. In J. B. Pride & J. Holmes (eds.) *Sociolinguistics*. Harmondsworth: Penguin Books.

Scherer, K. R. 1979. Voice and speech correlates of perceived social influence in simulated juries. In H. Giles & R. St Clair (eds.): *Language and social psychology*. Oxford: Blackwell.

Scherer, K. R. & Giles, H. (eds.) 1979. *Social markers in speech*. Cambridge: Cambridge University Press.

254   Jitendra N. Thakerar, Howard Giles and Jenny Cheshire

Scotton, C. M. 1979. Code switching as a 'safe choice' in choosing a lingua franca. In W. C. McCormack & S. A. Wurm (eds.) *Language and society: anthropological issues*. The Hague: Mouton.

1980. Explaining linguistic choices as identity negotiations. In H. Giles, P. W. Robinson & P. M. Smith (eds.) *Language: social psychological perspectives*. Oxford: Pergamon Press.

Scotton, C. M. & Ury, W. 1977. Bilingual strategies: the social functions of code switching. *International Journal of the Sociology of Language*, 13, 5–20.

Siegman, A. W., Pope, B. & Blass, T. 1969. Effects of interviewer status and derivation of interviewer messages on interviewee productivity. *Proceedings of the 77th Annual Convention of the APA*, 4, 541–2.

Siegman, A. W. & Feldstein, S. (eds.) 1978. *Non-verbal behaviour and communication*. New Jersey: Erlbaum.

Simard, L., Taylor, D. M. & Giles, H. 1976. Attribution processes and interpersonal accommodation in a bilingual setting. *Language and Speech*, 374–87.

Skevington, S. M. 1980. Intergroup relations and social change withing a nursing context. *British Journal of Social and Clinical Psychology*, 19, 201–14.

Smith, B. L., Brown, B. L., Strong, W. J. & Rencher, A. C. 1975. Effects of speech rate on personality perception. *Language and Speech*, 18, 145–52.

Smith, P. M. 1979. Sex markers in speech. In K. R. Scherer & H. Giles (eds.) *Social markers in speech*. Cambridge: Cambridge University Press.

1980. Judging masculine and feminine social identities from content-controlled speech. In H. Giles, P. W. Robinson & P. M. Smith (eds.) *Language: social psychological perspectives*. Oxford: Pergamon Press.

Smith, P. M., Giles, H. & Hewstone, M. 1980. Sociolinguistics: a social psychological perspective. In R. St Clair & H. Giles (eds.) *The social and psychological contexts of language*. New Jersey: Erlbaum.

Snedecor, G. W. & Cochran, W. G. 1967. *Statistical methods*, 6th ed., p. 271. Iowa: Iowa State University Press.

Snyder, M. in press. On the self-perpetuating nature of social stereotypes. In D. L. Hamilton (ed.) *Cognitive processes in stereotyping and intergroup behaviour*. New Jersey: Erlbaum.

Street, R. L. under review. Evaluation of non-content speech accommodation.

Street, R. L. & Giles, H. in press. Speech accommodation theory: a social cognitive approach to language and speech behaviour. In M. E. Roloff & C. R. Berger (eds.) *Social cognition and communication*. Beverly Hills: Sage.

Tajfel, H. 1974. Social identity and intergroup behaviour. *Social Science Information*, 13, 65–93.

(ed.) 1978. *Differentiation between social groups: studies in the social psychology of intergroup behaviour*. European Monographs in Social Psychology, 14. London: Academic Press.

Tajfel, H. & Turner, J. C. 1979. An integrative theory of intergroup conflict. In W. G. Austin & S. Worchel (eds.) *The social psychology of intergroup relations*. Monterey, Calif.: Brooks/Cole.

Taylor, D. M. 1976. Ethnic identity: some cross-cultural comparison. In J. W. Berry & W. J. Lonner (eds.) *Applied cross-cultural psychology*. Amsterdam: Swets & Zeitlinger.

Taylor, D. M. & Giles, H. 1979. At the crossroads of research into language and ethnic relations. In H. Giles & B. Saint-Jacques (eds.) *Language and ethnic relations*. Oxford: Pergamon Press.

Taylor, D. M. & Royer, S. 1980. Group processes affecting anticipated language choice in intergroup relations. In H. Giles, P. W. Robinson & P. M. Smith (eds.) *Language: social psychological perspectives*. Oxford: Pergamon Press.

Taylor, D. M., Simard, L. M. & Papineau, D. 1978. Perceptions of cultural differences and language use: a field study in a bilingual environment. *Canadian Journal of Behavioural Science*, 10, 181–91.

Thakerar, J. N. 1981. Speech accommodation: some psychological and linguistic parameters. Unpublished Doctoral dissertation, University of Bristol.

Thakerar, J. N. & Giles, H. 1981. They are – so they speak: non-content speech stereotypes. *Language and Communication*, 1, 255–61.

Triandis, H. C. 1960. Cognitive similarity and communication in a dyad. *Human Relations*, 13, 175–83.

Trudgill, P. 1974. *The social differentiation of English in Norwich*. Cambridge: Cambridge University Press.

Turner, J. C. & Brown, R. J. 1978. Social status, cognitive alternatives and intergroup behaviour. In H. Tajfel (ed.) *Differentiation between social groups: studies in the social psychology of intergroup behaviour*. European Monographs in Social Psychology, 14. London: Academic Press.

Valdés-Fallis, G. 1977. Code switching among bilingual Mexican-American women: towards an understanding of sex-related language alternation. *International Journal of the Sociology of Language*, 17, 65–72.

Watzlawick, P., Beavin, J. H. & Jackson, D. P. 1967. *Pragmatics of human communication: a study of interactional patterns, pathologies and paradoxes*. New York: Norton.

Welkowitz, J. & Feldstein, S. 1970. Relation of experimentally manipulated interpersonal perception and psychological differentiation to the temporal patterning of conversation. *Proceedings of the 78th Annual Convention of the APA*, 5, 387–8.

Wolfram, W. 1973. *Sociolinguistic aspects of assimilation: Puerto Rican English in New York City*. Washington, DC: Center for Applied Linguistics.

Winer, B. J. 1971. *Statistical principles in experimental design*, 2nd ed., pp. 375–8. New York: McGraw Hill.

Subject index

Author index